GUN DIGEST BOOK OF
SPORTING CLAYS

By
Jack Lewis
and
Steve Comus

DBI BOOKS, INC.

About Our Covers

AVANZA! That's a pretty exciting name for a gun, no doubt, but it's a pretty exciting gun for the game that has taken the shooting sports by storm—sporting clays.

Taken from the Italian *avanzare* (verb, to advance or move forward), the word Avanza describes modern, contemporary design-think on the part of Marocchi, one of Europe's outstanding gunmakers of fine competition shotguns. Imported by Precision Sales International, the Marocchi Avanza is available in two models for the discriminating shooter.

The upper gun on our covers is the Marocchi Avanza Sporting Clays shotgun. The beauty of this gun is its balance and weight—it's built on a slim 20-gauge profile that results in an amazingly fast and easy-mounting gun that has been engineered to shoot very comfortably, despite its weight of just 7 lbs. The Avanza Sporting Clays model is chambered for 3-inch 12-gauge shells, which means you can shoot 2¾-inch shells, too. The 28-inch chrome-steel barrels come with Interchoke interchangeable choke tubes in Improved Cylinder and Modified, but other choke tubes are optionally available. The barrels have top and middle ventilated ribs and a luminous red bar front sight and metal bead middle.

The action of the Avanza is the Marocchi monoblock boxlock with selective automatic ejectors, unbreakable firing pins, and 5½-lb. pull single selective trigger that's adjustable for length of pull. Barrel cycling is auto-mechanical for sequence and the safety is automatic.

The mirror-black finish on the frame is tastefully accented with the gold Marocchi name. The stock is of select walnut, as is the broad forend that's specially contoured for the sporting clays game, and the buttpad is specially shaped for easy, quick mounting.

The lower gun is the Marocchi Avanza field model that shares many of the same design characteristics of the Sporting Clays gun.

Available in 12- and 20-gauge, both with 3-inch chambers, and with either 26- or 28-inch barrels, the field version can be had with either fixed chokes or the excellent Interchoke interchangeable choke tubes. This all-steel lightweight uses the same 20-gauge profile frame, single selective trigger, auto-mechanical barrel cycling and selective automatic ejectors. Again, only select walnut is used for the stock and forend, beautifully checkered and fitted with a ventilated recoil pad.

If you're just getting into the exciting sporting clays game, or want a new gun for hunting, take a hard look at the Avanza—it really is a step forward.

Photo by John Hanusin.

Produced by

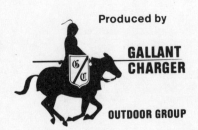

GALLANT CHARGER

OUTDOOR GROUP

Editorial Director
Jack Lewis

Production Director
Sonya Kaiser

Art Director
Bradley L. Wood

Artists
Gary Duck
Rueselle Gilbert

Copy Editor
Julie T. Rieman

Production Coordinator
Nadine Symons

Photo Services
Lori Morrison

Lithographic Services
Gallant Graphics

Contributing Editors
Chris Christian
Roger Combs
Barry G. Davis
Galen Geer
John Ross
Don Zutz

Publisher
Sheldon L. Factor

ISBN: 0-87349-125-4   Library of Congress Catalog Card Number: 91-71896

CONTENTS

INTRODUCTION 5

1. **BEGINNING OF A CHALLENGE** — Sporting clays went through a development phase before it was formalized in this country 6

2. **GETTING STARTED IN SPORTING CLAYS** — You probably have more of the needed equipment than you think 22

3. **WHAT, WHERE & WHEN TO SHOOT** — Sporting clays provides challenges not experienced in other claybird games 34

4. **GUNS FOR THE SPORT** — Single-shots and bolt-actions don't hack it — the other models can! 48

5. **SIGHT YOUR SHOTGUN** — Knowing where your scattergun shoots is a must for sporting clays 68

6. **UNDERSTANDING SHOTGUN BALANCE** — Here's a facet of scattergunning excellence that often goes ignored 74

7. **RETROFITTING FOR SPORTING CLAYS** — There are gunsmiths who specialize in making your favorite shotgun a sporting clays contender ...78

8. **THE TWO FACES OF SPORTING CLAYS** — The British and International styles have different courses — and demands 88

9. **LAY OF THE LAND** — Layouts for a sporting clays course are governed by terrain and imagination 100

10. **CLUES TO THE COURSE** — Depending upon your goal as a sporting clays shooter, there are certain facets to seek 112

11. **THE ORGANIZATIONS** — Shooters have a choice of styles and rules 120

12. **A MATTER OF INDUSTRY** — Outdoor-oriented businesses recognize the lure of sporting clays 130

13. **THE COST FACTOR** — Is sporting clays an expensive pastime? Check it against golf! 136

14. **TRAVELS & THE SHOOTER** — If you're serious about the sport, that means movin' on 144

15. **COACHES & INSTRUCTORS** — Just where do they fit into the scheme of this sport? 150

16. **CLAYS & STEEL** — Here's an objective look at how steel shot does in this game 160

17. **OF TARGETS & TRAPS** — Understanding the tools involved in the game can help your scores 168

18. **THE EXTRA-BIRD TECHNIQUE** — This trick is as much psychological as talent, but takes concentration 178

19. **THE MENTAL GAME** — Or what to do when you start to choke up 178

20. **CHEROKEE ROSE** — This Georgia shooting resort may be the finest in the nation 194

21. **MINI-COURSE, MAXI-RESULTS** — This layout has all the advantages and few of the costs of a large, commercial field 204

22. **WINNING THE CUSTOMER GAME** — Operating a successful sporting clays range is more than just throwing targets 226

23. **WISDOM FROM A CHAMPION** — "KK" Kennerknecht offers his thoughts on the right way to win, the wrong way to try 236

SPORTING CLAYS COURSES 248

INTRODUCTION

It is not often that a new sport — or new anything — bursts upon the scene as has been the case with sporting clays. That is the popular concept. However, the sport has been with us in one form or another for almost a quarter of a century.

It was imported from England originally in the Sixties by Remington, who brought over a British design expert to lay out a course at Remington Farms in Maryland. At that time — following a meeting with National Rifle Association and National Shooting Sports Foundation representatives — it was decided to call the sport "hunters clays," since the purpose was to more closely approximate hunting than was the case with skeet and trap shooting.

The effort suffered the doldrums until a group in Houston set about forming the United States Sporting Clays Association. That was followed by the National Sporting Clays Association, an offshoot of the National Skeet Shooting Association, which is headquartered in San Antonio.

These two organizations have worked hard at making the nation's shooters aware of the sport. And from that introduction, an entire shooting industry has been spawned!

Jack Lewis,
Capistrano Beach, California

Steve Comus,
Whittier, California

Tower shots are a virtual must for this particular game. But targets can be launched from the tops of barns, an old windmill or anything that allows high-angle shots.

SPORTING CLAYS' growing popularity is grounded in its closeness to actual hunting conditions — surprise flight paths, a variety of targets and similar hunting terrain.

This shotgun sport has roots deep in England's live-bird shooting that started sometime in the middle of the Eighteenth Century. Groups of Englishmen armed with muzzle-loaded guns went out into the fields to shoot live pigeons. The pigeons were trapped under hats, and when the gunner called, "Pull," a cord was jerked to knock over the hat releasing the pigeon. The first recorded formal "trapshooting" event was in 1793 and quickly spread throughout England and into the United States.

In 1831, the first formal live-bird trap event in the United States took place. Ten years later, its popularity subsided as non-hunters waged protests against shooting at live birds. Around the mid-1800s, glass ball targets hurled into the air by mechanical machines became popular in both countries, but never proved satisfactory. Besides being too hard, they had inconsistent flight patterns, were too costly and hard to clean. Combined with unreliable trap throwers, trapshooting still was in the premature stages. Inventors offered numerous modifications on trap throwers and glass ball targets — all with little success.

In 1866, Boston-born Charles Portlock improved a sling device used in England to hurl glass ball targets. He was one of the most influential figures in the movement away from standard use of live-bird targets. Another key figure was Captain Adam Bogardus who stimulated interest in glass-ball shooting with his exhibitions, using an improved trap that threw the balls in a more consistent flight pattern. Bogardus was the first to shoot one hundred straight pigeons in a Chicago tournament, and later broke 5000 glass balls at one of his exhibitions.

Finally in the 1880s, George Ligowsky of Cincinnati invented a flat disc target made of baked clay and pitch, which won instant approval in the U.S. and brought to a virtual end use of live-bird targets. He also established the first real consistent trap and target operation. The first U.S. clay target trapshooting championship was held in New Orleans, Louisiana, in 1885.

Experimenters everywhere introduced imitations of Ligowsky's clay birds, but an Englishman named McCaskey developed the benchmark for today's target about the same time Ligowsky introduced his in the U.S. McCaskey used river silt — later changed to limestone — and pitch. The limestone and pitch composition remains today because of its consistent hardness. Although there is no clay in the composition, the name "clay target" is unchanged. With these new marvels, trapshooting accelerated, London shooting schools became more influential in their growth, and sporting clays began its evolutionary process.

Despite these revolutionary inventions, trapshooting continued to frustrate many hunters. Among them was Charles Davies of Andover, Massachuetts. Davies was dissatisfied with trapshooting's lack of crossover and incoming shots of claybirds. In the 1920s, Davies, his son Henry, and friend, William H. Foster, set out to develop a shooting game that would incorporate more "hunting shots."

After many discarded ideas and failed plans, Davies set-

CHAPTER 1

BEGINNING OF A CHALLENGE

Sporting Clays Went Through A Development Phase Before It Was Formalized In This Country

LOW TOWER EVENT

At Remington Farms in Maryland, what is thought to be the first sporting clays range in this country was laid out.

tled on an eight-station semi-circle whereby birds were shot from two trap houses positioned at each end of the semi-circle, sitting at high and low levels off the ground. This introduced new angles and crossover double shots for more realistic flight patterns. The game was called "Shooting Around the Clock," which later was named skeet (Norse for "shooter"). The skeet machines threw targets in a fixed pattern of flight; whereas, trap machines threw targets that oscillated back and forth and flew in directions unknown to the shooter. Skeet also introduced more social interaction between shooters as only one squad member at a time shoots, while others wait their turn behind the station. This was carried over into today's sporting clays.

Sporting clays really developed in England at the time skeet was most popular in the U.S. Around 1925, the English were shooting a game called Sporting. Even before the 1920's, Sporting was preordained by some of Britain's top gun manufacturers on their private hunting grounds. Initially, Sporting never took off in England, but over the last twenty years, sporting clays, as it is called today, has become the most popular game in England and the trend has moved to the United States.

Sporting clays takes trap and skeet one step further. Added to this game is more challenge with simulated hunting terrain, surprise targets and target variety. The sport incorporates different game "species" at each station. One station may provide "passing ducks," another may have "flushing pheasants" or "rabbits" breaking cover. Participants also shoot at six different size clay targets that, when thrown, move at various speeds and react differently to the wind. Sporting clays gets even closer to actual hunting conditions.

Also attributed to sporting clays' development are the "quail walk" and "grouse walk," two games used in trap. In the quail walk, shooters walk a winding path through a

A few lengths of scrap lumber and some chicken wire were all that were needed to put together the shooting boxes. The boxes were meant to protect shooters on other posts.

At Remington Farms, the construction of shooting boxes was pursued as a means of limiting shooter's gun swing.

wooded or high brush area where traps are laid out, usually hidden behind shrubs or rocks. The puller, following behind, releases targets at surprise intervals. Targets thus emerge from both sides of the path, simulating the flight patterns of quail.

The grouse walk is similar. A pair of shooters walk shoulder to shoulder along both sides of a fence where the trap throwers are concealed. The shooter fires at the clay targets that emerge only on the side of the fence this individual is following. The targets are meant to resemble the flight patterns of grouse.

While a version of sporting clays had enjoyed a degree of popularity in England, it did not reach our shores until the late 1960s. Remington Arms probably was the first to recognize the potential of this game and to do something about it. The firm brought Chris Craddock, a British authority on range design, to Remington Farms in Maryland with the assignment to lay out a course. The Britisher took advantage of the hills, heavy woods and ponds to design a truly challenging layout.

Preparatory to introducing this adopted sport to American shooters, Remington invited the National Rifle Association and the National Shooting Sports Foundation to become involved. It was during a meeting of representatives from these bodies that it was decided to call the game "hunter clays."

"We were attempting to develop a game that would be of interest to the average bird hunter," recalls Dick Dietz, veteran press relations manager for Remington Arms, who was deeply involved in selling the concept to the firearms press. "Trap and skeet shooting, a lot of people felt, had passed beyond the means and abilities of the average shooter. They had become high-pressure games in which the amount of money one could spend on equipment had a good deal to do with what he could win. The fun had gone out of the games for Joe Shooter, who would bring his duck gun to shoot trap for fun, not a title and a place in the record books.

"Sporting clays — or hunter clays, as we called it then — is not the highly programmed, relatively predictable clay target game enountered in trap or skeet. Neither is it a game of perfection where tournaments produce a bunch of one hundred straights to be resolved by a lengthy shoot-off," Dietz specifies. "Winning tournament scores, even among top shooters, are generally in the 80s. Besides coping with varied and non-predictable targets, shooters must call for the target with their gun off the shoulder in a field position and can't mount the gun until the target is visible.

"One should not be put off by the competitive, tournament form of sporting clays," Dietz insists. "These are fine for those who like this kind of activity and they do help showcase and spread knowledge of the sport, just as pro-

In the late Sixties, when hunter clays was introduced, the thrower wasn't as well hidden as he is under present day standards. In this instance, Dick Dietz, Jr., acts as the thrower for a group of shooters visiting Remington Farms.

Some of the claybirds used in sporting clays are of a tougher material than those used in trap, skeet, but they still break when hit. (Below) Natural growth often is utilized as a means of hiding thrower and his trap.

fessional tennis and golf tours do for those sports. But you don't have to play the tournament game or get into an expensive equipment race and have the latest fad in specialized shotguns, ammunition or Yuppie-shooter clothing to enjoy or benefit from sporting clays.

"In fact, just the opposite is true for the larger majority of everyday field scattergunners. For this group, the sport has two major benefits. First, it provides a new and challenging opportunity to enjoy shotgunning throughout the entire year, not just during the limited time when hunting seasons are open.

"Second, sporting clays provides an excellent opportunity to improve your field shooting skills and techniques. While shooting stance and form for trap and skeet are somewhat artifically matched to those sports, gun handling techniques best adapted to sporting clays are exactly the same as those required for successful field gunning."

As late as July, 1989, Dick Dietz still was preaching — rightfully, in our opinion — from the same soapbox. In a letter to George Conrad, editor of *Sporting Clays* magazine, organ of the National Sporting Clays Association, Dietz said, "At long last, sporting clays looks like a valid growth opportunity for inanimate shotgunning. I think the tournament aspect is great, because it helps showcase and promote the sport. But I am concerned that it doesn't become a total 'elitist' sport with all sorts of special 'snobby' equipment and clothing. If it does, it will turn off the average hunter-shooter who is the only source of high-volume participation.

Claybirds are launched from hidden locations so that the similarity in challenge to hunting actual birds is maintained. Farmlands can be used to an advantage.

"I've been selling the concept of sporting clays at every game preserve I've been on for the past five years," Dietz wrote, "because sporting clays and game preserves are a natural marriage. Preserves have the necessary space and land locations where noise is not a problem and there are existing customers. The sport gives the preserve owner another income opportunity during live bird shooting seasons and something to attract customers during the half year when he can't put out live birds.

"For sporting clays to grow, there also has to be a not-too-expensive opportunity for the those who come in with a regular field gun of whatever kind and who are dressed in jeans and a jack shirt. If we restrict the game to people who look like a uniformed instructor, growth potential won't be any greater than that of registered skeet!"

The National Sporting Clays Association, incidentally, is an offshoot of the National Skeet Shooting Association. Both share the same headquarters in San Antonio, Texas.

The point that shooting preserves are ideal for incorporating sporting clays has been taken a step further by a number of Midwest farmers. Unused pastures and fallow farming ground have been — and are being — turned into sporting clays layouts with an eye to attaining instant cash that is not available from the farmer's grainfields until harvest time.

One farmer of our acquaintance pointed to a background of broken clays on a hillside, announcing, "That stuff marks the best-paying crop I've had on this ground in years!"

While farmers might realize additional funds by establishing such operations on their lands, the layouts can be established almost any place where it is safe to fire a shotgun. The important requirement, of course, is that there be a safety zone of at least three hundred yards in the direction the shooter is going to be firing from each of the shooting stations. In addition to farms and ranches, it is possible to install layouts at gun clubs, hunting clubs and there are instances of such land use even around the unused areas of golf courses; installations can be made in almost any area where there will be no danger of shot striking individuals, livestock or structures.

The best and most attractive layouts usually are in wooded areas featuring some hill or ridge from which high targets can be launched. If the terrain is suitable, the trap machines launching the targets can be hidden from the shooter's view. It is much more like game shooting when a target suddenly appears over trees or from behind a clump of brush.

The National Shooting Sports Foundation did some early investigating relative to this possibility and has come

Bales of straw or hay can be used to hide the trap, but this presents an obvious location. Shooter must stay within the confines of the low box during his shooting.

up with a number of suggestions a landowner might heed before setting up a course on his own wooded lands.

First, anyone planning a sporting clays installation should check with his insurance agent to determine what liabilities may be involved and how he should be insured. The landowner also should determine in advance whether there are local ordinances prohibiting such shooting facilites. Experience shows that locating such gunning grounds too close to residential areas is bound to lead to noise complaints — if nothing stronger.

The National Shooting Sports Foundation also cautions that such installations are not always compatible with livestock operations on the same ground. Hogs have been known to eat fragments of clay targets and suffer illnesses. Plastic shotshells have been eaten by cattle, so they should be picked up and carried away from the scene if livestock is grazing the terrain.

When no hills or ridges are included in the available real estate — in other words, the land is virtually flat — some type of tower should be erected to handle one or two trap machines, as the high target is an important challenge of the game. It simulates the circumstances often encountered in hunting waterfowl and dove. Needless to say, neither skeet nor trap can simulate such high altitude crossing or incoming shots.

If building a tower is impractical, it is possible to use barn tops, windmills or even water tanks as a substitute. The shooter can be down on a riverbed with the trap situated on a high embankment above him.

Several shooting stations can be set up to utilize a single tower. Situated in front of the tower, the shooter can get the high overhead incoming claybird. Moving to either right or left, he gets a chance at high crossing targets. With the shooter stationed directly beneath the tower, he also has a chance at high going-away shots. The last is similar to the angles presented by high ducks passing over from behind the duck blind.

When the land is flat, some clubs seek to obscure the origin of low targets by piling up brush, planting trees around the trap or even using hay bales as cover around the location.

If manual traps are used, it is important the operator be protected from stray pellets. This can be done by situating the traps behind a ridge or hill or by erectng some type of protection. Bales of hay are effective or one can use corrugated sheets of pellet-proof metal. Trap operators must wear shooting glasses for eye protection.

The National Sporting Clays Association is an offshoot of the National Skeet Shooting Association, as mentioned.

However, James Moore, a dentist in Houston, Texas, was instrumental in founding the U.S. Sporting Clays Association and in establishing rules for actual competition.

If you want to know more about this organization, which was founded in November, 1985, write to U.S. Sporting Clays Association, 111 N. Post Oak Lane, Suite 130, Houston, TX 77024.

The USSCA got off to a rousing start and, in the first year of its existence conducted two regional shoots and a national championship tournament. Growth since has continued at a record pace.

The USSCA has received acceptance and endorsement for the Shooting and Safety Program of the Boy Scouts of America as well as the 4-H Clubs and the NRA's Hunter Safety Program.

Sporting clays, as shot in the United States, is a far cry from the pastoral appearance of an English contest.

Course owner, designer and an instructor in sporting clays, Rick Spivey mounts his gun on a single "flushing pheasant" clay.

"IT'S BEEN said before, but I'll say it again: nothing that uses targets made of clay comes as close to hunting with a shotgun as the game of sporting clays."

Those are the words of Barry G. Davis, an outdoor writer who operates out of Merry Hill, North Carolina. In his career, he has spent a lot more years looking over his sights at live game than he has breaking clay targets. However, he has become an avid sporting clays shooter and we felt his observations worthwhile for those who are still thinking about this relatively new type of competition.

"Most of us who string words together for outdoor magazines, and who have reputations — often dubious, I might add — to uphold when in the field, are strong proponents of practice. Every year, before the start of hunting season, we preach 'practice, practice, practice.' Until only a few years ago, when sporting clays made its trans-Atlantic crossing from Great Britain, that 'practice' usually referred to a couple of rounds at the skeet or trap range, or slow, wobbly targets tossed with a hand thrower across an open field. It wasn't representative of hunting, but at least it "was something."

Hand-thrown targets have obvious limitations. And the problem with trap and skeet is their blatantly technical specialization. The average hunter with his well worn automatic or pump and briar-torn hunting vest, simply trying to get ready for the hunting season, can't relate to the regulars with their Mercedes-priced target guns and highfalutin', fancy 'accessories.' And, frankly, some skeet and trap shooters get perverse pleasure out of subtly intimidating someone who is obviously out of his element. I've seen it; you've seen it.

Flanking tower stations provide long, high crossing shots similar to pass shooting doves, geese or diver ducks. John Dunn III swings on this pair of targets. The amount of lead needed in such shots is deceptive to newcomers.

The icing on the cake usually comes after the shooting. If Junior was along to share the day with Dad, it was inevitable he'd ask why Pop missed a lot and the other folks didn't hardly miss at all? Any explanations, as legitimate as they may be, about how shooting with a mounted gun and being a robot in a fixed groove isn't the way it happens in the field; or how unrealistic it is having targets that always fly the same way at the same speed, do little to salve a beat-up ego. And you could almost guarantee that it would be a cold day in hell before he'd return to the range for another dose of humiliation.

For those of you who have gone through that, and made the same 'stick it where the sun don't shine' vow, let me tell you: Sporting clays ain't the same!

Here is a target game the average hunter can appreciate, and, best of all, do well at. It's a game in which getting "grooved" on a particular target presentation just doesn't happen, because the rules allow variables that make it next to impossible. This is a game where scores in the stratosphere are not the norm; where missing a number of targets during a round isn't confined to newcomers or the less practiced, and where regular field-type hardware doesn't instantly put you at an insurmountable disadvantage.

In fact, almost every hard-core duck hunter and bird hunter

John Dunn III takes a high crossing single at a flanking station at the tower field. Such birds are quite elusive.

Traps are hidden in heavy undergrowth in many layouts, but path of birds must be clear for proper launching.

I know who has shot it has gone back to shoot it again; many on a regular basis. Knowing the unique diversity of hunters, a consensus of agreement like that is rare. It also should tell you that sporting clays' stated purpose — to accurately simulate the types of shots in the types of conditions that an honest-to-goodness, sweaty and scratched hunter could expect in the field — has been achieved.

Even though sporting clays has grown by leaps and bounds in the past couple of years, the overwhelming majority of hunters still have yet to try it. However, before we get into a description of the mechanics of the game, the layout of a typical course, how the rules play into a hunter's hand, and some tips to make it even more enjoyable, let me make an important point.

Like every target game, there exists a segment of shooters concerned only with the competitive aspects. In sporting clays, thankfully, the segment is small. Most clays shooters — even those at the upper level of the game — are hunters first and foremost. They know what you, as a fellow hunter, are all about. They want you to succeed and get the most out of it.

If you are among the majority who still are sporting clays virgins, here's what it is. A sporting clays course consists of a number of "fields" layed out in the available natural terrain. It varies throughout the country, because the terrain itself varies. Fields set along ponds and swamp edges, cut into gaps in thick woods, or through and along hedgerows and treelines are typical. Anything goes, however, as long as the main criteria of simulating a legitimate shot at game is met.

Strategically placed around these fields are designated shooting stations, the idea being to offer a wide variety of angles at the targets being thrown. Generally speaking, a typical course will have ten or more fields and thirty-plus shooting stations — all of them not being used during a normal round. The variety, however, enables constant changes in order to keep a course "fresh." No two courses are identical, though there are universal similarities like a tower field, "fur and feather," and "driven grouse."

What you can expect is an endless variety of quartering shots, both right to left and left to right, high and low, incomers and outgoers at various heights and speeds — and some target flights that are impossible to describe in one or two words.

Beyond the standard, safety-oriented regulations, which are always paramount, sporting clays' two principal rules favor hunters. Unlike trap and skeet, the gun must be held in the low position, its butt visible below the armpit, and it cannot be mounted until the target is thrown and visible. The second rule allows for up to a three-second delay between the time the target is called for and when it's thrown. Both put a premium on fluid gun mounting, one of the keys to being a good shot on live birds, and the latter wreaks havoc with those accustomed to getting into a "timing groove" like quality shooters do in skeet and trap.

Targets are presented in a number of ways: singles; simultaneous pairs in which both targets are thrown at the same time; following pairs where one target is thrown immediately after another; or report pairs where the second bird is thrown at the sound of the shot at the first bird.

Rick Spivey takes a single at the quail flush station. Like a real quail, one never knows whether it will go left, right or straight.

The shooter knows ahead of time what's coming, but that often doesn't make it any easier.

There are differing opinions on the value of pairs for hunter practice. An authority of sorts recently proclaimed that only singles should be shot. Pairs tend to confuse the shooter, and do little to help develop field skill and technique, he complained.

Everyone's entitled to their opinion, and mine disagrees almost entirely with "singles only." It may be okay for the first round ever tried, but after that, pairs lend the necessary realistic spice to keep it interesting. A covey flush of quail or huns, a small flock of ducks or geese coming into the decoys, a pair of early-season grouse flushing in the alders all present multiple targets, and hunters have to work at being adept enough to handle the confusion. Every hunter I surveyed who has shot sporting clays wouldn't go back if it was singles only.

In addition to singles and pairs, there are also different kinds of targets. Besides the standard clay pigeon, there's the midi, which is one-third smaller and flies faster; the mini, which is one-third again smaller than the midi, and looks not much bigger than the period at the end of this sentence when it's thrown. The battue is a domeless target without a stabilizing rim that will fly erratically when kissed by a breeze, or look like the edge of a razor blade when it's not. And the "rabbit" is a flat, thick-rimmed target made to be bounced along the ground like a bounding bunny. Because of the increase in degree of difficulty, midis, minis and battues most often are reserved for tournament-level shooters pushing the envelope.

The trap machines, themselves, are specialized units. Most are operated manually and are fully adjustable with dual arms that permit slight variations in angle from one target to the next. Unlike the automatic traps seen at regulation U.S. trap and skeet ranges — and the little backyard throwers many hunters have used — sporting clays machines can be cranked up to throw targets much faster and farther.

Regulations and intentions are a good foundation, but the proof in the pudding is how clays stacks up to the real

Rick Spivey works a nearly vertically thrown single at the so-called springing teal station, a real challenge.

thing. Let's shoot through a few of the typical fields and stations to give you a better idea.

Virtually all clays courses have a tower field; some have more than one. Heights range from twenty-five feet or so and up. A normal setup employs a pair of traps; one at the top of the tower, one at the base. Shooting stations are laid out adjacent to the tower — and even from a platform ten feet up on the tower itself.

The flanking stations take high, crossing targets thrown from the top machine. This resembles long-range shooting at high-flying doves as they cruise a feeding field, pass shooting at diving ducks crossing the edge of a big water spread, or even at geese that have become decoy shy from heavy pressure. Don't be surprised if, on a simultaneous pair, you break the trailing target when you were shooting at the lead one. Most hunters miss long shots by failing to incorporate enough lead, and the tower field is quick to make that clear.

The platform station, where the targets blast out literally from beneath your feet, is quite similar to the hard-driving flush of big-field, Midwest pheasants propelled by a typical twenty-mile-an-hour Great Plains tailwind. Hesitate and the second bird of a pair is long gone.

Another typical clays field/station is the "quail flush." The shooter sets up fifteen yards or so directly behind a well concealed and protected trap. At the call, a pair of targets are thrown either ninety degrees left, ninety degrees right or straightaway. There's no way to see or know which until it happens, and it's just like moving in over a covey point where edge cover meets the woods. You have a general idea where the birds will fly, but nothing's certain until they bust out from under the dog's nose. The key is being prepared to take them, no matter what the direction, and it's a prime example of the need for proper body mechanics and flexibility on the swing.

Proper foot placement and fluidity in the hips and torso are critical, because everything in the art of wingshooting literally revolves around them. Unlike skeet and trap, where muscle moves become memorized and precise, because target flight and speed never vary, clays places a

Shooter zeroes in on an overhead outgoing single at the stand known as the beaver pond. This area also is used for low over-the-water shots that shatter confidence.

huge emphasis on smooth, spontaneous reaction; the same quality necessary to kill birds in the field.

The driven-grouse sequence has a European origin. Incoming targets are thrown directly overhead. It wouldn't be bad if the station was set back sixty yards, but most courses have it well within forty. Your reaction time and gun-mounting skills really are put to the test. If your swing blots them out, the targets should inkball. Unfortunately, many shooters — yours truly included — have a tendency to lift their heads off the stock to follow the flight path, and that's a guaranteed miss.

Another customary field is the springing-teal event, where single and double targets are thrown near vertical in a small opening in the woods. Visibility is no problem, but tempering your swing to match the quickly decreasing speed of the targets is. Break the first one on the way up, the second at the crest of flight, and you're in business; wait 'til they start falling, and you're in trouble. Pulling a gun muzzle below a horizontal plane is much more difficult than pushing it above.

A particularly challenging true-to-life station is the woodcock. Here the trap is hidden downslope in the woods. The targets are thrown in a fashion somewhat similar to springing teal, except that they are hidden, off and on, throughout their flight. The brief "windows of opportunity" you have are almost identical to shooting grouse or woodcock in dense, second-story growth.

I really focus on this field before an extended trip to grouse country in order to fine-tune my rhythm, reaction time and hand/eye coordination. It's paid multiple dividends, particularly in dense, early-season coverts where the spruces, paper birches and alders make you feel like you are shooting in a dimly lit grade-school cloakroom. The only thing that could make the station more realistic would be to have someone smacking you with branches just as the targets are thrown!

Duck hunters also are given their fair share of opportunities. One of my favorite fields at a course I regularly shoot is called the wood duck hole. Three trap machines and six stations are set around half of a beaver pond. Shots range from slowly settling incomers — just like ducks dropping into a decoy spread — to overhead outgoers that start from behind the shooter and escape into a stand of cypress trees, like wood ducks hurtling through flooded timber.

The variety of target presentations possible at all of the stations are too numerous to mention, but they cover almost everything I've ever seen while hunting puddle ducks. You may not get wet and cold, but your duck shooting skill is definitely tested.

Fur and feather is a virtual standard at every regulation sporting clays course. Here, a rabbit target is bounced along the ground in front of the shooter, and, at the shot, a low-flying, crossing target is launched along the same path. The rabbit can be tricky, because you never know how it's

High-angle shots, whether incoming or outgoing, call for an adjusted stance and rotating hip action!

going to bounce. Some skim the ground, others hop up and down like a kangaroo on steroids. The trick is to not ride it too long, or your swing will exceed the point where it can be controlled. Pick the spot where you want to break it ahead of time, then break it right there! That's how to do it. The problem is sometimes the rabbit has a mind of its own.

There are other fields and stations on every course that test you on quartering shots, outgoers and crossers, through cover and wide open, fast and slow. The variations are infinite, but I think you get the picture. A normal round of fifty targets takes anywhere from an hour to two hours to complete. Depending upon the course, the cost will range

from $15 to $25. Granted, that's proportionately more than trap or skeet, but the variety of target presentations alone makes it worthwhile.

Sporting clays also doesn't require you to outfit yourself with specialty stuff in order to immediately gain something from it. It occurs the second you slip the first shell into the chamber of your favorite bird gun.

For a hunter new to the game, his field gun usually will do just fine. In fact, a shooting instructor/friend suggests a newcomer only makes things more difficult if he doesn't use it.

My first rounds were shot with a well traveled side-by-

Cover and obstructions all are part of hunting, and are recreated in this game. Shooter prepares for quartering target appearing in gap in woods line.

side field gun with a straight stock, double triggers and interchangeable chokes. Since then, I've moved to a Marocchi Avanza Sporting Clays O/U, because it has a more appropriate balance, yet still retains the quickness I like in a gun. However, I still shoot the side-by-side occasionally, particularly just before hunting season.

Improved cylinder, the choke of choice for most bird-hunters, is suitable for ninety percent of the targets on a standard clays course. Sporting clays rules limit loads to 1⅛ ounces of #7½s, 8s or 9s; you can compensate for longer targets by shooting #7½s rather than the usual #8s. The only other things you'll need are common-sense items like eye protection, ear protection and something in which to tote around your shells. A belt-style shell bag is convenient, but a bargain-basement alternative is a carpenter's apron. It ain't pretty, but it works. And when you're taking your first taste of clays, pretty doesn't matter.

More important than the accessories and hardware is approaching the game with an open mind. The average first-time score for an experienced field shot is eighteen to twenty-two out of a round of fifty. At first, it's depressing, but remember, missing is no big deal; *everyone* misses at clays, some just more frequently than others. To put it into perspective, I've seen a former All-American, who's normal average is eighty percent, shoot below sixty percent. It happens. And when you're practicing to improve your field skills, the final score is not the end-all and be-all. It's what you've learned that counts.

A range-owner friend of mine put the value of sporting clays into perspective when he said, "Seventy-five years ago, a man could learn to shoot in the field. Bag limits were high or didn't exist at all, game was readily available, and the inevitable misses and mistakes — the greatest teachers of all — were not critically important.

"Today, the world has changed; hunting is a completely different ball game. The average hunter will see only a few birds in a normal day, and the odds are next to nil that he'll ever get sufficient chances on live game to improve, let alone perfect, his shotgunning technique.

"If he doesn't invest at least a little bit of time in realistic practice, then the few opportunities he does get will end in failure. And if there are enough frustrating days of failure, it won't be long before he gives up hunting all together. As a group, it's something we hunters simply can't afford to let happen."

For those of us whose principal interest lies in the hedgerows and coverts, the marshes and fields, there is a sportsman's obligation to bring the few opportunities we get to a clean and fruitful conclusion. Becoming a better field shot is the best way to fulfill the obligation, and sporting clays can help make it happen. The bottom line: It's as close to the "real" thing as you can get.

CHAPTER 2

GETTING STARTED IN SPORTING CLAYS

Most sporting clays ranges in the United States are new and in excellent condition. All welcome beginners to the sport, with plenty of coaching and advice available to get the shooter started. Most will find standard skeet/trap guns adequate.

SPORTING CLAYS is new and growing rapidly in popularity in the United States, although developed about sixty years ago in England. Said to be America's fastest growing sport, there are about four hundred sporting clays facilities around the country. More are on the way, as interest continues to grow.

The sport offers several challenges to shooters, whether they are hunters looking for warm-up practice before the seasons open or skeet and trap shooters who want something different in the way of challenge. The course is supposed to simulate hunting habitat and situations as realistically as possible. Several different types of clays are thrown in actual habitat, mirroring rabbits and various

You Probably Have More Of The
Needed Equipment Than You Think!

Each sporting clays course is influenced by the terrain and geographical considerations; no two are alike. Experienced clays shooter Chuck Stapel, above and right, shows how and where targets are expected to appear.

game birds that may be found in the area.

In some ways, the sporting clays game resembles skeet and trap shooting, but is more exciting because of the wide variety of throwing patterns. Similar to golf, sporting clays provides a course to be followed by the shooter. The more the shooter practices — again, similar to golf — the better he or she should become.

No two sporting clays courses are exactly alike, because the terrain and habitat will vary from one geographic location to the next. Furthermore, the shooting stations at any course may be varied from one day to the next, depending upon local conditions, weather and shooters' desires. The United States Sporting Clays Association, (USSCA) does determine that a course will have ten stations which simulate the flight or run of game such as rabbit, duck, quail, dove, chukar, geese, pheasant or other local upland game birds or waterfowl.

Starting out in the sport requires a certain amount of basic equipment, but the trap and skeet shooter already will have the necessities. Almost any shotgun of 12-gauge or smaller bore will do the job — with the exception of a single-shot, single-barrel gun, of course. Official rules do not permit anything larger than 12-gauge, so leave that 10-gauge boomer at home.

The type of shotgun seen most commonly on the course is an over/under skeet gun. However, the beginning sporting clays shooter need not go out and purchase the most expensive imported, customized over/under to be successful. Any gun suitable for trap or skeet shooting will do the job. Special stocks, ported barrels and built-in recoil-reducing devices may be tested, and perhaps added to the gun case at a later date.

While the over/under shotgun is the most popular gun for sporting clays, it is not the only type seen on the course. Slide-actions, autoloaders and side-by-sides are used successfully in this sport. Many feel the autoloader is easier on the shooter through at least a hundred rounds over the course, and a proficient pump-gun shooter can score on doubles as quickly and easily as most over/under shooters.

The beginner should keep in mind though, that the original concept of sporting clays was to simulate and practice for bird and small-game hunting, so any shotgun that feels comfortable may be used in the game. The rules permit no more than two rounds to be loaded at a time; this applies to pump-action and autoloading shotguns.

Nor does the sporting clays shooter have to shoot only a 12-gauge gun. Those seeking greater challenge are shooting 20-gauge and even .410-bore shotguns in the game. The lighter shotguns have the advantage of swinging faster for better follow-through — in the hands of some shooters. Shooting a good score at sporting clays is never easy, but adding the additional handicap of shooting the course with a diminutive .410 would be a challenge. But it has been done.

Part of the enjoyment of any sport is improvement as time goes on. Keeping score adds to the competition and progress. Each station is equipped with a handy gun rack.

At the Passing Mallards station, the shooter is looking up a hill, awaiting targets thrown from behind brush.

A wooden frame at each station defines and restricts the range of barrel swing permitted for safe shooting.

Most beginners to the sport probably will want to try it first with a 12-gauge shotgun — most likely an over/under. Barrel lengths of twenty-six and twenty-eight inches seem about right for most. Look for barrels choked for skeet, trap or improved cylinder. If interchangeable choke tubes are part of the shotgun, chokes in the aforementioned persuasions should be installed.

Chokes or even complete barrels may be changed during shooting competition, but the change must be done only between fields, not between different stations on the same field. Competitors may shoot different guns and attempt shots at various targets with different guns or perhaps the guns of another shooter. But guns are changed only between fields and not between different stations on the same field.

It always is a good idea to pattern the gun the first time it is used, because different chokes may be more suitable for some shooters. Some barrels print their shot patterns in different areas and configurations than others, using the same ammunition. The shooter should know and not guess where the shot string is likely to go for every shot.

Most shotgun manufacturers now are producing smooth-bores expressly designed for sporting clays shooting. Among the features are slightly lighter weight for faster swing and a slightly weight-forward balance to the gun. Many manufacturers and importers also are offering optional barrel porting to reduce the amount of felt recoil to the shooter. A

Cloherty, right, demonstrates what the correct sight alignment for sporting clays shooting should look like. Most gunners will do well with a single-bead picture.

John Cloherty is a Southern California shotgunner and certified USSCA instructor. He also offers trick shooting exhibitions at various Southwestern shotgun ranges.

rubber recoil pad would seem essential, but it should be solid to maintain maximum shooter control, smooth gun mounting and quick second-shot recovery. Beginners, as well as all shooters, should make sure the gun fits. Length of pull should be short enough that the butt does not become hung up beneath the arms or on the biceps on the way to a fast mount.

Some experienced clay shooters remove the front sight bead from the top of the barrel rib, if one is mounted on the gun. Instead of the typical figure eight sight bead alignment, the shooter sees only the center bead on top of the rib. The shooter should not see any of the top of the rib while taking a good shooting position. Doing so usually will cause the shots to go too high above the target.

The head should be in a comfortable, relaxed position on the stock, without straining too far forward on the cheek piece. If the length of pull is too short, the head and eyes will be too far forward. No two shooters are exactly alike as far as head shape and size, arm length, shoulder width and other physical factors are concerned, so gun fit should be worked out carefully between the shooter and a knowledgeable coach or fellow shooter.

Barrel ribs, rib width — tapering or not — sight beads and other sighting options are a matter of shooter choice. If whatever the shooter finds comfortable works well when shooting skeet or trap, the same configuration should do well for sporting clays. Most target shooters will prefer not to have an automatic safety on the gun, but if this shooting is intended as a warm-up for hunting seasons, a gun with that feature can be used on the sporting clays range.

The beginner should plan on firing a considerable amount of ammunition to learn the sport just as he or she would when learning trap or skeet. The official course consists of a hundred shots. During sanctioned competition, only factory ammunition may be fired, but reloads are permitted during informal shooting or practice by any shooter.

Roger Combs shows good sporting clays form with the right elbow well up, the butt into the shoulder, head straight and the body balanced equally on both feet. On all targets, the gun must swing smoothly through.

Right: Patricia Wallig swings on a doubles target.

When shooting 12-gauge ammunition, loads must not exceed 1⅛ ounces of lead or plated lead shot. Maximum powder charge cannot exceed 3¼ dram equivalent. Shot size should not exceed number 7½ nor be smaller than number 9. Several ammunition companies are producing special sporting clays ammunition, just as some make special skeet or trap loads. Any legal factory load will do the job, if that is what is on hand. The first-time shooter may wish to experiment with rounds of 7½s, 8s and 9s to determine which works better. Later, some sporting clays loads can be tried, remembering that different loads will act differently through different guns.

Once the gun and ammunition have been selected, there are a few more essential pieces of gear the sporting clays shooter must — or, at least should — have. Depending on the weather, a shooting vest or jacket is something most shooters would not want to be without. An upland game shooting vest or jacket will do as well as a special skeet or trap shooting coat so long as the shoulder area has adequate padding.

Most shooting vests have two or more large pockets for carrying loaded shells in one side and empty hulls in the other. Many shooters carry a shell bag in addition to or instead of carrying shells in pockets. Shell bags usually will

Most, but not all, sporting clays is shot with over/under guns in 12-gauge. Gun must be broken and unloaded when out of box.

accommodate at least a hundred rounds — four boxes — of ammunition. Sporting clays stations always are some distance apart, depending on the terrain and course layout, so there may be considerable walking involved. Shooters should find it restful to carry shells in a bag that can be placed on the bench while shooting.

Official USSCA rules recommend but do not require the use of ear and eye protection for all shooters. Professional shooters never shoot without both, and every shooter should consider them mandatory. Eyes and ears always should be well protected. Shooting glasses may be plain or ground to prescription. They can be of almost any color that does not distort colors and lenses should be made of any strong, shatter-resistant material.

Hearing protectors also should be worn when shooting or when near other shooters. If the shooter's head and gun stock configuration permit, many believe that ear muff-type protectors are the best to wear. But not everyone can wear them when shooting shotguns. Commercially made ear plugs of rubber, plastic or sponge foam are the common types. A step beyond standard plugs is the E.A.R. Insta-Foam custom-made protectors. These are made of a special fast-hardening foam which, when installed correctly, actually conforms to the inside of individual ear canals. These plugs offer excellent sound protection for most people and do not interfere with shooting technique.

Many sporting clays courses are laid out over rugged terrain, typical of that found in upland or small-game fields. Footing can be unsteady from one station to the next — not at all like the manicured fields and paths of the skeet range — and good footwear is recommended for beginners and experts alike. In some areas, it pays to watch for rattlesnakes while walking from one area to the next. Hunting boots add a feeling of security under such circumstances and tend to add to the realism of pre-season practice.

On the course, the clay targets may be presented to the shooter from almost any direction, height or speed. Given the appropriate terrain, targets may fly from high above the

Chuck Stapel has shot the Moore-N-Moore Los Angeles sporting clays course many times and demonstrates the preferred position for the targets. Shotgun is unloaded.

At this station, both targets fly from behind bushes on the high right of the shooter.

Here, the shooter shows poor form as he lifts his cheek from the stock in an effort to see the oncoming targets.

shooter or originate from beneath a steep hill on which the competitor is standing. They may be fast or slow and often are affected by the prevailing winds. Some will sail out of sight over trees, bushes or nearby hillsides, if missed by the shotgunner.

John Cloherty is a Southern California trick shooter and certified USSCA sporting clays instructor. He shoots a lot of sporting clays throughout much of the West and has watched and coached hundreds of shooters. He has some helpful hints for beginners and more experienced sporting clays shotgunners.

Cloherty's first admonition is to obtain a shotgun that fits the shooter. This, he says, is essential, because the wrong gun will cause poor results and discourage the beginner. An improperly fitted gun also will tend to cause too much felt recoil and transmit pain and even injury to the shooter.

With the right gun and at least a hundred rounds of ammunition in bags and pockets, wearing the appropriate clothing, the shooter is ready to pay the nominal fee and shoot sporting clays. Most courses are laid out so that one or more of the stations are visible from the club house. It is the shooter's option as to which station he will use to begin the course. The stations are numbered from one to ten, but there is no need to take them in order. The shooter may start at ten and work down, begin in the middle or select any station of choice, as long as each station is shot.

The shooter should take a firm stance in the box or stand. The ground may be rough or loose and firm footing is essential. Plant the left toe — assuming you're a right-hand shooter — toward the area where the clay is expected to be broken. Starting out with the body turned too far in either direction will cause the shooter to twist his or her torso out of balance when the barrel follows the claybird. Other shooters or partners who have shot the course before usually are happy to pass on their experience to novice shooters and may be able to point out the expected "kill" zone.

The shooter's knees should be bent slightly, the weight balanced over both feet. Beware of leaning too far into or out of a good skeet shooting stance. Many sporting clays stations have a wood or metal framework or cage surrounding the shooter. The frame usually is there to keep the shooter from swinging too far in any direction and thus endangering shooters at other stations. Until one has become used to such a station, some beginners may tend to lean too far forward in an effort to "get out of the box." The shooter soon learns there is plenty of room to swing the barrel and make the shot.

The shotgun butt cannot be mounted at the shoulder before the shooter sees the target. The butt must be visible below the armpit and above the belt line. Most will want to press the stock against the body as far forward as possible

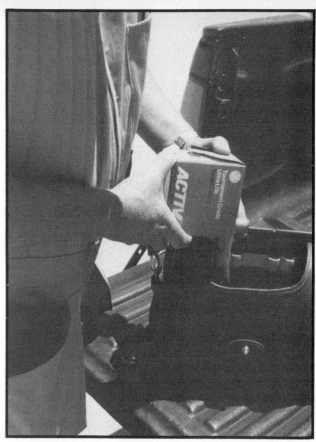

A standard round of sporting clays will require at least a hundred rounds of ammunition. While the shells may be in vest pockets, a shouldered shell carrier is handy.

The range manager may use his imagination when setting up shooting stations, including the use of an old duck boat.

The message of the sign on the stern of the boat is always good to remember. Gun action should be unloaded and open.

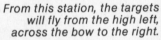

From this station, the targets will fly from the high left, across the bow to the right.

for a quick mount just beneath the shoulder pocket. For a right-hand shooter, the right elbow should be raised as high as is still comfortable in the ready position.

Still using our right-handed shooter as an example, the left-hand should be placed on the gun's forend quite far forward. Extend the left forefinger straight along the side of the forend as in pointing. Instructor Cloherty insists the technique is to actually point at the target with the left forefinger as it passes into view.

"Swing slowly," says Cloherty. "Be calm. Don't rush the shot."

Most beginners tend to rush the shot, swing too fast and overestimate the speed of the claybird. Sporting clays is so close to real bird shooting that most shooters get a rush of

The dry land boat is hung from four posts and springs to simulate the feel of a craft in water. Patricia Wallig takes a practice swing to feel the boat's action before shooting.

adrenaline when they call for the bird, often tensing up and swinging erratically. They also may tend to climb up on the stock, pushing the face and cheek too far forward on the cheek piece, changing the sight alignment.

Calling for a look at the clay targets without shooting the first round is appropriate etiquette. The first-time shooter especially will want to become familiar with the trajectory of the targets. The clays, by the way, may be colored green, white, red, black or any other color the range manager thinks appropriate. The rabbit target often is a thin, black disk, considerably faster than the standard saucer-shape claybird.

The gun's action must be open as the shooter steps into the shooting stand, which usually measures slightly less than a meter on each side. If the station is in a circle, it should measure one meter in diameter. The shooter must stand with both feet within the limits of the stand, loading two rounds when ready, always keeping the muzzle pointed in a safe direction. The gun must be held in both hands, the gun clearly off the shoulder and the stock touching the body under the armpit. The position must be maintained until the targets are in sight.

Upon the call, "Ready!" or "Pull!" by the shooter, the trapper has from zero to three seconds to release the clay

A shotgun from the seated position seems a bit awkward to most gunners, but it is a realistic shot for duck hunters. The intent of the sport is to simulate actual hunting situations and the spring-mounted boat bounces at slightest movement.

targets. The shooter may mount the gun only when the targets are in sight. If the targets are controlled electrically, a member of the squad may activate the push-button activator. Otherwise, the call must be loud enough for the trap operators to hear before they release the clays.

Once the clays are in sight, the gun is mounted and the shooter fires at all targets — including the rabbit clay, if appropriate. Some stations are true doubles; both targets are released at the same time and the shooter must hit each in either order. At some stations, the second target is released "on report," or as the sound of the first shot is heard by the trapper. Other doubles come following shots; the second target is released after the first, regardless of a

hit on the first. In simultaneous pairs, the shooter may fire at either of the targets first, and if the first is missed, the second round may be fired at the first target. Of course, if the second target is not shot at, but the second round breaks the first target, the second target is scored as a miss. On some doubles, the targets will virtually cross trajectories at some point. If a shooter breaks both clays with one shot, the score will be two kills.

Targets that appear already broken or do not fly from the trap in the obvious trajectory of others are called "no bird" and are not engaged by the shooter. The shooter then calls for another target.

As mentioned, instructor John Cloherty favors a slow,

It is estimated that a challenging sporting clays course may be set up on about ten acres or more of land. As the popularity grows, one expects to find more of them.

Safety rules are clearly posted in several areas throughout most sporting clays courses. When not shooting, the gun must always be kept open and unloaded.

RUSTLING GUNS
NO SMOKING
OPEN & UNLOADED
SHOOT ONLY IN BLINDS
DO NOT SHOOT CHIPS
STAY ON WALKWAYS
NO ALCOHOL ON COURSE
THINK SAFETY

steady barrel swing when shooting sporting clays. He also favors the "through" swing, the muzzle starting slightly behind the target, swinging through and in front of the claybird as the trigger is squeezed. To do this effectively, the swing must follow the trajectory of the target exactly. If the barrel wavers slightly above or below the line of the target flight, a miss is likely.

"Think of the shot string as a three-dimensional thick stream, not as a pattern on a sheet of paper," Cloherty says. "If the muzzle is slightly above or below the target, the claybird is not likely to meet up with any of the shot. But if the gun is fired when the muzzle is just ahead of the bird, some percentage of the shot has a good chance of breaking the clay target.

"The swing must be smooth and accurate. Pass through the target before the trigger is squeezed. Keep the muzzle swinging after the shell has been fired. A lot of beginners want to stop the muzzle as the trigger is pulled and the target flies past before the shot string arrives to connect with it."

The correct technique is to concentrate on the target to the exclusion of everything else. The shooter must learn to concentrate hard on the flying clay and not allow focus to shift from the barrel to the target and back. Attempting to align the barrel with the target will result in a miss. The sight focus of the barrel should be slightly fuzzy, but the claybird should be sharply in focus. Snapping the focus to the muzzle, even for an instant, costs fractions of moments and probably a lost bird. Such lack of concentration is common with many beginning sporting clays shooters, according to Cloherty.

As with any other hand/eye-coordinated sport, plenty of practice is necessary for better scores. The novice should not be discouraged by a series of missed targets. With a properly fitted gun, correct loads and equipment, better scores will follow. Watch the claybirds, concentrate on the targets and listen to experienced sporting clay shooters; "dead" birds will follow.

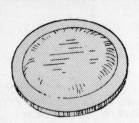

CHAPTER 3

WHAT, WHERE & WHEN TO SHOOT

WHEN ONE considers all of the possible combinations and permutations of target presentations in sporting clays, it is mind boggling. Simply put, there are an infinite number of possibilities. However, it is not necessary to list or discuss them all, because most are nothing more or less than variations of the basics.

Basic target presentations in sporting clays are incoming, going away, right-to-left crossers, left-to-right crossers, rising, falling and quartering. That is simple enough, but when it comes to shooting a station, one learns instantly that most presentations are combinations of two or more of the above — simultaneously. It is a four-dimensional reality.

Sporting Clays Provides Challenges
Not Experienced In Other Claybird Games

For example, an incoming target also might be quartering, while it is coming in. The same is true for the going away target. Or the target might be incoming, quartering and rising or dropping, all at the same time. The possibilities go on and on.

Hence, to be reasonably successful, the shooter must learn to "read" the targets — to see exactly what the target is doing. This differs from some of the other forms of clay target shooting in a number of respects. For example, it is possible in some types of trap shooting for the shooter to "read" the trap and know with a degree of certainty exactly which target presentation he or she will get.

And even in the forms of trap shooting where reading the trap itself is not possible, there are comparatively few variations of target presentation relative to the shooting position. For example, one knows automatically that all trap targets will be rising as they leave the trap and that they will fly outward within a defined horizontal arc from the trap.

Similarly, skeet shooters know in advance that the target will fly within an established line from each trap each time they are thrown. Hence, in skeet it is not only possible but virtually mandatory for the shooter to "read" the course.

All of this is moot in sporting clays, because no two courses are the same and it is only coincidental that a shooter would ever find exactly the same combination of factors on a given station from one course to another. Couple that with the natural variables of wind, lighting and cover, and sporting clays takes on new dimensions.

Steve Comus is one of those folks with an inquiring mind, so we asked him to take a hard, long look at what goes on at the various stations and with the differing targets. This is his report:

"In sporting clays, it is imperative that the shooter read the target, as opposed to shooting the trap or the course," he concludes.

Since most sporting clays target presentations are patterned after the characteristics of some kind of bird or upland game animal, field hunters and waterfowlers generally do at least passably well when introduced to the game.

However, there is simply no way that a clay target can duplicate exactly something that is alive. To accommodate this sort of difference, the target presentations on most sporting clays facilities are actually somewhat more difficult than are similar presentations by actual living things.

Here is where the competitive shooters and the casual participants part company. Casual shooters — most of whom are also hunters — rely primarily upon instinct shooting. This particular brand of shooting is pretty much what it sounds like: The shooter uses natural coordination to see the target, swing the gun and pull the trigger.

However, as the target angles and presentations become

When shooting crossing targets, pay close attention to target's flight to be certain it's not rising, falling.

more complex, the instinct-only shooter begins to drop scores. That is why, for example, that people who are good field shooters have no trouble scoring consistently in the sixties and even seventies (out of one hundred targets) on most courses. Yet, those same shooters find that registering significantly higher scores on any kind of a consistent basis seems ever elusive.

Here is where basic shooting techniques come into play. The higher up the scale the competitive shooters get, the more they find they need to be able to use any or all techniques, depending upon what they encounter on a course.

In addition to the basic instinctive approach, there are essentially two major shotgun target shooting techniques in sporting clays. There is the come-from-behind tech-

Sporting clays often use bodies of water in presentation of shot. Hooking, incoming clay imitates decoyed duck.

nique in which the shooter spots the target, shoulders the gun and begins the swing from behind the target, tracking it all the way. Then, it is merely a matter of accelerating the swing to make the gun swing through the target and, as the barrel pulls away, squeeze off the shot — continuing the follow-through swing, of course.

This technique is rather easy to remember by reducing the concept to the Four Bs — Butt, Belly, Beak, Bang! This is by far the most commonly encountered technique in sporting clays and is the method most often used by top competitors like world champ A.J. "Smoker" Smith from England.

The other basic technique is a form of sustained lead, much like that used in skeet shooting. In shooting this technique, the shooter never allows the barrel to be behind the target. Rather, the shooter looks at the target presentation and decides where in the flight it should be broken. Then, before calling for the target, the shooter positions the muzzle of the gun so it is pointing at a spot just beneath the line of flight and about halfway between the trap and the point where the shot will be taken.

Then, when the target is launched, the shooter visually picks up the target and begins the swing as the gun is mounted. Instinctively, as the target and the muzzle of the gun come into the proper relationship to each other, the shot is taken and the target breaks.

This technique takes a little more practice to perfect than the come-from-behind method, but it is an essential basic for anyone considering serious competition. The reason is simple. This technique allows a quicker shot than any other. Some target presentations simply do not allow the amount of time it takes to shoot them consistently any other way.

When the surrounding terrain is varied in nature, course can include targets that follow the ridges and valleys,

The sustained lead technique has become most well known in sporting clays circles as the "Move, Mount, Shoot" approach, which is espoused by world champ John Bidwell of England.

Regardless which technique is used, there are some basic things a shooter can do when getting set up in the shooting cage that can help increase the number of targets broken. The most important thing does not even require that the shooter be in the cage. It is the act of determining what the target's actual flight presentation is at each station.

For example, a great many courses may seem more difficult than they really are, simply because the shooter is deceived by the presentation. The shooter may think a particular target is a simple right-to-left crosser. But if it also happens to be quartering slightly at the same time, or going up or down at the same time, shooting it like it was a simple crosser will result in a miss.

Terrain factors like foliage or hills really can confuse shooters. Here, a target might look like a simple crosser because its line of flight follows a terrain feature. However, by looking closely, it becomes apparent that the terrain feature is going uphill or downhill. That means the target not only is crossing, but it also is rising or falling at the same time.

Once the actual presentation is determined, the shooter steps into the cage and prepares to shoot the station. Remembering what the presentation looks like, the shooter points the main part of his or her body (the belt buckle is a good aiming point) at the spot where the target is to be broken. From that point, configure the body for the necessary swing, as well as adjust the head so the target can be seen at its earliest point in the presentation. Then, it is simply a matter of calling for the target and shooting it.

For a detailed look at the ways to shoot the various basic forms of target presentations, consider each individually. This also will allow for consideration of the many variations.

INCOMING

A pure incoming shot would see the trap directly in front of the shooting cage; it might also be above or below the cage. Also, a pure incoming target would typically fly directly overhead or fall short and in front of the cage.

To shoot this type of presentation, the shooter merely needs to stand facing the trap directly, hold the gun in the low position and call for the target. When the target appears, mount the gun and shoot. If it is a presentation in which the target goes overhead, the come-from-behind technique works superbly. If a "dying quail" or "decoying duck" sort of presentation, in which the target falls short of the shooting station, it might be best to sustain the lead. Otherwise, as the target falls it can be obscured from view by the barrels of the gun — and missed.

More often than not, however, incoming presentations in sporting clays are not simple and pure incomers. Instead,

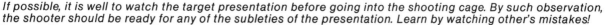

If possible, it is well to watch the target presentation before going into the shooting cage. By such observation, the shooter should be ready for any of the subleties of the presentation. Learn by watching other's mistakes!

It is important to be ready to break a clay target at the best spot in its flight. To increase your success, it is critical that you, as the shooter, be ready to slap the trigger before you consider calling for target.

they are quartering incoming presentations in which the target is approaching the station at an angle. Also, that angle would rarely intersect the station itself. Rather, the target would be coming toward the station and angling right or left, actually passing the station a distance out from the shooter. On tournament-level courses, this target also is likely to be rising or falling simultaneously.

It is quite easy to miss when shooting such a compound target presentation. Not only would one need the amount of "lead" indicated by the speed and distance of the incoming shot, but there needs to be a right or left allowance for the quartering angle of flight, as well.

It is relatively simple to determine how much to allow, assuming the shooter recognizes that such a compound allowance is needed. However, if the shooter has not looked closely and determined the flight path properly, he or she could shoot the entire station and never hit a target. This is often what happens when the shooter obviously doesn't

Shooter at left is in the cage. Others in the squad are watching to see what target will do in their turns.

have a clue about what is going wrong. Hence, when a target presentation seems totally elusive — when it is anything but an absolute incoming or going away target — chances are it is being missed either from behind and/or from one side or the other.

GOING AWAY

To a certain extent, going away target presentations call for movements that are the reverse of those for incomers. But only to an extent. Physical limitations dictate that there cannot be as many variations of a true incomer as there are for going away shots. The reason is simple. If the trap was right in front of the shooter, the trap and/or trapper would be shot. For going away presentations, this is not a factor.

Trap shooters usually do well with sporting clays going-away target presentations. So do upland bird hunters. For these shots, the shooter again stands in the cage, pointing the body at the spot where the target will be broken. Then, the shooter configures the stance so the target can be spotted visually and the gun is put into motion for the shot.

Most going-away presentations also see the target rising or falling simultaneously. For going-away risers, it is essentially a flushing pheasant or traditional trap shot proposition. To shoot it, simply spot the target visually, bring the muzzle of gun up to the target and shoot, continuing the gun follow-through, of course.

However, going-away targets that also are falling can be quite challenging. Follow-through is critical. The shooter not only must maintain an arc that stays on the line of target flight, but also must adjust timing correctly or the target will be missed, the shot pattern going high over the target.

Again, there is rarely a totally straight going-away presentation. Most have some degree of quartering angle as well — with a rising or falling aspect not uncommon. To the degree that the target is quartering, the shooter must

Brian Ballard, a member of the U.S. Shooting Team, shows proper way to prepare for sporting clays target. He watches carefully to spot target at earliest moment.

Sporting clays shooters start at the low gun position, bringing the gun up and on line in one smooth movement when a target has been released and spotted.

It is important to configure the shooting stance to be able to hit targets, whether high or low.

compensate in gun-to-target relationship. Otherwise, the target will be missed, most commonly from behind and from right or left, depending upon which way the quartering angle is going.

CROSSING SHOTS

Classic crossing shots are those encountered on stations two through six on a typical American skeet field. In sporting clays, the major differences are the varying distances, as well as the compounding factors like simultaneous rising, falling or quartering characteristics.

Also complicating such shots on many sporting clays courses are terrain features like the sides of hills, trees or other visual obstructions. These limit the time and distances at which the target can be seen and shot.

When time allows, the come-from-behind technique is classic for such shots. Or, for those who have perfected the procedure, hitting true crossers can be done like a machine with the sustained-lead technique.

For these shots, however, it is critical that the shooter's body be pointed toward where the target will be broken. This way, the swing is both easier and more consistent. With crossers, it is much easier to determine if there is a rising or falling characteristic in the target flight. However, the more subtle any quartering angle might be on crossers, the more technically demanding the presentation becomes. When any kind of crossing target is missed repeatedly, there are normally some quick remedies that should put the shooter back on track.

Most shooters miss crossers because they shoot behind the target. This is the result of a failure to match the speed of the target, or because the shooter failed to follow through with the swing. This is when the shooter does everything right until the moment of the shot, then stops the swing of the gun when the trigger is squeezed. It is called "dead gunning" and it guarantees a miss.

If the shooter does the swing and follow-through correctly and the target still doesn't break, the problem is likely complicated by some undetermined degree of quartering or rising or falling. Look carefully at the target flight, determine

Unlike traditional claybird games, sporting clays makes use of natural terrain. Note that women are joining the ranks and competing. (Below) While competition can be a serious matter, new friendships tend to be important, too.

Some stations may present a high degree of difficulty due to hills or bushes obscuring the target most of time.

Rising shots call for the shooter to be able to swing a gun on line with the target, pass through, then shoot.

which other factor or factors also are involved and allow for them as well. Suddenly, what had been a seemingly impossible target to hit becomes an easy break.

RISING TARGETS

Most sporting clays courses have at least one true rising target presentation. It often is called the Rising Teal station. Here, the target or targets (there are both singles and pairs) are launched essentially straight up into the air from the trap.

If it is not broken on the way up, the target here continues its upward flight, slowing as it goes and then peaking out at a particular point. Then, it begins falling. Since it is almost impossible for any trap to throw targets exactly straight up, they tend to go up in a slight arc and fall in a slower and more pronounced opposite arc. They may also be incoming slightly or going away slightly at the same time.

There are several ways to shoot these presentations. Most of the time when they are missed, it is because the shooter rushed the shot. If the target is to be broken on the way up, the technique is simple. Point the body in the proper direction, call for the target and, as it comes into view, begin moving the gun as it is being mounted to the shoulder. Then simply come up from behind and, as the gun continues to pass through the target, shoot.

If the target hangs at its highest point, and if the shooter's

Above: Sides of shooting cage can obscure target in its initial flight. (Upper right) Shooters watch the targets before going into the cage to determine the flight path.

Right: Shooting cages are designed to limit swing of the shooter for safety purposes, but this limitation can make matters difficult as it determines shooter's stance.

timing is good, it can be broken as a dead-on spot shot as it peaks.

There is still another way to shoot this particular target presentation which, for some reason, seems to escape the imagination of many shooters. This factor also can come into play when pairs are shot at such a station and there is time to break only one of the targets as they go up. That means the second of the pair will have to be shot as it falls in an arc. If the shooter opts, the falling shot here is really not all that difficult.

To hit the target while it is falling, the shooter must remember that, as much as the target was losing velocity steadily as it went up, it will be gaining velocity almost as steadily for most of its drop. So, a pronounced form of come-from-behind technique works well. Merely spot the target visually, come from behind it and keep on track with it. As the gun accelerates through the target, shoot it.

The single most complicating factor in this approach is

U.S. Shooting Team member Brian Ballard, a left-hander, has no problem in hitting clays, because he has developed the basic shooting techniques and is always in position to hit targets at most breakable point.

By hiding traps behind trees and bushes, the course can be designed to obscure in-flight targets from shooter. That means the shooter has to spot the flying target as it appears and shoot it. Fast reflexes are a great help.

the fact that the target is rarely falling straight down. It is arcing down and, with the shotgun held normally, it is virtually impossible to track a target smoothly through a downward arc. That is why shooters who casually attempt such shots find themselves hitting some, but missing a lot. It is virtually impossible to repeat with any regularity the kind of spot shooting it would take to hit the target consistently as it arcs downward. Yet, by canting the gun with the top of the barrels pointed in the direction of the falling arc, the gun can track the target easily for the downward trip, and the shooter can choose the spot for the break almost casually.

If there is a strong wind blowing when the Rising Teal station is shot, it is often much easier to improve scores if the shooter has the technique to hit the falling/arcing target rather than having to rely upon hitting the target only on its upward path.

Other rising and falling characteristics of target presentations have been discussed elsewhere as adjuncts to still more flight variations. Hitting any of them is not nearly so difficult once the shooter recognizes that they are a part of the presentation. But if they are a factor and that factor is not taken into consideration, certainly the target will be missed every time — or at least enough of the time to make the score anything but outstanding.

Consistency, after all, is the essence of good shooting anywhere, anytime and under any conditions.

SPECIALTY TARGETS

Unlike some of the more traditional clay target shotgun sports, sporting clays often involves the use of specialty targets. Most common is the *rabbit,* which is launched so it bounces along the ground in front of the shooter.

Physically, the rabbit clay target is somewhat different from the traditional domed targets encountered in trap and skeet. The rabbit target is the same diameter as normal clays — 110mm — but it is much beefier in its construction and is more like a plain disk with a thick edge. This design allows it to bounce along the ground without breaking.

To add degrees of difficulty to rabbit presentations, course designers often obscure much, it not most, of the target's path from the trap with obstacles like berms, bushes or straw bales. There often will be ridges constructed along the ground to make the target bounce even more erratically than it would normally.

tion by timing an ambush intersect when the target is launched. Also, it is typically a quick presentation, which means the shooter must see the target at the earliest point in its presentation, get on it and shoot it. Although the shot may be a variant of a spot shot, gun follow-through is critical. To hit this presentation, the shooter must focus solely on the target, thus enabling the gun to stay on track, even when the target bounces.

Another specialty sporting clays target is the *midi,* so named because it is medium-sized at 90mm in diameter. It is configured with the standard dome design and its flight characteristics are similar to those of the full-size clays. Because they are smaller and lighter than the full-size 110mm targets, though, the midis do fly faster.

Midis most often are presented as part of a pair of targets — a pair in which one target is standard size, the other a midi. If the shooter is not paying close attention at stations

Even when there are no bushes to limit the shooter in getting ready for target, walls and other obstructions may be used to limit the shooter's ability to see the target coming; it also determines where target is hit.

Usually, the rabbit presentation is a form of crossing target, with fairly radical quartering angles not uncommon. The rabbit target may be part of a "Fur and Feather" station in which the rabbit is one part of a pair and an aerial clay imitating a quail or pheasant is the other.

Since the rabbit target routinely bounces differently each time it is thrown, it is impossible to "groove" this sta-

where midis are mixed with other size targets, there can be major problems. First, the midis fly a little faster than do the regular targets. This means that during flight a simultaneous pair of targets flying through the air from the same trap will follow divergent paths.

But even more than the speed and rate of fall difference between midis and full-size targets is the shooter's perception of what is happening. If the shooter does not recognize a midi for what it is, he or she can easily assume the target is actually a lot farther away than it is. This is enough to make the necessary perceived lead to change, resulting in a missed clay.

Next in the lineup is a target called a *mini*. It is 60mm in diameter, which means that it is noticeably smaller than a midi and just slightly larger than half the size of a standard clay. Many shooters liken shooting the minis to trying to hit a screaming aspirin. Actually, they do sort of look like black aspirins zinging through the air.

Even though they go quite a lot faster than the standard targets, the minis are not that difficult to hit so long as the shooter concentrates on the target and shoots what is presented. It simply means moving the gun a little faster while following all of the other normal shooting techniques. Aside from the fact that it is smaller and going a little faster,

tue is unquestionably the most different. It is the standard 110mm-diameter clay, but it is not domed like a normal target. Instead, it has an almost wavy side profile — much like a small phonograph record that has warped.

This wave, coupled with the extremely thin side profile of the target, causes it to go through the air edge-on for a distance after leaving the trap, then hook and fall. This flight pattern is much like waterfowl coming in for a landing. Often the stations where battues are shot are named things like "Decoying Mallards."

Because the battue target is so thin when viewed from the side, it is virtually unbreakable on a consistent basis until it goes into its banking and falling arc. Hence, the shooter rarely has problems seeing the targets and being ready for them. In fact, one of the mistakes shooters often make is to try to shoot the battues too soon.

It is better to allow these targets to "develop" or con-

Women are finding sporting clays to be a challenging game at which they can compete on a level with men.

the most difficult aspect of mini shooting is visually spotting the target in the first place. When thrown against a dark background, the mini can be extremely difficult to see.

Like the midi, the mini is also often thrown as part of a pair. It might be paired with a standard target, or even another mini.

In the realm of specialty sporting clays targets, the *bat-*

tinue their flight until a full presentation is made. In the case of battues, this is when the entire round top profile of the target is visible. Then they look much like falling garbage can lids and are eminently breakable. The secret to hitting them consistently is to swing the gun on line with the flight of the target and continue with a good follow-through.

The last of the more common specialty targets is the *roc-*

One learns to stand as far forward in the shooting cage as possible so as not to limit swing of barrel.

Quick follow-up shots are routine in sporting clays. One must break the first target, get on the second.

There is plenty of time in walking from one station to another to discuss challenges at various shooting areas.

ket. This clay target looks much like a compromise between a standard domed target and a rabbit target. It is 110mm in diameter like the standard or the rabbit, but from the side it has only a slight dome when compared to the standard clay.

The rocket leaves the trap exceedingly fast, but slows more quickly than does the standard domed target. As its deceleration increases, the rocket begins to fall at a faster rate than the standard clay, so it presents still another modified form of arc. Compounding the presentation on some courses are distractions like foliage or other things that block the shooter's view for part of the target's flight.

When the rocket is launched as part of a pair, it might travel in front of, say, a standard target for part of the flight, then fall behind as it goes through the air. If the shooter is located in a spot where he or she has to allow the targets to develop fully before taking the shot, the target that looked like the proper one to shoot first when it came into view is actually the one that should be shot second. For any but the most seasoned competitors this can cause the shooter to make a last-second change in the initial target shot, interrupting the entire swinging process and resulting in two missed targets!

Sporting clays is a study in angles, speeds and optical deception. So long as the shooter keeps this fact in mind and concentrates at each station, the degree of perceived difficulty can be lessened.

It is understanding both the types of presentations and the targets for what they really are, rather than what they appear to be, that separates high scores from the rest.

CHAPTER 4

GUNS FOR THE SPORT

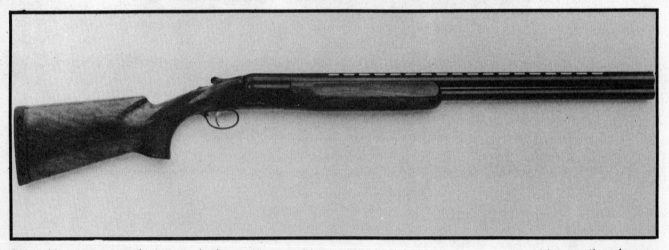

Perazzi is among manufacturers who have come up with guns that have been especially designed for sporting clays.

WITHOUT QUESTION, the over/under and semi-auto shotguns dominate sporting clays. The two major reasons are both simple and straight-forward. Over/unders and semi-autos offer the ability to make two quick shots and they feature an unmistakable single sighting plane.

Certainly, there are other more subtle factors which make these two gun types preferred, but the essential consideration is the fact that they simply are easier for most people to shoot well and quickly.

Of these two types, the over/under is more commonly the choice of serious competitors. A combination of reliability and ease of maintenance are the major contributors to that choice.

Steve Comus is an investigative type — as well as a staff editor for *Western Outdoors* — who has done a good deal of looking down a gun barrel at sporting clays. We asked him to look over the shotgun scene and offer some personal evaluations. Here is what he has to say:

Recognizing that over/unders and semi-autos are the actions of choice for the more frequent sporting clays shooters, firearms manufacturers are responding with an increasingly large number of models which they designate as "sporting clays" or "sporting" guns.

Depending upon the company and particular guns involved, these sporters range from only slightly modified field guns to some rather highly evolved clay target configurations. Virtually all guns designated by the manufacturer as sporting clays models feature interchangeable choke tube systems.

Because the target presentations in sporting clays range from only a few yards to occasional long shots — and everything between — it is common for shooters to opt for more or less bore restriction, depending upon the specific station. Interchangeable choke tubes make this sort of fine tuning easier and simpler than using different barrels, or even different guns while shooting a particular course.

It is both common and permitted for sporting clays

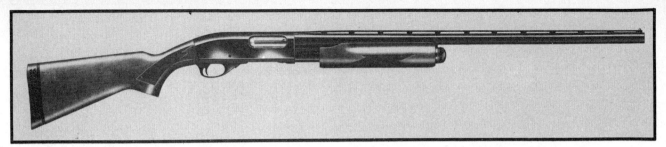

With proper choking, Remington's Sportsman 12 pump action is adequate for sporting clays, though a trifle slow.

Single-Shots And Bolt-Actions Don't Hack It — The Others Can!

Trick shooter John Cloherty, a AA level sporting clays competitor, favors a Benelli Montefeltro semi-automatic.

shooters to change chokes, barrels or even guns between stations. However, once the shooter is in the station, he or she is limited to using just one rig.

It is in this arena of concern that over/unders are preferred over any of the single-barrel alternatives by a number of shooters. Two barrels gives them the option of using one amount of choke restriction for the first target and a different degree of restriction for the second shot. One type of situation where this comes into play is the "fur and feather" station on many courses. At this station, the "fur," or rabbit target, might be sent bouncing along the ground close to the shooter, while the following "feather," or flying target, might be thrown or "flushed" from a greater distance and present a longer shot. At such a station, the shooter might opt for a fully open bore on the rabbit target and a more restricted choking for the aerial target. With a single barrel on a semi-auto or pump gun, the shooter would be physically forced to shoot both targets with the same choking.

Increasingly, guns made specifically for sporting clays also feature a forcing cone (the abrupt restriction in the barrel just fore of the chamber) which is extended or "relieved." Simply, this means that rather than a short stepdown in internal diameter, the reduction from the chamber

to the main bore is more gradual. This not only tends to contribute to more uniform patterns, but it also reduces the violence of the recoil; there is not so sharp a hit to the shoulder.

Internal bore work on some of the more highly refined sporting clays guns goes even farther. For example, some feature oversize bores — a phenomenon sometimes referred to as "back boring." This also tends to reduce perceived recoil and it contributes to a higher degree of control over patterning.

When overboring is done in conjunction with finely tuned choke tubes, the shot pattern can be highly manipulated to produce more precisely what an individual shooter might want for a specific shot presentation.

Another feature that is almost universal on any gun which is either specifically designed for sporting clays use, or one which is altered for it, is the configuration of the butt. Whether the butt is rubber or just checkered wood, the heel (top) of the butt is radiused in a contour which precludes it from snagging or hanging up on clothing when the gun is put to the shoulder. The reason is simple. Sporting clays shooting calls for the shooter to start with a "low" gun, which means the butt of the gun must be held below the shoulder until the target is called for. This differs from the more traditional American trap and skeet which allow the gun to be mounted at the shoulder when the shooter calls for the target.

Barrel porting is another increasingly common feature on the more highly refined sporting clays guns. Porting is simply the cutting of holes or slots into the barrel or barrels several inches before the muzzle. The angle at which the holes or slots are cut, combined with the number of them and their configuration, determines how much they dampen actual recoil and how much they reduce barrel jump.

In sporting clays, where shooters routinely shoot doubles or pairs of targets, reducing the amount of barrel jump can have a significant effect on a shooter's score, simply because when the barrel jumps less in recoil from the first shot, it is easier and quicker to get onto the second target. Further, when hundreds of targets a day are involved, the reduction in barrel jump also means less trauma to the shooter's face when the gun recoils.

Regardless of the kind of shotgun used, interchangeable chokes are the hot ticket for sporting clays. Screw-in chokes shown are part of retro-fit on a Remington 1100.

Over/unders are the preferred guns for this sport. One reason is that the simple designs tend to preclude a lot of maintenance work.

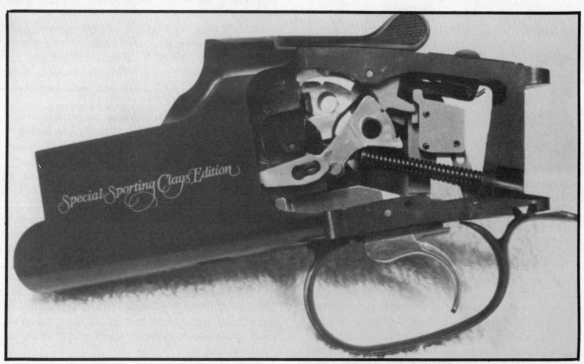

Certainly, top shooters often use guns which feature all of these sorts of refinements. Whether they are really necessary for most sporting clays enthusiasts is more a matter of personal preference and degree of involvement in tournaments than anything else.

Shooters often become tempted to look at the guns being used by top competitors and automatically assume those would be the best for them. Perhaps so, but frequently not. There is a world of difference between the needs of the occasional recreational shooter and those of the serious, top-ranked competitor.

Since sporting clays shooters come primarily from the ranks of hunters, it is common to see both pumps and side-by-side double-barrel shotguns in use at fun shoots or for more casual weekend course work. No need for mystery here. They are used because they are the guns those shooters also use when hunting upland game or waterfowl.

Hence, slide-action shotguns and side-by-sides are definitely suited to the sport. In the hands of shooters who know how to use them well, they perform admirably for shooting clays. In fact, at all but the top levels of competition, an accomplished pump gunner should not feel a bit handicapped at most kinds of sporting clays stations and one who shoots a side-by-side well should expect his or her score to be no less than it would be with any other action design.

For different reasons, neither the pump nor the side-by-side is encountered often at top competitions. For a shooter

All American Rick Kennerknecht uses the MX3 Perazzi Special Sporting over/under to shoot crossing targets. He has found that handling dynamics of the over/under make it ideal for the game.

who really knows how to use a pump gun efficiently, most sporting clays target presentations represent hittable combinations. However, on some of the really close and quick stations on some courses, the pumper is at a slight disadvantage.

What does this really mean? Over the years, it has become apparent that on a tournament level course, a shooter using a pump gun could expect to average one or two fewer broken targets out of a hundred than that same shooter would expect to average with a semi-auto or over/under on the same course.

That's not bad at all, considering the fact that until the shooter reaches the top rankings, the shooter himself or herself would be inconsistent by at least one or two targets per one hundred anyway. What this means is that for all but the absolute top shooters, there is no reason to expect that overall performance will be less with a pump-action gun.

As for side-by-side doubles, the reason they are encountered relatively infrequently on most sporting clays courses is that they represent a relatively small percentage of the total number of shotguns. In other words, they are seen less simply because far fewer shooters own and use them.

To accommodate any of these perceived disadvantages, a number of specialty shoots are evolving in conjunction with other shoots, or specialty events held in their own right. At many shoots, there now are pump gun classifications which means that those using pumps are competing

against other pumpers. The same is true for side-by-side shooters. There often are side-by-side classifications or even special side-by-side shoots.

Proper barrel length is a matter of much discussion among sporting clays shooters. Simply put, there is no single "best" choice for all target presentations, but there are some generally accepted norms.

When sporting clays first appeared on the American scene, skeet guns with twenty-six-inch barrels were common. The thought was that, since many of the shots are quick, it would be advantageous to use a short, quick-pointing gun. But as shooters experienced an increasingly wider variety of shot presentations — many with targets at longer distances or featuring crossing targets which required a longer and smoother swing — the cogniscenti started using longer barrels.

For over/under shooters, those lengths went almost immediately to twenty-eight inches and were followed rather quickly by thirty-inch barrels. In Europe — and to a degree in the Unted States — some of the more experienced shooters began showing up with even longer barrels: some were thirty-two inches and there were even a few thirty-four-inch guns.

The pendulum began to swing back a bit and at this point in the game, over/under sporting clays guns typically have twenty-eight or thirty-inch barrels.

There was not nearly the degree of change among semi-auto and pump gun shooters when it came to barrel length and there are a couple of reasons for this phenomenon.

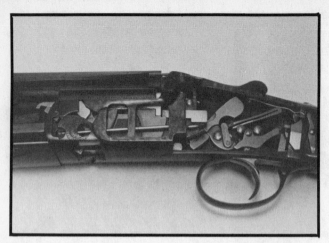

This full cut-away of the Perazzi MX3 over/under shows the simplicity of the design, a factor that makes these stack-barrel shotguns so popular for sporting clays.

First, the action itself on a semi-auto or a pump is much longer than the action on an over/under or side-by-side double. What this means is that a twenty-six-inch barrel on a semi-auto, for example, offers about the same length of sighting plane as a twenty-eight-inch barrel on a break-open gun. Hence, semi-autos and pumps used in sporting clays started out generally with twenty-six or twenty-eight-inch barrels and remain at that level, even though there are some thirty-inch tubes in use.

Another reason semi-auto shooters were not as tempted to alter their barrel lengths so quickly is that the addition of two inches of barrel length on a semi-auto does not as drastically affect the handling characteristics of the entire gun as does the same increase in length on a break-open double gun like an over/under.

Not only is the actual weight virtually doubled with a two-barrel gun when the same length is added, but the distribution of weight in relation to balance is magnified with a double than with a semi-auto.

A closer look at the types of actions and how they are used in the sport can help explain why the various types are used widely or more rarely.

OVER/UNDERS

From its handling dynamics to its virtual total reliability, the over/under shotgun is without question the dominant type used in sporting clays around the world. Of all its characteristics, the way an over/under handles is by far the biggest reason why it is chosen, almost to the exclusion of other types, by the hard core shooters.

By virtue of its design, the over/under is inherently easier to make into a well balanced gun. Equally important is the fact that the design also makes it relatively easy to alter the points of balance. In sporting clays, for example, it is better to have a gun which is slightly barrel heavy than it is to have one which is either absolutely neutrally balanced or butt heavy.

The reason is simple. Most of the targets shot in sporting clays involve the swinging of the gun as opposed to simple pointing or spot shooting. The presentation is more frequently comprised of compound angles, rather than classic straight-aways or risers encountered in some of the other shotgun sports.

Whether the shot calls for a sustained lead or a come-from-behind attack, the swing of the shotgun tends to be smoother and the follow-through tends to be more consistent if the gun is slightly barrel heavy than if the balance is any other way.

Although sporting clays closely approximate the full range of shots encountered in field hunting, it is still a clay target game. This means the shooter routinely will fire more shots in a shorter period of time than would be the case in hunting. This means, in one demonstrable way, that an ideal sporting gun logically would be somewhat heavier than some thoroughbred upland game gun. Again, the over/under lends itself well to the sport in that most production 12-gauge over/unders are at least slightly heavier than many of the purer upland hunting guns.

Slightly heavier guns for sporting clays accomplish two goals simultaneously. They reduce felt recoil and they cut down the aggregate effects on the shooter of being pounded with repeated shots. This translates into two benefits to the shooter. Reduction of felt recoil minimizes the tendency to flinch and miss targets, and preventing the build-up of pain allows the shooter to concentrate more fully on shooting and less on discomfort.

Lucio Sosta, manager for Perazzi USA, uses hand reaming tool to relieve the choke on an older over/under. Retro-work by qualified gunsmith can upgrade such guns.

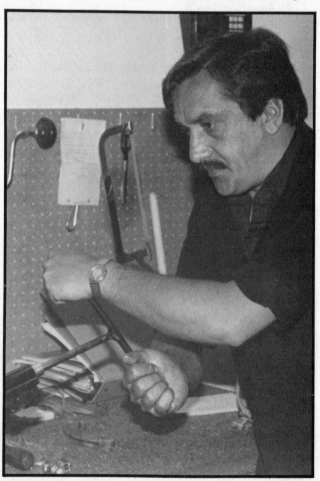

Rick Kennerknecht finds an over/under works well for demands of sporting clays.

Although these two factors may appear at first rather obtuse to some who have not experienced extended courses of fire, they are both real and quantifiable when it comes to tallying scores. It is not uncommon for sporting clays shooters to fire one hundred or more shots in a morning or afternoon. Certainly, for the more advanced shooters, it is not odd to see them firing two hundred or more shots in a day. They also find themselves involved in shoots involving two consecutive days, so recoil can definitely be a factor.

Another design factor inherent in over/unders is the position of the barrels relative to the shooter's hands and eyes. The importance of these relationships cannot be

Browning's BPS pump with interchangeable tubes is a good bet today.

Remington 870 is preferred pump action for clay game

Because gas-operated semi-autos deliver less perceived recoil, many female shooters prefer them for sporting clays. A Beretta 303 semi-auto is being fired here.

toward the target with the index finger of the leading hand, both the finger and the barrels will always be pointed in the same plane as the target — assuming proper hand/eye coordination. In fact, a great many shooters hold the gun in such a way that the index finger of the leading hand is literally pointing at the target.

When shooting pumps or autos, for example, the barrel is always somewhat above the leading hand. Although this distance is relatively minor compared to the increasing size of the pattern as the shot travels farther from the barrel on the various shots, making consistent hits is a matter of angles. This means a minor miscalculation or inconsistency at the gun is only magnified as the distance to the target increases. This becomes a problem at those times when that angle of disparity at the gun itself is more than the angle at which the pattern of the shot increases.

The buttstock configuration on most sporting clays over/unders involves some degree of pistol grip, as well as a relatively flat or even low comb. Certainly, the exact dimensions necessary are a factor of the shooter's personal body configuration, but for most purposes, a general field stock works well — again, because the kinds of shots encountered generally approximate field shooting.

Straight-grip stocks are more rare in sporting clays than are pistol grips or semi-pistol grips for a number of increasingly subtle reasons. As much as a straight grip may be ideal for shots at flushing upland birds in the wild, it is a hinderance when attempting some of the incoming or quartering shots presented routinely on sporting clays ranges. A straight grip limits the compound gun movements needed for these shots more than does a pistol grip. Further, a pistol grip — especially those which also include a palm swell

overstated. Since sporting clays involve an extremely wide variety of types of shots, it is correspondingly important for the gun to shoot right where the shooter is looking. Certainly, this also is the ideal for field hunting guns, but is not always the best bet for some of the other shotgun sports. For example, in trap, the shooter might prefer that the pattern be a bit higher, because all of the targets in that game are risers.

Starting with the leading hand (left hand for right-hand shooters), the position of the fingertips on a properly fitted gun are at or extremely near the horizontal line between the stacked barrels. This means that, if the shooter "points"

Bernardelli now is coming on strong with special shotguns designed specifically for sporting clays competition. This Model 115S from the Italian manufacturer is finding shooter favor.

Former Olympian and world record holder Dan Carlisle shows his sporting clays form with Beretta sidelock over/under. (Left) Quick-pointing side-by-sides are not used in sporting clays as much as are some of the other shotgun actions.

— make it easier for the shooter to hold the gun in exactly the same way from shot to shot. And consistency is the essence of any form of target shooting.

The reason buttstock configuration is so critically important is that it determines to a large degree how well the shooter will be able to point, swing and shoot the various types of target presentations. Part of this built-in physical determination is how the gun appears — or doesn't appear — to the shooter at the moment of the shot.

Here is another reason why over/unders are so popular among sporting clays shooters. Although the shooter of a properly fitted sporting gun may not be consciously aware that he or she sees any part of the gun at the moment of the shot, the eye does pick up the barrel/rib and the mind automatically aligns everything properly.

Because the over/under features a single top barrel/rib, it simplifies the perception for the shooter. In a lesser

sense, it also precludes the obscuring of a crossing target by a right or a left barrel, as might be the case from time to time with a side-by-side double. Certainly, this is a relatively minor concern, but it is real nonetheless.

Another reason over/unders are fine choices for sporting clays is that credible production models are generally available in the price ranges most shooters can afford. The market is focused primarily upon basic over/unders with price tags ranging from just under $1000 to about $2000 — depending upon a number of features.

Although the initial buy-in for an over/under may be higher than for an auto, for example, the long-term low-maintenance characteristics of over/unders — coupled with the ease with which a shooter can retrieve empties for reloading — can make them a less expensive alternative in the end.

It is in the realm of low maintenance and incredible reliability that over/unders really shine for sporting clays shooters. Aside from the routine cleaning and occasional lubrication at the pivot point, there really is no maintenance needed for over/unders. They typically shoot tens of thousands of rounds without a hint of a problem. And, when they do need attention, over/unders are relatively simple — but not always easy — to repair. They have relatively few moving parts and springs, so there is literally less that can go wrong.

Since over/unders also make fine hunting field guns, they are a logical and a good choice for shooters who also hunt and who do not care to have a different gun for each type of use.

SEMI-AUTOS

Semi-auto shotguns are extremely popular and effective for sporting clays. In addition to offering the shooter the ability to get off two shots quickly, semi-autos are less expensive than over/unders. Further, a great many hunters who also shoot sporting clays use the same semi-auto shotgun for both applications.

Since semi-autos generally cost about half as much as a basic over/under, they are totally logical choices for any but the most advanced sporting clays shooters. In fact, there are a few among the top shooters who routinely use semi-autos in competition.

Keeping the working parts of a semi-auto clean can lessen the probability of a mechanical malfunction, but it cannot preclude it. Most semi-autos encountered in sporting clays shooting are gas-operated, as opposed to recoil-operated models. The reasons range from the fact that gas guns deliver a softer felt recoil to the greater availability of gas guns on the market.

For gas-operated semi-autos, the most important area to keep clean is at and around the gas port, which is typically located on the bottom of the barrel about a foot in front of the action. Gases created when the shotshell goes off bleed from the barrel, through the port and activate a piston. This, in turn, operates the bolt and action of the gun.

If the port becomes plugged or severely restricted, there is not enough gas bled off to the piston to cycle the action properly. Or if the piston and/or its seals are too dirty or are faulty, the cyling process is impeded. Whenever this type of impediment is pronounced enough, it can cause the gun to malfunction. Most often, this occurs in the form of failure to cycle the spent shell out and to feed the second shell into the chamber from the magazine.

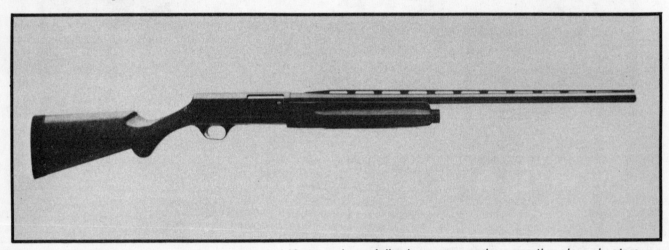

Browning's A-500G semi-automatic, gas-operated 12-gauge has a following among serious sporting clays shooters.

Sporting clays requires a low gun position when target is called for, so the butt of the gun needs to be smooth and rounded to avoid catching in clothes when mounted.

The major drawback with semi-autos is their lower degree of functional reliability. They are, after all, a form of machine with comparatively many parts. From time to time, semi-autos do malfunction and it is the spectre of malfunction which causes many shooters to opt for over/unders instead. Confidence is a major element in success and anything which will contribute to a higher confidence factor is desirable. Whether that added confidence level justifies the difference in price is a personal matter for each shooter.

With so many different types of shots presented in sporting clays, gun design has to fit the challenge, as is the case where this shooter is in a "goose pit," shooting at clays that resemble decoyed geese.

Of course, there are a number of other rather common causes of malfunction among semi-autos. These can range from jams in the feeding process involving the magazine cutoff assembly to weak return springs in the action. If the bolt and interior of the receiver become dirty enough, mere friction can make the action sluggish enough to work improperly.

Semi-autos also are more finicky when it comes to the ammunition itself. Although many semi-autos now on the market shoot all intensities of loadings without any adjustments, some guns do not feed lighter loads as well as heavier ones; some semi-autos will not feed reloads as well as they do new factory ammo. Although all of these concerns can be addressed individually by the shooter, they also happen to be things which one need not consider with a fixed breech gun like an over/under, pump or side-by-side.

Traditionally, shooters are at least as concerned with perceived potential problems as they are with actual problems. This means that even though the actual number of mechanical malfunctions in properly maintained semi-autos may be small, the fact that those numbers are larger than for break-open guns weighs heavily in the consideration of many shooters when choosing a particular type of gun.

Some companies market semi-autos specifically designed for sporting clays use. These guns typically have interchangeable choke tubes and a radiused recoil pad. Increas-

ingly, they also have — either standard or as options —relieved forcing cones and ported barrels.

Because most semi-autos on the market were initially designed for hunting, they are as a group configured well for sporting clays. Their design allows them to be pointed and swung both quickly and smoothly and the second shot is as quick as another squeeze on the trigger. For any number of reasons, a semi-auto is a good choice for shooting sporting clays.

PUMPS

In the United States, pump-action shotguns are a fact of life in any type of smoothbore shooting. Sporting clays is no exception. When it comes to fun shoots and local activities, pump shotguns are encountered routinely in sporting clays circles. However, on the competition front, pumps quickly disappear. The real or perceived handicap in shooting simultaneous pairs of targets with a pump is the primary contributing factor here.

It has long been alleged that a pump shotgun can be shot faster than can a semi-auto. Although this may be true in a scientific sense, it almost never is a real-life fact, because there are almost no shooters around who can shoot a pump more quickly and maintain accuracy.

However, there are many accomplished pump shotgun shooters and they certainly are at no disadvantage with most target presentations. But in high-level competition circles, where one or two targets can make a major difference, shooters invariably opt for either a semi-auto or over/under.

Those who do use pump shotguns for sporting clays can find themselves causing a common problem — short pumping or "short shucking." This is when they are in such a hurry to pump the action that they don't pump it all the way back before pushing the slide forward for the next shot. When this occurs, the spent shell is not ejected and it becomes jammed between the face of the bolt and the ejection port. Familiarity and practice can reduce the number of times short-shucking is a problem, but when it rears its head, it always means a lost second target.

In an effort to address the concerns of pump gun shooters as well as interest newcomers to the sport, there are a growing number of pump gun classifications within organized

Some of the cages used in sporting clays tend to be quite elaborate in construction, but are no less challenging.

shoots, as well as special pump gun shoots, in sporting clays.

Aside from the competitive area, there is no question that a good pump shotgun is a credible sporting clays gun. In fact, many shooters find that a pump adds another element of enjoyment to a relaxed day of sporting clays shooting.

There is far less special configuring and retrofitting practiced with respect to pumps in sporting clays than with over/unders or semi-autos. But, there are a few features which can help make a pump shotgun a better performer on the sporting clays course.

Since many pump guns initially were used for hunting, it is common for them to have full-choke barrels, but there is almost never a station on a sporting clays course at which a full choke is needed. Hence, a pump shotgun used for sporting clays should have at least a relatively open choke. As with other designs, interchangeable chokes make total sense. When in doubt, use an improved cylinder choke.

Aside from that, the pump gun should fit the shooter and the top of the butt should be radiused to keep it from snagging when the gun is being mounted.

In practice, about the only kinds of target presentations which categorically would put a pump gunner at a disadvantage are those which feature fast doubles targets which are visible for extemely short periods of time. These typically are the ones which zap through openings in heavy vegetation or which disappear quickly behind a hill or other obstruction. These targets are normally hit by spot shooting, as opposed to any noticeable sort of swing.

Any of the target presentations which involve swinging the gun also allow enough time for a pump gun user to operate the action and hit the target. In fact, some shooters find that the operation of the slide forces them to put the gun back on target better for the second shot than would be the case with a semi-auto or break-open gun.

SIDE-BY-SIDES

As classically proper as the side-by-side double-barrel shotgun might be, it never has become a major factor in sporting clays in the United States and is currently not a major factor anywhere in the world in that sport. The side-by-side suffers more from a general lack of use in any shotgunning as the Twentieth Century draws to a close, than from any other factor. Simply put, there are relatively few side-by-sides in use when compared to the other gun configurations.

Price has been one of the foremost reasons for the comparatively fewer number of side-by-sides in use. They are generally more expensive than other types of guns. Beyond initial price, side-by-sides as a class of guns also suffer from another inhibitor when it comes to sporting clays. Through the years, the side-by-side evolved significantly and many of these double guns are thoroughbreds which are designed specifically for the hunting of flushing upland game. That means they are light so they can be carried with ease in the field and that they feature straight grips and splinter forends.

Because these game guns are light in weight, they can hammer the clay target shooter even on a standard one hundred-target course. They also typically have rather short barrels, like twenty-five inches, and when combined with the short

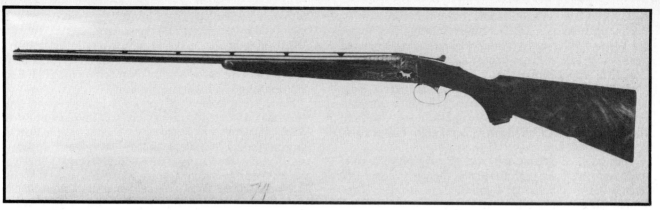

The Winchester Model 21 is a classic that one doesn't see too often on sporting clays, but it should be adequate.

break-open action, provide a highly whippy shooting package. As much as this might be just the ticket for woodcock and bobwhite quail in the wild, it is an inhibitor when trying to shoot stations where the gun must be swung in a compound arc.

During the evolution of the side-by-side, there also was developed a longer, heavier type of double which traditionally was found more often in duck blinds and goose pits. This design, which typically features both a form of pistol grip and some form of fuller "beavertail" forend, is better suited for sporting clays, because it performs better on the full range of target presentations and certainly is far better on the swing shots.

Assuming that the barrels have fairly open chokes — and that is quite an assumption when it comes to 12-gauge doubles — these guns actually are suited quite well for sporting clays shooting. Whether they have double or single triggers is really not a substantive consideration, because the individual shooter can become familiar and proficient with either system.

Although this might be fine for shooters who already happen to have such a double gun, there are both real and perceived problems and considerations which would preclude most shooters from procuring a side-by-side double just to shoot sporting clays.

As was mentioned earlier, price is a consideration and a good side-by-side represents a major investment. Further, there are few credible side-by-sides which either feature or can be retrofitted with interchangeable chokes.

And, as importantly, shooters who have not traditionally used side-by-sides are often overwhelmed with the sight picture they think they get when they look down the top of both barrels. In fact, if the gun fits properly, the shooter is consciously unaware of the horizontal expanse across both barrels, but the spectre is enough to psych out some otherwise potential side-by-side users.

There are only a few kinds of target presentations encountered in sporting clays for which a side-by-side is less well suited than are over/unders, pumps or semi-autos. These include the low or dropping targets which also are quartering or crossing. At times, the configuration of the side-by-side barrels can obscure the target — that brief period being right at the time of the shot.

The side-by-side offers the same level of low maintenance and high reliability as the over/under — a definite plus. Assuming the side-by-side is well made and fits the shooter well, there is no reason it could not be considered a credible sporting clays gun.

As with pump guns, there is a trend in sporting clays now for events to feature special classifications for this specific design. Also, there are growing numbers of side-by-side sporting clays shoots.

Side-by-sides are not seen often in sporting clays. One reason is that the barrels all too often are thin and cannot be reworked to accept screw-in chokes. Model 201 Classic Doubles side-by-side is improved/modified.

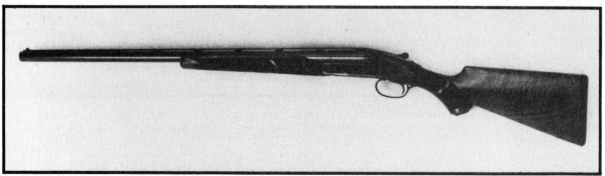

SPORTING CLAYS GUNS

American Arms markets a Silver Sporting over/under in 12-gauge with twenty-eight-inch barrels and chambered for 2¾-inch shells. It has interchangeable choke tubes.

Beretta offers three over/under sporting shotguns in Models 682, 686 and 687. Barrel lengths are twenty-eight and thirty inches. These are primarily 12-gauge guns, but the 687 Sporting also is available in 20-gauge. Also from Beretta is the Model 303 Sporting semi-auto. This is a gas-operated semi-auto.

Bernardelli is getting into the sporting clays market more seriously each year. Currently, there is a Model 192 over/under designated for sporting clays use. For those who might want a side-by-side double for sporting clays,

Bernardelli's Model 112 with interchangeable chokes is one of the better choices on the market.

Browning is one of the major players in the sporting clays gun market. In their line are three sporting clays over/unders, all based on the Citori action: the GTI, Special Sporting and Lightning Sporting.

There are a number of options available in this line, which include everything from barrel porting to spare barrels. Interchangeable choke tubes are standard and the Special Sporting model is available in two-barrel sets. For pump-gun shooters, the Browing BPS with Browning's Invector choke tubes is a credible choice, as are the various Model 12 reproductions Browning has been marketing for the past several years. These are in 20, 28 and .410, but work

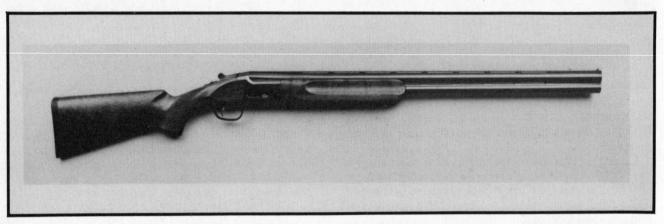

Browning is another manufacturer that has noted interest in sporting clays and has climbed on the bandwagon. This is the maker's GTI Sporting Clays model, which is a no-nonsense shotgun built for hard use, not as decoration.

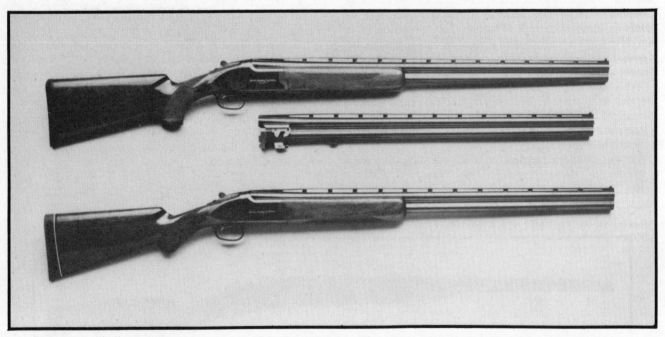

Adding to its line of shotguns specifically for sporting clays, Browning has reworked their Lightning model to conform to what competitors are demanding. The Special Sporting Clays version (top) has this extra barrel, too.

fine for most sporting clays applications.

Classic Doubles (now out of business) offered a Model 101 Sporter over/under which was marketed with one or two sets of barrels which were twenty-eight and thirty inches. Interchangeable chokes were standard in this 12-gauge model. These guns can be found on the used-gun racks occasionally.

Krieghoff markets a 12-gauge over/under K-80 sporting

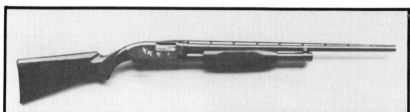

MX3 Special Sporting and the Mirage Sporting. Barrel lengths are generally 29½ inches and have interchangeable choke tubes. Some longer barrel options are available. As is the situation with most Perazzi guns, there is a seemingly endless variety of special options available to the shooter.

Although Remington does not currently market a gun specifically designated for sporting clays, that firm's Model

Browning's re-creation of the old Model 12 pump-action has developed interest in the gun, but this 20-gauge is not likely to be used in truly serious competitions.

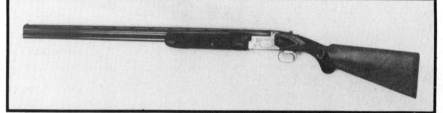

A host of over/under models have made the scene since sporting clays was introduced in the United States. It originated among British shotgunners.

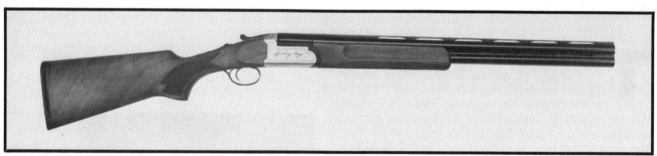

When Savage Arms reorganized and began new production, one of the first guns in the line was the M312 Sporting Clays.

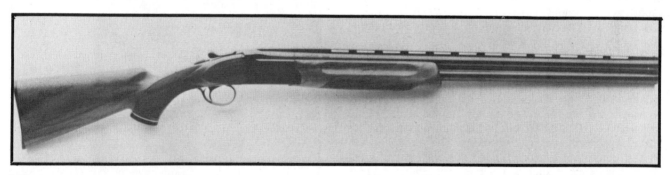

Weatherby — better known for big-bore rifles — also has gotten into the act with the Orion Grade I shotgun. This model has been reworked for sporting clays competition.

clays shotgun with twenty-eight-inch barrels. Choke tubes are standard and as is the situation with any of Krieghoff's guns, there are a number of grades and special options available.

Laurona offers the Model 85 MS Special Sporting over/under with twenty-eight-inch barrels and an interchangeable choke tube configuration for the bottom barrel.

Perazzi markets two basic sporting clays models — the

1100 and 11-87 semi-autos are encountered so widely on sporting clays courses that they deserve mention here. Most of those used for sporting clays also feature Remington's interchangeable choke system.

Of the pump guns encountered on sporting clays courses, Remington's 870 is by far the dominant type — again, with the Rem Choke system.

Savage is also marketing an over/under 12-gauge sporting clays gun called the Model 312. It has twenty-eight-inch barrels and features interchangeable chokes.

Weatherby has introduced a sporting clays over/under which is a variant of that company's Orion series. It features interchangeable chokes and is available in 12-gauge.

Marocchi's Avanza Model Is Designed Specifically For Winning At Sporting Clays!

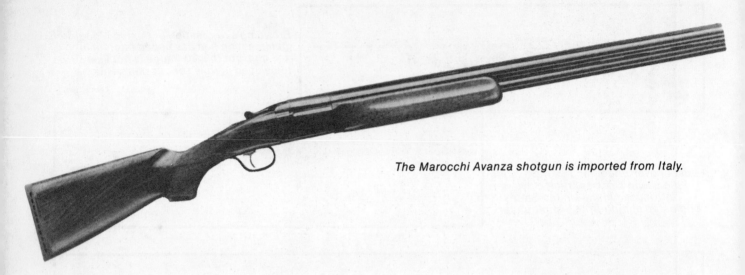

The Marocchi Avanza shotgun is imported from Italy.

THE SEARCH for the perfect — or at least a good — shotgun for sporting clays shooting usually centers around a 12-gauge over/under. Barrels are twenty-six to thirty inches long with 2¾-inch or three-inch chambers, ventilated top and middle ribs and a single, selective trigger. The gun will weigh a bit less than the average trap or skeet shotgun and most likely will be equipped with interchangeable choke tubes.

The selected gun need not be all of the above. Plenty of sporting clays targets have been broken by shooters using 20-gauge or .410-bore guns and by shooters using autoloaders or pump-action guns.

Experienced slide-action gunners can easily "kill" the doubles so common with sporting clays shooting. Autoloading shotguns will function as fast as any over/under for that second shot. According to the rules of the game, however, no more than two rounds may be loaded in the gun for each station's targets, so the pump and autoloader have no magazine-capacity advantage. The primary advantage to guns other than over/unders is in the familiarity felt by the shooter, if such a gun has been shot for years past.

No matter the style, the primary requirement of a satisfactory sporting clays gun is that it fit the shooter correctly. Nothing is more important when choosing a gun for the sport. The potential sporting clays gun should be tried out at the range before any money changes hands. But before that, the buyer should rely upon the help of a knowledgeable gun dealer or fellow shooter to help ensure the gun will fit.

A typical over/under designed and built specifically for the sporting clays game is the Marocchi Avanza, manufactured in Italy and imported into the United States by Precision Sales, (P.O. Box 1776, Westfield, MA 01086). The

A stylized M and the words Avanza Sporting Clays are imprinted on the bottom of the shotgun's action.

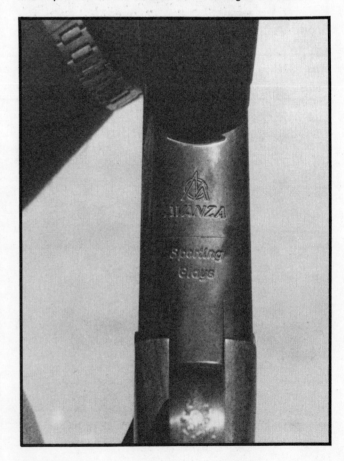

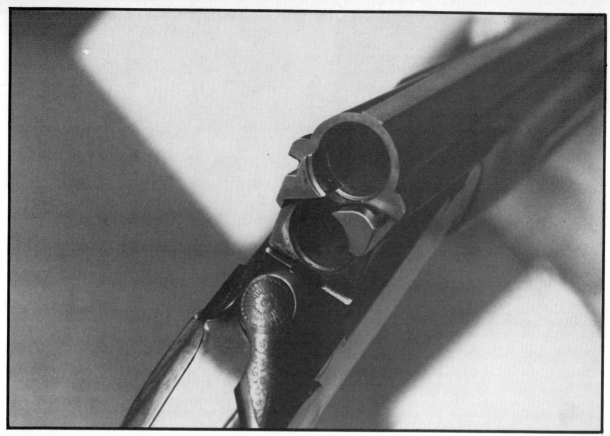

The Marocchi Avanza will accept either 2¾- or three-inch shells in its chambers. Gun features automatic selective ejectors, auto-mechanical barrel cycling and unbreakable firing pins. Locking bolt is lightly engraved.

sporting clays model was first introduced in late 1990, a modification of the company's earlier field model.

The 12-gauge Avanza's European walnut stock has a rubber recoil pad on the butt, usually considered mandatory for most target shooters. The stock and forend are cut-checkered for a firm grip with both hands. Length of pull is adjustable within a three-eighths-inch range, because of a trigger adjustment feature. The trigger will slide back and forth along its rail inside and near the top of the trigger guard for positioning. This is done quickly and easily by pressing inward on the spring-loaded button at the base of the trigger. With the release button held in, the trigger moves in either direction along the rail to the desired position. The shooter may experiment with various lengths of pull to find the most comfortable location for his or her style of shooting.

Both chambers are three inches, so either standard or three-inch magnum shells may be fired through the gun, although only 2¾-inch loads are permitted on the sporting clays course. The Avanza also may be used for upland game hunting.

The preferred choke for sporting clays will vary from shooter to shooter — and from gun to gun. Those who already own a skeet-choked shotgun probably will want to leave it the way it is. Many shooters prefer skeet barrels for any clay target. For the Avanza, the tested tube combo for clays was an improved cylinder in the bottom barrel, modified in the top. This is because, under normal conditions, the bottom barrel fires first. Usually, the nearer target is

Sporting Clays model features interchangeable choke tubes which are screwed into gun's muzzle.

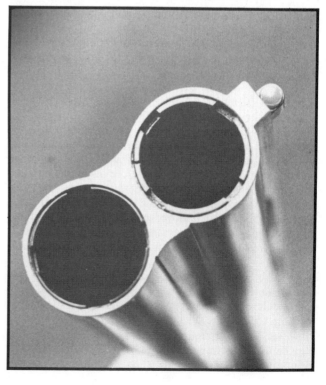

The Avanza Sporting Clays model was designed specifically for the new sport. It has the weight of the Marocchi 20-gauge, but is chambered in 12-gauge. Weight and profile permit faster swinging and follow-through.

engaged first and the slightly wider shot spread on the first shot is more appropriate. The second shot most likely will be farther away, to be engaged with the tighter choke.

The safety lever atop the receiver's tang also is the manual barrel selector. In the normal position with the safety to the right, the first pull of the trigger fires the bottom barrel. Without any further contemplation, the internal mechanism of the gun will select the top barrel to fire upon the next trigger pull.

This can be reversed, at will, if you wish to fire the top barrel first. Placing the safety lever to the left of the tang will cause the top barrel to fire first. This feature may be used when— depending on the sporting clays layout — the first target is launched at a distance and flies away from the shooter, while the second target may be closer. The shooter will know the target trajectories before stepping up to the shooting box and can adjust the gun accordingly. The Marocchi will continue to select the same barrel to fire first until the safety selector is moved to the opposite side position.

The Avanza Sporting Clays model was designed expressly as a 12-gauge gun, weighing and profiling the same as a 20-gauge for faster swinging and quicker mounting. The gun has a slightly heavier forend and a little more weight forward than the earlier model.

The rules of the sport prohibit mounting the gun before the target is in sight. The target is called, but the shooter must wait until the trapper has released the clays and that may be up to three seconds after the call, at the trapper's descretion. Most shooters will try to get the gun shouldered

The butt is equipped with a ventilated rubber recoil pad.

and into shooting position in the fastest possible time.

The gun butt must be visible below the armpit in the ready position, until the target is visible. A rubber recoil pad is necessary for shooting comfort, but it should be firm and smooth to avoid being caught on the shooting jacket or vest as it comes up to the shoulder. The rubber should offer some recoil protection, but must not permit the gun to roll, rotate or bounce against the shoulder, especially when trying to execute a fast second shot.

The Marocchi Avanza Sporting Clays over/under has a

vented rubber recoil pad fitted to the butt of the walnut stock. The pad is straight with slightly rounded toe and heel. The black rubber pad measures five-eighths-inch thick. The stock grip and forend are nicely checkered in what appears to be hand-cut work. The diamonds are neat, sharp and even, with little evidence of any run-overs along the borders.

All exterior metal work is dark blue with some engraving on the trigger guard, around the receiver and rear of the chamber, along the tang and top of the locking bolt lever. The word *Marocchi* appears in gold on the right side of the receiver, while *Avanza* and *Sporting Clays* is engraved on the bottom of the receiver. With the action open, one may examine the machine jeweling work on both sides of the barrel monoblock. The serial number is stamped inside the left side of the receiver rail and is visible when the action is open.

The top and middle ribs are ventilated. The top rib tapers slightly from the rear to the muzzle, and is matted to reduce glare along the sight plain. The front sight bead is a translucent ruby color, probably made of plastic, and the middle bead is a smaller brass pin.

On the left side and top of the silver-colored trigger is a spring-loaded button which is used to lock the trigger in position. The shooter may experiment with all of the trigger positions to determine which trigger location seems best. Other guns, such as the Browning sporting clays over/under, supply a similar adjustable system with their models.

The adjustable trigger feature puts the length of pull of the Avanza at from fourteen inches to 14⅜ inches. Specifications put the drop at the comb as 2¼ inches and the drop at the heel as 1½ inches. Unloaded, the gun weighs six pounds fourteen ounces, reflecting current designer think-

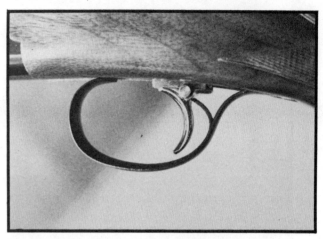

The adjustable trigger is an important feature of the Avanza. In effect, moving the trigger to front or rear changes length of pull to accommodate most shooters.

When the action is open, the jeweled area below the chambers is visible. When new, opening, closing action is stiff.

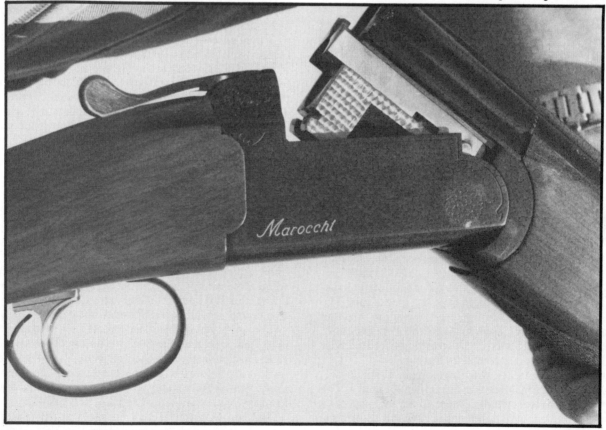

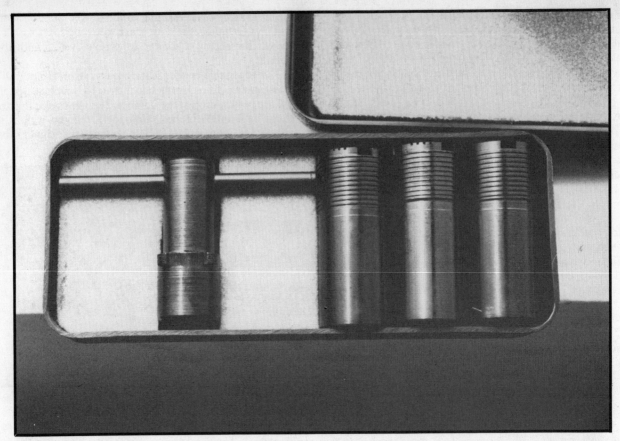

Neat plastic container, above, holds three unused choke tubes and T-handle choke wrench. In all, five threaded interchangeable chokes are included with the Avanza Sporting Clays model. At the range, gun swings smoothly, below, with weight forward. Ventilated top and middle ribs are visible; top barrel rib is grooved to reduce glare.

ing that a sporting clays gun should be a bit lighter in weight for faster swinging.

The Avanza is furnished with a set of five interchangeable choke tubes and wrench, all fitted in a special case. The steel *Interchokes,* as Marocchi terms them, are threaded on top to match the threading in the barrels. The five choke tubes are marked full, modified, two are improved cylinder and the cylinder choke completes the choices.

The tubes are marked with tiny notches along the forward rim in patterns denoting the amount of choke. The two with improved cylinder, intended for most sporting clays, are marked with four notches. The full choke tube

has one mark, three for modified, and there are no marks on the cylinder choke tube.

A light coating of gun oil should be added to each tube before it is installed and each should be tightened inside the muzzle with the wrench to avoid damage to the threads or to the barrels when the gun is fired. Moderate pressure with the choke wrench is enough to lock in the tubes correctly. The interchangeable chokes permit the gun to be used for purposes other than sporting clays, although the gun is designed primarily for that sport.

The barrels measure twenty-eight inches and the gun is forty-five inches long overall.

After a few familiarization shots, the gun and ammunition were tested on the pattern board to determine which choke tube seemed best for sporting clays shooting. It is important for the shooter to know where the shot pattern of the selected ammunition is printing before the gun is used for clay targets. Some shooters will prefer to put the two improved cylinder tubes in the barrels so both pattern the same. Others may wish to install chokes which will provide a wider pattern on the first shot and a slightly tighter pattern on the second, usually longer-range shot.

The safety slide places itself on safe each time the action is broken open, with the S visible on top of the tang. The slide must be pushed forward until the S is covered after loading and before firing. Some experienced sporting clays shooters may have their gunsmith eliminate this feature from their guns for the fast sporting clays action.

The gun was put through its paces at the Moore-N-

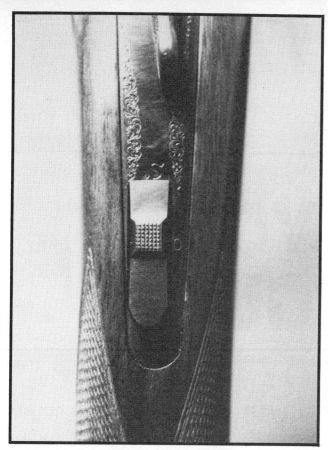

Tang safety lever also acts as a manual barrel selector. In the normal, centered position, the bottom barrel will fire first. Moving the lever to the right, uncovering the O, the internal mechanism will select the top barrel first.

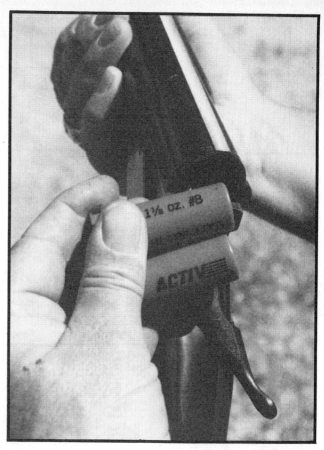

Ammunition manufacturers such as ACTIV are producing special sporting clays loads to keep up with the interest in the sport. Most use 7½ or 8 shot, minimum loads.

Moore sporting clays range in San Fernando, California. Like most sporting clays ranges in the United States, the facility is relatively new and is laid out in some rugged canyons and hills to test shooters' skills. Shotgunners from throughout the Southern California and Los Angeles area find challenges aplenty at the course.

The facility has ten stations with clay targets designed to simulate small game such as rabbit, duck, quail, dove, chukar, geese, pheasant and pigeon. The speed, angle of flight, trajectory and release points are all designed to emulate the flight or run of live game. Natural habitat is utilized as much as possible and all targets are released from traps invisible to the shooter. To maintain the challenge, the course is changed every two weeks. Most shooters are able to expend their hundred rounds through the course in about an hour and a half.

ACTIV Industries of Kearneysville, West Virginia, is producing special sporting clays loads. The hulls and wads are of plastic, and loaded with 1⅛ ounces of #8 shot, just about right for most sporting clays shooting. The Avanza seemed to like the diet of ACTIV ammunition throughout several sessions of claybird shooting.

The gun is light enough to be carried all afternoon without undue fatigue. It mounts to the shoulder quickly and smoothly, with no snags caused by the rubber recoil pad. As mentioned, the pad is slightly radiused at heel and toe to avoid being caught in a shooting jacket or vest.

The middle sight bead is smaller than the front bead and the ideal sight alignment is to have the rear bead lined up exactly with the front. The figure eight picture familiar to the skeet shooter is not the most desirable for sporting clays, according to some instructors. The top rib draws the aiming eye directly toward the target for maximum concentration.

The gun is designed to be slightly weight-forward for a better swing and smooth follow-through. This feature shows up especially well during fast doubles shooting. The shooter must concentrate fully on the target with no distractions from the design or action of the gun. The Avanza accomplished all those things.

Because test shooting was with a new gun, the break-open action was a bit stiff, but this should smooth itself out after a few more range sessions. The automatic selective ejectors functioned as they were designed: empty hulls were ejected smartly to the rear while unfired rounds were lifted from the chambers, but not ejected. Firing pins are manufactured to be unbreakable and there were no problems during the sessions at the range.

The Marocchi Avanza is an attractive sporting clays over/under shotgun, imported from Italy. It is well designed and balanced for the fast sporting clays action attracting more shooters every day. The gun should take the shooter successfully through thousands of rounds, as he or she goes from beginner to expert.

CHAPTER 5

SIGHT YOUR SHOTGUN

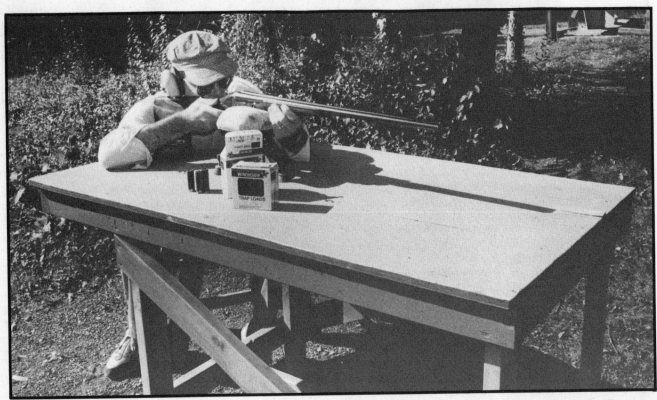

John Ross benchrests a Parker Reproduction 12 gauge. For the most accurate pattern, position the front sandbag so it suports both the barrel and receiver of the shotgun. Resting the barrel on the sandbag means high patterns.

NOT ONE in a dozen hunters, probably not one in a hundred, ever patterns his or her shotgun. Shotgun shooting is supposed to come naturally; that blessed hand and eye coordination which allows some shooters to swing a shotgun and nail a bird as easily as Mickey Mantle once smacked a homer.

"I'm not a good shot and I admit it. When it comes to rifles, I work hard to improve the odds. Loads are tested thoroughly from the bench before I go hunting. Why not? You improve your chances of scoring on game by knowing exactly where your rifle shoots," admits John Ross, a New Jersey shooting enthusiast.

Knowing Where Your Scattergun Shoots Is A Must For Sporting Clays!

To learn how you perform with the gun and load, face 90 degrees from stationary target. Have a friend cry, "Bird!" then mount and swing the gun toward the target, shooting as the muzzle crosses the aiming point. It's revealing!

"But I've burned plenty of powder pushing shot at various fowl, feathered and ceramic, without once sitting down to find out where or how well my shotguns and shells were shooting.

"I suspect I'm not alone. On a recent sporting clays outing, where we were all, again, properly humiliated, I asked the guys in the squad: 'Ever pattern your shotgun?' The collective response was a chorus of mumbled negatives. The consensus was when it comes to sporting clays, you either hit 'em or you don't."

In addition to doing a whale of a lot of shooting, John Ross is one of those inquiring-mind fellows who wants to know the "why" of things as well as the "how." For that reason, we asked him to come up with some methods of checking out where a shotgun shoots — and what to do about it if it's less than satisfactory.

Here's what he has to offer:

"Wait 'til you shoot the pond course," one shooter said. "You can tell how your gun shoots there." What can you tell from a string of shot stinging water to a froth? Maybe whether you centered the object at which you shot, but not much more. Not only is such an exercise futile, but it can be dangerous. Those little round shot can ricochet from the water's surface.

In sporting clays, it's imperative that you know where your shotgun shoots and how you shoot it — two different things — at a variety of ranges. The first step is patterning the gun with the ammo you'll use on the course, generally 1⅛ ounce of #8s or #9s.

What I always suspected about shotgun patterning is true. It's drudgery. You've got to count each one of those little pellets inside a thirty-inch circle. A typical 1⅛-ounce load of #8s holds 452 shot. Counting them is boring, but there is no other way.

I take that back. If you've got a four- or five-foot square steel plate and a gallon of whitewash, you can make yourself a dandy patterning board. Coat the plate with whitewash, fire a shot and you can clearly see where each pellet

Ross inspects Hornady's shotgun target. When snapshots are made at patterning paper, Ross suggests triggering the shot just before the bead swings by the bird. He has learned a good deal about steel, lead and modern chokes.

strikes. Most gun clubs ought to have such a plate, but they probably don't, because idiots — obviously not club members — would try out rifle and handgun loads on it.

Testing a shotgun and load requires three separate series of targets. First of all, you want to find out how the load performs in your shotgun. Then you want to learn how you and the shotgun perform with the load.

The first series of targets is no fun. They require you to sit at a shooting bench, rest the action or forearm — but not the barrel — on a padded rest, sight as carefully as you can down the barrel at an aiming point, using a six o'clock hold. Then you squeeze the trigger with as much consistency as you can muster.

You'll take a pounding. The average recoil of a standard 1⅛-ounce 12-gauge field load has almost twice the average recoil of a .30/06 loaded with a 180-grain bullet.

Five shots per load is the minimum acceptable number of rounds you need to test to obtain a valid indication of the performance of the load. The NRA and others use a minimum of ten shots per load.

It's always a question. At what distance do you pattern a shotgun? Forty yards is the standard. At that distance the number of shot within a thirty-inch circle will equate with percentages that define performance of full, modified, improved cylinder — and other — chokes.

Forty yards is fine for the flush station on the woods walk where the double comes up from behind the brush pile. It's just like regulation trap, only you've got a few trees around to distract your perspective. But the bouncing bunny shot is little more than fifteen yards out and the

optimum range for incoming clays seldom exceeds twenty-five yards.

According to Larry Nailon of Clearview Products (Box 12160, Oklahoma City, OK 73157), a master at tuning barrels and chokes for sporting clays, a shotgun should deliver one hundred percent patterns — or close to it — at each distance where one expects to make the shot. A fifty

TABLE #1							
APPROXIMATE SHOT COUNT PER WEIGHT — LEAD							
Size:	9	8	7½	6	5	4	2	BB
Ounce								
¾	439	308	262	169	128	101	68	37
⅞	512	359	306	197	149	118	79	44
1	585	410	350	225	170	135	90	50
1⅛	658	462	393	253	192	152	102	56
1¼	731	513	437	281	213	169	113	62
1⅜	804	564	481	309	234	185	124	69
1½	877	615	525	337	255	202	135	75
1⅝	951	667	568	396	277	221	158	81
1⅞							169	94
2							180	100
2¼								112

Note: Data from Lyman Shotshell Handbook #2 and Federal Cartridge Company. Actual number of shot/ounce varies with brand and lot.

percent pattern at forty yards can be pretty tight at twenty yards! It's worthwhile to pattern each barrel/tube/ammo combination at ranges of twenty, thirty and forty yards.

Also, you might find, as I have, that the tube marked improved cylinder gives a better pattern than the ones marked skeet or modified. And try different loads as well. You will count patterns until you see them in your sleep. Once you know how your gun shoots, then you can concentrate on how you shoot your gun.

That's the purpose of the second series of targets. Set up a patterning target at an appropriate range. Stand so you are facing ninety degrees from the target, but point your lead foot in the direction you plan to shoot. Hold your shotgun as you would if you were on a sporting clays course — gun off your shoulder with two inches of stock tucked under your arm with the barrel pointed slightly upward. Have a partner say, "Bird!" Raise the shotgun, swinging toward the center of the target as you do. As the barrel reaches the aiming point, squeeze off a shot.

This approximates mounting a shotgun and factors in the problems of stock fit, vision and swing into the equation of how you perform with a given shotgun and load. Using this technique, work your way through barrel/choke combinations, again at the distances of twenty, thirty and forty yards.

Awhile back, another gun scribe wrote a piece about how you could pattern your shotgun at ten yards, then project performance out to the distance where you expected to hit your bird. Unfortunately, that writer's imagination was better than his knowledge of ballistics.

He assumed the path of a charge of shot to be a perfect cone, with straight sides. It isn't. More likely, shot flares away from the center of the charge as distance increases from the muzzle. Thus, the path of a shot charge looks more like the bell of a trumpet than a straight-sided cone.

Wind drift is another factor, especially with light shot used in sporting clays. According to Nailon, the difference between shooting with a ten mile-per-hour wind and shooting against it can be fifteen percent pattern density.

Part of the problem in patterning a shotgun has been finding suitable targets and a way to set them up. Hornady (P.O. Box 1848, Grand Island, NE 68801) offers a shotgun

patterning kit for about $10 that includes five targets, stakes and cardboard backing on which to clip the targets.

This is a good rig. Printed on square sheets of heavy paper is a thirty-inch ring containing a concentric 17.5-inch inner circle. The target is divided into quadrants with a drawing of a duck at the center. Additional targets with doves or pheasants can be ordered.

Standard patterning targets employ a 21.1-inch inner circle surrounded by an 8.9-inch outer ring. This divides the area of a thirty-inch circle into two equal areas of roughly 350 square inches. Hornady's target puts one-third of the area, 240 square inches, inside the center ring and two-thirds in the outer circle.

In either case, by comparing the number of shot in the inner circle against the number in the outer ring, you can determine pattern density. You should have more hits in the inner circle than in the outer circle. We'll come back to evaluating patterns in a moment.

To set up the Hornady patterning kit, insert two of the three stakes through the die-cut tabs in the cardboard backer. Slide the third stake through a pair of cutouts on the top of the backer. Push or gently pound the stakes into the ground; then, with the paper clips provided, put a target on the front of the backer. It's that simple!

I use a lot of shotgun targets and, for that reason, usually make my own. Go to a paper supplier (found in the phone book) and buy a fifty-pound roll of thirty-six-inch-wide brown kraft wrapping paper. The cost should be about $35 and it should keep you in targets for years.

Cutting the paper into three-foot lengths provides convenient and cheap thirty-six-inch square targets. Fold each target in half, in half again, then in half, but diagonally, so you have a triangle.

When you open the target, you'll see that the folds mark forty-five-degree radians, dividing the target into eighths. Place a bright orange aiming dot where the vectors intersect. Folding targets into triangles also makes them easier to handle. Ever wrestled with fifty sheets of three-foot-square wrapping paper flapping in the wind?

My patterning board is a three- by four-foot sheet of three-eighths-inch plywood. It lasts for about two hundred rounds. I drive a couple of cheap, forty-eight-inch metal fence posts into the ground and wire the board against them. Then I staple my targets to the board. Unfortunately, the best way to evaluate shotgun patterns is based on the premise of one shot per target. But on each target, there's a host of useful data.

TABLE #2
APPROXIMATE SHOT COUNT PER WEIGHT — STEEL

Size:	6	5	4	3	2	1	BB	BBB	T	F
Ounce										
¾	236	182	144	118	94	77	54	46	39	30
15/16	295	228	180	143	117	97	67	58	49	37
1	315	243	192	158	125	103	72	62	52	40
1⅛	354	273	216	178	141	116	81	70	58	45
1¼	394	304	240	197	156	129	90	77	65	50
1⅜	433	334	264	217	172	142	99	85	71	55
1½	472	364	288	237	187	154	108	93	78	60
1⅝	512	395	312	257	203	167	117	101	84	65

Note: Data from Federal Cartridge Company. Actual number of shot/ounce varies with brand and lot.

TABLE #3
PERCENTAGE PATTERN — CHOKE

(Based on percentage of shot charge striking within a thirty-inch circle at forty yards.)

70% - 80%	=	Full Choke
65% - 70%	=	Improved Modified
55% - 65%	=	Modified Choke
50% - 60%	=	Skeet No. 2
50% - 55%	=	Quarter Choke
45% - 50%	=	Improved Cylinder
35% - 40%	=	Skeet No. 1 (Cylinder)

Fred Newhouse pulls a pair of doubles from an Outers trap mounted on a spare tire. The trap can be used to throw straightaway or crossing claybirds. This all is a help when one is attempting to determine where shotguns shoot.

The first step is to label the target with the following information: gun, gauge, choke and/or barrel, load, distance and date. When you get home, spread the target out on a flat surface. If your target's pre-printed, circle each shot with a dark-colored fine-point pen. Count and record the number of shot in each section of the target.

If you use wrapping paper targets, you'll need to make a couple of accessories before you can evaluate patterns. The biggest problem is drawing twenty-one-inch and thirty-inch circles. Here's how I do it, though you may have a better way:

Drive a flat-head nail through the center of a half-sheet of three-sixteenths-inch plywood. Put a piece of duct or similar tape over the nail head, lest you scratch the dining room table and incur the wrath of you know who. (When you know who read this, she exclaimed, "What are you doing with plywood on my dining room table?" I told her it was okay, because I put down a table cloth first!)

With a hollow punch, make a hole in the center of the aiming point on the target, then place the target over the nail which sticks up like a spindle through the piece of plywood. Punch and stack as many targets as the nail will hold.

Using a yardstick as your compass, draw a line down its center. Along the centerline, drill holes just a little bigger than the nail at one inch, 11½ inches and sixteen inches.

Place the hole at one inch over the nail on top of a target. Stick the point of an old thick-lead pencil or medium felt-tip pen through the hole at 11½ inches and scribe a circle. Do the same at sixteen inches. Cutting off the yardstick at eighteen inches makes your homemade circle drawer easier to swing.

If you folded the target into quarters, then diagonally in half again — and if you draw both circles — your target will be divided into sixteen segments of equal area.

Circle, count and note the number of hits in each segment. Add the number of strikes in each segment in the inner circle, then do the same for the hits in the outer ring. From the accompanying pellet count tables, find the number of pellets per weight of the shot size tested. I've included numbers for both lead and steel shot. Divide the total number of hits in the inner ring by the total number of shot in the charge. This gives you the percentage of hits in the inner circle. Do the same for the number of hits in the outer ring.

Adding inner and outer percentages gives you total pattern percentage. Compared against Table #3, you can determine whether the load performs as a full, modified, improved cylinder choke, et cetera. It's nice to know whether your full-choke bore is producing improved cylinder patterns or vice versa.

Compare the percentages in the inner and outer circles. If you use the twenty-one-inch inner and nine-inch outer circle system, the percentage of a good pattern will be significantly denser inside the inner circle.

With Hornady's system, density in the inner and outer rings should be about equal. If half the charge strikes inside the center ring, the pattern is appropriately more dense in the middle. Remember, Hornady's inner circle covers one-third of the area of the target.

But if there are more shot in the outer ring and the counts are distributed evenly in the sections of the outer ring, then you have a pattern that looks like a donut. Blown patterns aren't common with today's loads, but they do happen, particularly with handloads driven at velocities that are too high.

Look again at the number of pellets in each segment of the target. By comparing counts per segment, you can tell if the load is patterning evenly or if it's weighted in one direction. For instance, if there are significantly more pellets in those sections in the top part of the target, then the load may be shooting high. This is why shooting five targets with each load/choke/distance combination is a must. If four of the five targets show even distribution, but one does not, you probably held off-center for that·shot.

If three patterns tend to be weighted with more hits off in one direction, then either the load or the gun is not shooting where it's pointed.

It is not uncommon for a shotgun not to shoot where you point it. Said another way, given all the variation of loads (light, heavy, target, magnum, lead, steel, ad infinitum), why expect that a barrel will deliver all loads to the same point of impact at a given distance?

To check the difference between point of aim and center of pattern, get a thirty-six-inch square piece of cardboard and cut a thirty-inch circle in the middle. Move the circle around the target until as many shot as possible are enclosed within the circle. Trace the outline of that circle on the target and compare the difference from the original circle you scribed with the yardstick.

With a carpenter's square, you can easily determine the center of the circle you've just drawn. Make marks at fifteen inches on the outer edge of both arms of the square. Place the marks on the line of the circle. The outside tip of the right angle at the center of the square marks the center of your new circle. Put a round sticker on that point. Now you'll know whether the load and shotgun shoots high, low, left or right. By carefully comparing targets that you shot from the bench with those you shot swinging the gun, you can see how you tend to shoot.

The major problem with this type of shotgun patterning is that it only records shot distribution in one plane which is perpendicular to the axis of the bore. It assumes that all shot arrive at the target at the same time, which we know is not so. Shot strings out after leaving the muzzle and, in some cases, a shot string can become six feet long by the time it reaches the target. However, most pellets are grouped in the first couple feet of the string.

The third and final step in learning where your shotgun shoots is to take those loads that perform best, buy a box of claybirds and get together with a buddy who can use a hand trap. Have him throw series of straightaways, crossing, high and low birds. Practice shooting them, always beginning with the shotgun in the unmounted position. Before

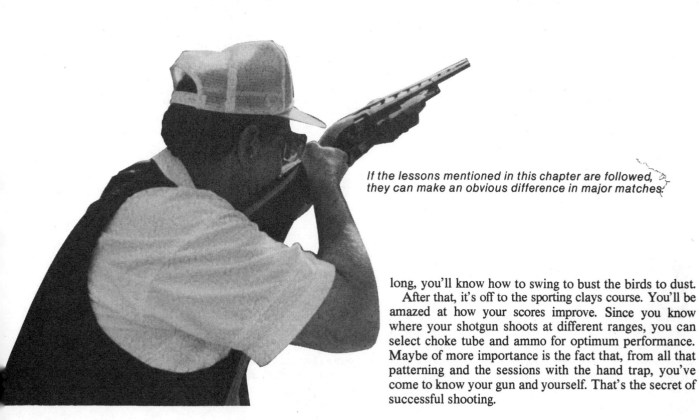

If the lessons mentioned in this chapter are followed, they can make an obvious difference in major matches.

long, you'll know how to swing to bust the birds to dust.

After that, it's off to the sporting clays course. You'll be amazed at how your scores improve. Since you know where your shotgun shoots at different ranges, you can select choke tube and ammo for optimum performance. Maybe of more importance is the fact that, from all that patterning and the sessions with the hand trap, you've come to know your gun and yourself. That's the secret of successful shooting.

CHAPTER
6

UNDERSTANDING SHOTGUN BALANCE

Lloyd Woodhouse, shotgun coach of our Olympic shooting team, checks the new trap bunker at the Olympic Shooting Center in Colorado. Many thousands of claybirds are shot by team here.

SHOTGUN BALANCE all too often is dismissed simply as comfort rather than a serious fault that is correctable. "My exploration of balance in shotguns began in a twenty-four-hour truck stop on a dead-of-winter morning. Several of us were starting an eastern Colorado goose hunt and one of the hunters was Lloyd Woodhouse, shotgun coach of the U.S. Olympic shooting team. With him was the Colorado NRA field representative, George Nyfler," recalls Galen A. Geer.

Geer has been a serious shooter for most of his life — including a tour in Vietnam that was even more serious — but he admits that the matter of shotgun balance was one about which he was vague. Here, he reports the development of his understanding:

The group included my brother, Wayne, and my brother-in-law, Shawn Cruzen, who had been sleeping in the back seat with my springer spaniel, until Wayne eased his Blazer into a parking space in front of the truck stop restaurant off U.S. 50 near Lamar, Colorado. We had planned to meet

Here's A Facet Of Scattergunning Excellence That Often Goes Ignored Through Ignorance Of The Need!

Nyfler and Woodhouse for breakfast at 4 a.m. to start the hunting day. Shawn scratched the dog's ears while I scanned the parking lot for George.

"They're here," I said, then stumbled out of the Blazer. We pushed my dog, Grettel, into the back seat and closed the door. We had more than two hours before dawn, time for a hearty breakfast and some "get acquainted conversation" with Woodhouse. A minute after introductions were completed, the five of us trooped inside for breakfast.

With our first cup of coffee poured and orders taken by a bleary-eyed waitress, I relaxed and looked at Woodhouse. He had asked us to call him Woody.

"Woody," I said, looking for something to say or ask that would spark conversation, "what would you say the most important single link is in shotguns that a shotgun hunter or a sporting clays shooter should look for when gun buying?"

I was prepared to begin a discussion of the variables of shotgun stocks, barrels, chokes and even gun handling. Instead, Woody quickly said, "Balance."

"I am not sure I understand," I said.

Woodhouse adjusts one of the traps in the bunker for practice by Olympic hopefuls.

"Balance," Woody repeated. "There are a lot of things that go into making a gun fit, but in the end, it is the balance of the shotgun which sets it apart as one that brings out all the abilities of the shooter. If a shotgun hunter's guns are balanced and fitted to him, he will shoot them well. When it comes to balance, a shooter who has to handle each gun a little different because the balance varies from gun to gun, will find he is fighting with each gun, because of the difference in balance. The shooter's chances of becoming proficient with all of his guns is limited because of the balance."

We spent the day hunting. Woody killed some ducks in the afternoon. I missed a pheasant and a goose and spent a lot of time thinking about "balance." Several times I talked with Woody about "balance," trying to clear in my mind how balance is a connecting thread between different shotguns owned by the same shooter. I also was thinking about some of my misses on sporting clays.

Over the next few months, I spent more time looking beyond shotgun fit to understand balance. In May, I visited with Woody at the Olympic Shooting Center on Fort Carson, near Colorado Springs. We again talked about balance.

Woody explained that balance is achieved with shotguns by following steps to correct a gun's fit.

"When buying a new shotgun," he explained, "everything begins by knowing what to look for in the gun."

The first criterion, Woody believes, is for the buyer to mount the gun, as he would for hunting or claybird shooting, while a friend checks for "cast" in the gun.

"All guns — even models made by the same company — will have a slightly different cast to them. It may be a little; it may be a lot. It is a slight manufacturing variation in the gun."

A gun's natural cast should not be confused with cast-off, which is the deliberate angling of the buttstock of a shotgun, either right or left, to make the gun easier for a

Woodhouse shows how the balance of this shotgun is found. This is not to be confused with balance of the shooter!

Cory Fritsch, one of the young shooters attending a summer shooting program, is taught to locate balance.

right- or left-hand shooter — depending on the cast-off — to mount. Building a specific cast-off into a custom-built gun — and even some rack guns — is common in Europe. Cast-off is not common in American-made guns and is, in fact, avoided by U.S. manufacturers.

"In American guns, the variation is slight," Woody said, "but cast will affect shooting."

To check your own guns for cast, first make sure the gun is unloaded, then have a friend stand in front of the barrel while you mount the gun exactly as you would for shooting.

"If the eye of the shooter is not in line with the top of the barrel and the bead, then the cast is off," Woody explained.

If the eye is to one side or the other, the cast can be corrected. A simple, but often effective means of correcting cast is to remove the buttstock, then place thin shims or spacers between the wood and the metal to move the stock and align the eye properly.

There also is the "pitch" and "drop" of the gun. Pitch is the angle of the buttplate and is measured at the muzzle end of the gun by standing the gun flat on the buttplate next to a wall with the action or receiver touching the wall. The distance from the wall to the top of the muzzle is the pitch. Normally, pitch is between two and three inches, depending upon barrel length.

To raise or lower the pitch of a gun, shims can be placed under the heel or toe of the buttplate. The effect will be to raise or lower the pattern by altering the fit of the buttplate to the shoulder, raising or lowering the shot pattern.

Drop appears twice on the shotgun stock. There is drop at the heel and drop at the comb. The "heel" of the shotgun is the top of the buttplate where it meets the buttstock. Drop at the heel is the distance between the gun's heel and the gun's line of sight. The less the amount of drop at the heel, the less recoil felt by the shooter. In other words, the straighter, or more in line with the gun's action the buttplate is, the lower the felt recoil on each shot.

Drop at the comb is critically important, because it is on the comb where the cheek of the shooter meets the stock, becoming the rear sight of the shotgun. If the comb drop is wrong, the shooter's eye will not be on the shotgun's line of sight. A proper drop to the comb will put the shooter's eye right on the line of sight of the shotgun when the cheek is firmly placed on the comb. A high comb will place the shooter's eye above the barrel, and when shooting, the barrel will be pointed over the target. On a low comb, the eye is looking into the receiver and the shot pattern will be low.

"The eye," Woody said, "must be on line with the barrel. When the shooter looks down he should see the bead, not a shortened barrel or the back of the receiver."

It takes only a few humbling misses either in the field or on the range before a good shooter realizes there is a problem and corrects those faults. Most shooters — while they understand these areas of shotgun fit — do not carry the shotgun fit a step further to include balance.

Woodhouse points to the difference between the balance of the gun and where shooter's leading hand is placed in order to achieve the proper balance for shooter.

While Cory Fritsch holds his shotgun in position, the Olympic coach checks for balance and fit of the gun.

Lloyd Woodhouse checks the cast of the shotgun for the young shooter attending the summer program.

"If these gun characteristics are considered from the start of a search for a new gun," Woody explained, "and the buyer gets as close as possible to a good fit, then has final adjustments made by a gunsmith, a custom fit on a shotgun off the rack is possible. But, if a competent shooter still is missing targets, even with a properly fitted gun, there must be a problem.

"Balance becomes the key to unlocking the gun's and shooter's potential. A gun can fit in every respect, but without balance to hold the elements together, the shooter still is fighting the gun on each shot."

To discover whether a gun has proper balance, the shooter mounts the gun while picking out a distant target at the same time a friend is watching closely from the side and front.

"It may be hard to see, but the sign of trouble with balance is a porpoising muzzle," Woody said. He demonstrated the balance problem using one of his younger shooters, Cory Fritsch, who was attending the summer shooting camp program at the time.

"Balance is the last factor in a gun's fit, because without good balance, the shooter is spending valuable time trying to steady the muzzle and find his target," Woody said. "If all other factors are corrected, but the muzzle moves from side to side, up and down, even in a figure eight, the gun is not balanced.

"Balance is not the balance of the piece like a scale, but the balance between the point where the forestock is held for support and where the gun is gripped by the shooting hand.

"This is a balance between muzzle, action and stock that allows the shooter to bring the gun up smooth, fast and on target without having the target disappear and reappear due to muzzle movement."

To be a successful shooter — whether bird hunting or shooting claybirds — a shooter should not shift shooting styles and positions from gun to gun to compensate for different balance or fit. A solid and comfortable position that allows maximum control of the gun is required first. The forearm can be extended, as is common with most skeet shooters, or at an angle, as in most trap and upland bird shooting positions — but the guns must be fitted to that position of the shooter and balanced.

The ideal balance is one that, at the point where the hand grips the forestock of the gun, has just enough weight forward to allow the other hand to bring the gun up smoothly, as if the leading hand is serving as a pivot for the shotgun. The mount should be done without additional movement of the gun or hands for position. Proper balance allows a smooth pivot of the gun on the leading hand, while unbalanced guns cause the shooter to jerk and punch the gun rather than mount it.

"Balance can be achieved on a gun once fit is established. If a gun is stock heavy, weight can be removed from the stock. A muzzle-heavy gun needs weight added to the stock," Woody explained.

Balance, then, is a single connecting thread between different shotguns owned by the same shooter. In the fraction of a second after the gun is mounted, the human brain is trying to line up the target and the shotgun, while calculating speed and angle. One can be disoriented by a shotgun that is not balanced and that is porpoising.

"Every aspect of the gun can be perfect," Woody said, "the cast, pitch, drop, length of pull — every detail except balance, because the shooter's gun is muzzle- or butt-heavy. Instead of coming up and staying in one comfortable position, the gun is moving back and forth. Even a fraction of an inch will throw the shooter off. Balance is a key that is often overlooked in gun selection and shooting."

When I left the shooting center I was thinking about my own guns. Balance, I realized, explains why I often favor one or two guns over others. I decided to check my shotguns for balance that afternoon and corrected two guns.

If you check your own shotgun, you may find the balance is off. To correct balance, take the gun to a gunsmith you can work with to correct the fit first, then the balance. The gun may need ounces shaved out of the inside of the stock, or weight added to offset a heavy muzzle to balance the gun for you.

Once fitted and balanced, a shotgun you just couldn't hit with may suddenly become a prized target taker!

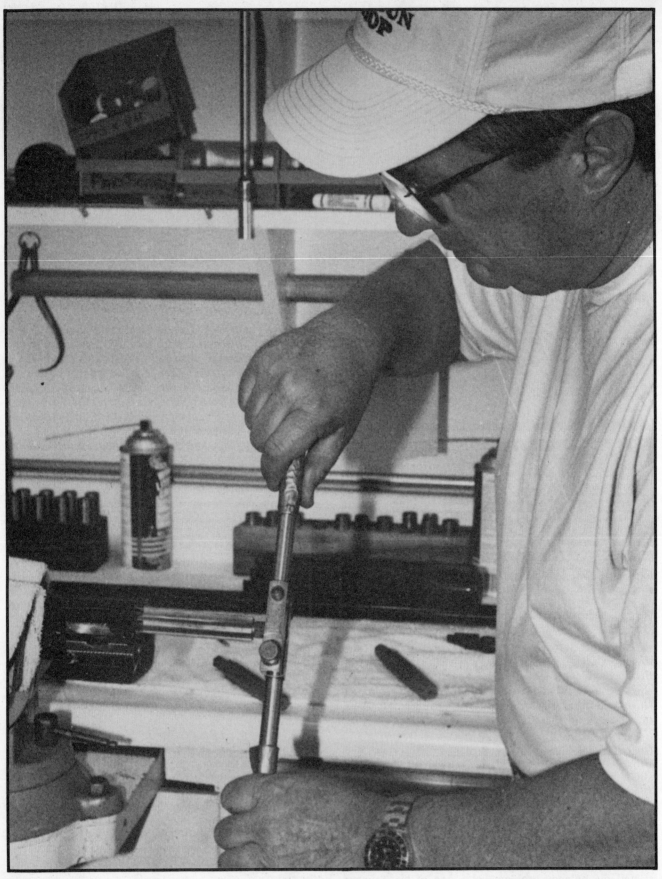

John Dickman of The Shotgun Shop uses a hand-reamer to relieve forcing cones on a set of over/under barrels. Reaming the part of the barrel where the chamber ends and barrel begins is common for sporting clays guns.

CHAPTER 7

RETROFITTING FOR SPORTING CLAYS

There Are Gunsmiths Who Specialize In Making Your Favorite Shotgun A Sporting Clays Contender!

I F NOTHING else, sporting clays has triggered an entirely new genre of aftermarket industry. Gadgets and goodies abound that are designed and produced primarily, or solely, for shooting sporting clays. A major segment of this aftermarket phenomenon is the mushrooming of specialty gunshops whose primary source of income is generated by retro-work on shotguns for sporting clays shooters.

Literally, from one end of the gun to the other, there are things that can be done to fine tune a shotgun for the sport. Starting at the muzzle end, there is choke work and sights to consider. Choke work generally falls into two categories: Opening up the integral choke in the barrel or the installation of an interchangeable choke tube system.

The more simple of the two choke modification processes, of course, is the opening up of a tight, integral choke. An example encountered routinely is the opening of a full choke to either an extremely light modified restriction or to improved cylinder. Full chokes are needed rarely, if ever, in shooting sporting clays. This is not to say the sport cannot be shot with a full choke, because it certainly can. The point is that such a high degree of restriction and its resultant narrow, dense pattern simply are not needed.

Some of the world class sporting clays shooters, however, do opt for modified choking in their guns. Former world champ John Bidwell of England, for example, uses modified choking in both barrels of his over/under Browning. This makes sense for top shooters, because they are able to hit repeated targets without the need for a wider pattern "edge" to account for scores. Generally, when they miss, it is not by just a little bit. When they miss, it usually is be-

cause they either misread the target presentation, or made some relatively basic shooting error. In such situations, a pattern that is a few inches wider normally would not do them any good.

But by using the same chokes all the time, those shooters can simplify life for themselves in that they are not bothered with worries about what might or might not be the "best" choke to use for a particular presentation. They can spend that time and effort concentrating on their game. But these are exceptional shooters, and it really is not proper to suggest that some of the things that work for them on the world circuit have any relevance to the needs and concerns of the other 99.9 percent of shooters.

Most shooters can improve their scores at sporting clays by at least several targets per hundred if they use an improved cylinder choke rather than a full choke — or even a modified.

Relieving an integral choke in a shotgun barrel is simple, but when done properly, is not particularly quick. Mechanically, it simply is a matter of reaming out some of the restriction in the choke. It is a multi-step, time-consuming project. In a best-case scenario, the gunsmith and the gun owner will determine what choke characteristic is desired. This means they will concern themselves with pattern density, pellet distribution within the pattern and center point of impact for the pattern. All of these factors can be manipulated via a choke job.

For starters, it really is not necessary for a shooter to concern himself or herself with the working terms such as "full," "modified" or "improved cylinder." These terms not only have different meanings to different people under

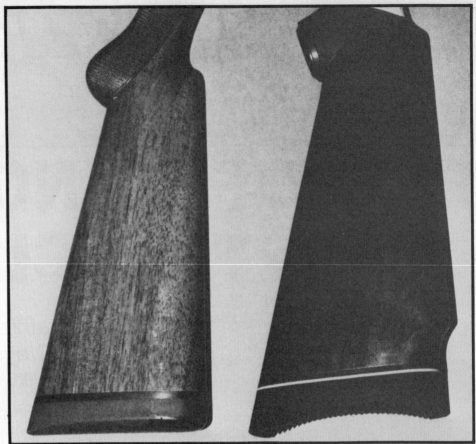

Sporting clays guns such as one at left are formed so they don't snag or hang up on clothing as the gun is mounted. Trap gun butts are configured to help shooter hold the gun in same position each time gun is mounted, as with the gun at right.

different circumstances, but are far too vague for someone who is taking the trouble to have a choke fine-tuned.

When chokes are discussed, the various terms, like "full," are discussed correctly in terms of the percentage of pellets that hit within a thirty-inch circle at forty yards. That's fine. But such a system really should be considered more like a sticker price on a new pickup truck than anything hard and fast. For example, if the gun shoots typically irregular patterns with holes in them large enough for targets to fly through, then it really doesn't matter how wide the pattern is; consistency will remain an elusive quantity in shooting.

Hence, it is the quality of the pattern that really is important — and there is only one way to determine that. It is to pattern the gun with specific ammo. Don't lose track of the fact that, when a choke is fine-tuned, it is a "custom" project. And there is no reason for this procedure to be quick-and-dirty. It may as well be done properly.

So, if the choke in the barrel is "full" from the factory, and the owner wants it opened up, the gunsmith logically would begin by measuring the inside of the barrel to determine exactly how much restriction there is between the main barrel and the choke. Barrels even from the same maker and in the same model can vary significantly, both in their internal barrel dimensions as well as in the degree of restriction. The gunsmith first must determine what exists on the shotgun.

Remington's design specifications are a good general set of standards to use when discussing chokes and that sort of thing, because that company's numbers are right in the middle of what are typically considered proper for the various designations. For example, Remington's production standard for 12-gauge bore diameter is .727-inch. Certainly, it is common to find 12-gauge bores with other dimensions like .729, but .727 is a good "standard."

Based upon the .727-inch standard bore diameter, Remington's standard dimension for a full choke is .036-inch restriction. That means that the choke constricts down .036 from the .727. Again, whether it is some other maker, or even on some of Remington's guns, there are acceptable pluses and minuses. It is not uncommon to encounter a "full" choke with .032-inch restriction. Nor is it terribly uncommon to find a "full" choke with .040-inch restriction.

For modified choke, Remington's standard is .018-inch restriction from the .727-inch bore; for improved cylinder, the company's standard is .009-inch restriction.

In general terms, this means Remington has decided that, on a production basis, the objective of achieving full-choke performance is achieved best with .036-inch restriction. That objective, in Remington terms, is to deliver seventy percent of the pellets in a load within a thirty-inch circle at forty yards. Similarly, the company's objective with a modified choke is to deliver sixty percent of the pellets within the thirty-inch circle at forty yards, and for the improved cylinder is to deliver fifty percent of the pellets within that thirty-inch circle at the same yardage.

Back to the retro-work in the gun shop. If the barrel to be

Installation of a radiused butt pad is another of the common retrofit projects often done by John Dickman.

done is full choke, and the shooter wants improved cylinder, the gunsmith might ream the inside of the choke area from say .036 constriction to something like .015-inch. Sometimes, it might not even be that much for the first effort. Then the gunsmith will pattern that barrel with whatever load he and the shooter have determined should be used as a benchmark loading. Depending upon how the pattern develops, the gunsmith may need to continue opening the restriction to achieve the desired percentage of pellets in the pattern. If the desired percentage is fifty, and if at .015-inch the delivered percentage is fifty-six, then the gunsmith might take out another .002-inch of restriction, then pattern it again. This .002-inch opening-up could continue repeatedly until the desired performance is achieved.

During this procedure, the gunsmith should be paying attention to some of the other factors, as well. For example, if the barrel is not centering the pattern well, it can be "adjusted" during the reaming procedures. Certainly, there is a limit to how much adjustment can be achieved this way, but the subject here is fine tuning, not barrel bending. And there are subtle ways to massage the inside of the choke area to alter the distribution of pellets within a pattern — again, to a degree only.

It is important for the shooter to have the barrel patterned with exactly the same loads that normally will be used. Different loadings can pattern quite differently, even through the same barrel.

So much for opening up and fine tuning a fixed choke.

More frequently, when shotguns are retro-worked for sporting clays, the shooter opts to have the barrel modified for an interchangeable choke tube system. This makes sense in a variety of ways. First, it gives the shooter more

Fine tuning on such actions as this Beretta, as well as trigger mechanisms, is another retro job done on guns.

latitude by enabling him or her to change the restriction to suit individual needs. This allows total fine-tuning of the level of restriction and characteristics of pellet distribution. And, from station to station, the shooter has the option of picking precisely the pattern characteristics desired.

For shooters who might also use the sporting gun for hunting, the interchangeable choke tube systems make further sense in that they allow the luxury of being able to adjust the choking characteristics for the use of steel shot, as well as for lead shot. A word of caution, however. Not all interchangeable choke tubes are designed to handle steel shot. Check with the manufacturer before using steel shot in such tubes. Most of the tubes now being manufactured by the major companies will handle steel, but some will not. Certainly, a great many of the earlier production tubes were not designed to handle the harder steel payloads. What this means is that continued hammering by shooting steel loads can cause the tubes to bulge. This could mean

problems, including the inability to change them anymore.

One of the better known companies in the interchangeable choke tube business is Briley in Houston, Texas. Even though this firm is more than just a maker of interchangeable shotgun choke tubes, it is that product line that has made Briley one of the top operations of its kind in the nation.

One type of offering that separates Briley from the rest of the interchangeable choke tube crowd is the development of long, thin and strong tubes for guns with thin barrels. Using Space Age materials, these thin choke tubes will handle steel shot with ease.

Such tubes can be fitted into many of the older guns with the thinner barrels — the ones designed for lead shot a long time before anyone considered any need for any other type of shot. For these kinds of guns, like some of the Belgian-made Browning Superposed over/unders, it is either Briley tubes or no tubes — and no steel use, at all.

Like any major gun retro-fit company, Briley does a full

This close-up veiw of a reamer illustrates how it can be used to relieve forcing cones on Beretta over/under.

line of shotgun procedures, including normal things such as lengthening the forcing cones just forward of the chamber to help improve patterning with many kinds of loads and to cut down on felt recoil. Also in the realm of reducing felt recoil, this company does porting of barrels to reduce or eliminate muzzle jump. In fact, Briley can even go so far as to totally replace barrels — something that is becoming popular for some of the better vintage side-by-sides that originally came with twist-steel Damascus barrels. When the twist barrels are replaced with ones of modern metals, many of these classics can be put back into operation.

But when it comes to barrel porting, there is an operation in Southern California that is rewriting the book. The place is simply called The Shotgun Shop. It is located in the City of Industry, a suburb of Los Angeles. This shop has patented a procedure it calls Lazer Porting — something that differs in a number of ways from the more traditional methods.

Typically, ports — small holes — in the shotgun barrel were drilled. Different numbers and patterns of these holes, located between four and six inches from the muzzle,

served to bleed off powder gases when the gun was fired.

Since the holes were located in the upper part of the barrel, the force of the escaping gas would push the muzzle downward when the gun was fired. By controlling muzzle jump, the ports reduced or eliminated much of the felt recoil to the shooter, because the gun would not jump up and into the shooter's face. This kind of porting did little, if anything, to reduce the rearward thrust of the gun. The primary objective, in addition to reducing felt recoil, was to keep the muzzles from jumping up during recoil. This permitted a quicker and more effective second shot.

On pumps and autos that feature a single barrel, the ports in such a system are located on either side of the rib atop the barrel. On over/unders, some shooters prefer to have just the bottom barrel ported, while others opt to have both barrels ported. When both barrels are ported, it is not uncommon to have the top barrel ported somewhat differently than the bottom barrel. There are reasons for this.

Porting just the bottom barrel accomplishes the goal of

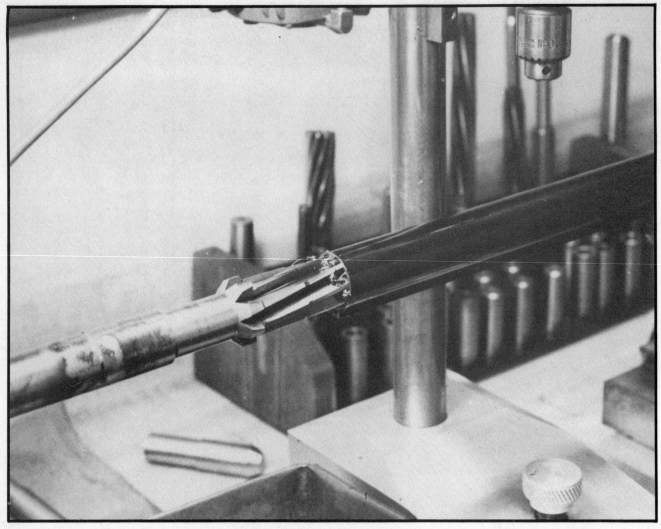

Remington barrel is being reamed before interchangeable tubes are fitted. Opening up chokes or installing such interchangeable tube systems is another of the common retro procedures being done on sporting clays guns.

assuring a more rapid recovery from the first shot so the second shot can be taken more quickly. Typically, the bottom barrel of an over/under is fired first. However, some shooters prefer to have the top barrel ported, as well, in a double effort to reduce perceived recoil. This may not seem like such a major consideration, but during long days of competition — when targets are counted by the hundred — any help is welcomed. And when a shooter is faced with two or more straight days of competition, it really makes a difference.

Effective porting, however, is much more than just drilling a few holes into a shotgun barrel. The angle at which the holes are made, as well as their placement on the barrel, is critical. Many shops that do a lot of porting use established jigs to help duplicate hole placement and drilling angle.

But Bill Houston and John Dickman at The Shotgun Shop developed a process for porting that precludes most of the negative possibilities when it comes to altering a barrel. For example, the drilling process could result in small scratches and nicks in the bluing. This could easily mean re-bluing — more time and money. If the barrel isn't

positioned correctly, one or more of the holes might be drilled at slightly the wrong angle, or at imprecise intervals. The drilling process can also result in barrel heating and torquing during the process. These are all points for potential problems.

Following a lengthy research and development effort, Lazer Porting came on the scene. These ports are rectangular, rather than round, and run lengthwise on the barrel. Depending upon where they are placed and how many of the rectangular ports are used, the recoil characteristics of the gun can be determined. But that's not what makes Lazer Porting so different. After all, oblong ports can be cut with a mill.

What separates Lazer Ports is the fact that they are really not "cut" or "drilled" at all. Rather, they are electronically installed at the molecular level. This means the barrel never gets hot, and the ports can be made totally consistently, time after time. This is just one example of the strides being made in aftermarket retro fitting of shotguns. guns.

Continuing rearward on a shotgun, the next popular pro-

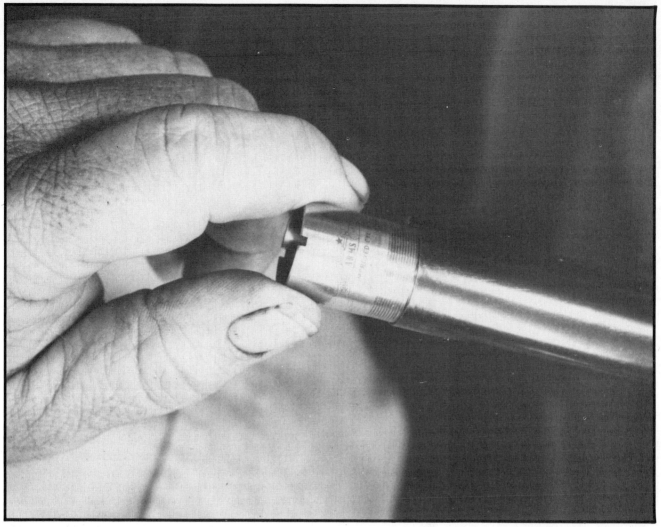

Once the muzzle area of the barrel is prepared, threaded, interchangeable choke tubes can be screwed into place.

cedure is to "relieve" the forcing cone just in front of the chamber. Typically, shotguns come from the factory with short, abrupt constrictions where the front end of the chamber meets the rear portion of the main bore. And there are times when a short forcing cone here is needed. For example, when paper and/or felt wads are used in shells, the shorter forcing cone helps prevent powder gas blow-by when the gun is fired. This is a particularly acute problem in extremely low temperatures. And, to a degree, it is a factor with plastic shot cup/wad combos in extremely low temperatures, as well.

Under normal conditions, the concave bottom of a plastic wad is forced out when the shell is fired, forming an effective gas seal. Hence, it is not necessary to have an abrupt forcing cone, because the expanded base of the wad fills any gap as the wad is forced from the shell and into the barrel proper. In fact, lengthening of the forcing cone often contributes to better patterning when plastic wads are used, because longer, gentler constrictions from the chamber to the bore allow the payload and wad to undergo less trauma there. With lead shot, this often means fewer pellets

deformed by being hammered against a radical constriction. Additionally, it means a reduction in the sharpness of recoil, because the payload is squeezed more gently into the main bore, rather than being choked into it. This reduction in recoil sharpness is even more pronounced when steel shot is used for two reasons. First, steel loads normally are going out faster, and second, steel doesn't deform like lead, so any abrupt restriction really accentuates the hammering effect.

Other barrel modifications made on sporting clays guns might involve altering the rib atop the barrel. This can mean anything from replacing the rib totally to reshaping the one that already is there. Some shooters prefer a really wide rib like the ones often used on trap shotguns. Other shooters prefer thin ribs. Still others opt for tapered ribs that are thinner at the muzzle than at the rear of the barrel. Other modifications of ribs include procedures like altering the top surface of the rib to reflect or absorb light in different ways.

Then there are the bead "sights" often found on shotguns. Some shooters opt to have beads removed totally. Others

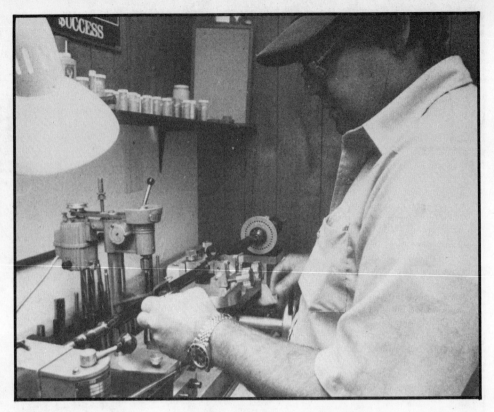

Gunsmith Stan Fitzgerald cuts ports in the barrel of a shotgun. Porting is a common procedure to aid in eliminating barrel jump and felt recoil. The shooter can get onto the second target of a pair with much greater speed.

want a larger or smaller front bead, or one of some other color — white, silver, gold or red. Some shooters prefer two beads as found on trap shotguns. When two beads are used, the back bead located near the middle of the barrel is smaller than the front bead. When the gun is mounted properly, the two beads form a "figure 8," with the small bead located at the bottom of the large bead.

So much for the barrel.

Retro jobs on the action can be simple or complex. Usually, the procedures might involve nothing more than fine-tuning the action. A term used here is "slicking-up" the action, and it is what is sounds like. Action parts are polished and fitted for smoother function. Generally, it is too expensive to have much fine-tuning done at the factory on production shotguns.

The trigger mechanism on a sporting clays gun is critical. Too often, shotgun shooters overlook or down-play the importance of a well made, finely tuned trigger. Consistency is the name of the game, and it is impossible to be consistent with a soft, hard or spongy trigger. The shooter must know exactly when the gun is going to go off, and the trigger pull must not tend to jerk the gun off target or put it out of the proper swing.

Sadly, a great many shotgunners have no idea what difference a good trigger can make, simply because, in their entire lives, they never have experienced one. Good trigger mechanisms that are adjusted properly can be expensive propositions, because there is a considerable amount of highly skilled handwork involved. But a good trigger can make the difference of one or two targets per one hundred or more, if the trigger is really bad. That may not sound like a lot, but to a serious shooter, an average of one or two targets less can be the difference between winning or losing — or between one classification and another. This is important.

The stock also is a must-fit proposition. No one can hit consistently with a gun that does not fit properly. It's that simple. For American trap shooters, overall stock configuration is somewhat more simple than for sporting clays shooters, because in American trap, the target is called for when the gun already is mounted. Since sporting clays requires a low-gun position when the target is called for, the stock not only has to fit well lengthwise and in comb height, but it also has to to be shaped so it doesn't hang up on clothing during the mounting process. Simply put, there are more motions involved in sporting clays and more variables to consider in stock configuration.

This is not to suggest that American trap stocks are simple. They are not. However, they do not have as many critical angles and thicknesses and corner radii to worry about as do sporting clays stocks. Since most shotgun stocks come in two pieces, let's first consider the forend. All of the general types of forends are found on sporting clays courses.

To a large extent, whichever type fits the shooter's hand the best is the one to have. However, diminutive, splinter-type forends generally are not a good idea, since rapid successions of shots heat up the barrels in sporting clays. A semi-beavertail or full beavertail forend design usually is a better bet.

For aesthetics, some shooters opt for a reversed-curve "schnabel" tip on their over/under forends. Beyond aesthetics, there are only two major dimensional factors to consider when it comes to a forend. First, it should be large enough around so the leading hand has control of the gun. Second, it needs to be long enough so that when the leading hand is held in the proper place, the forend is under it. Other than that, the exact length is not critical to the performance of the gun.

For the buttstock, a hand-filling grip for the trigger hand

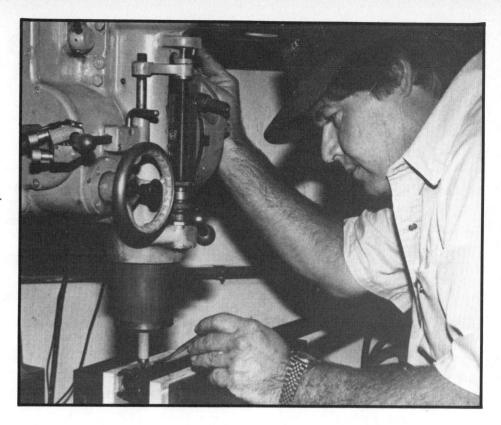

Detail work is another facet of retro work. Here Stan Fitzgerald polishes and jewels shotgun parts.

also is a must. Because sporting clays involves shooting just about any degree of angle — with virtually every kind of swing imaginable — most shooters prefer a semi-pistol grip or a full-pistol grip. Among them, a tighter pistol grip usually is more effective. Certainly, straight grips are encountered in sporting clays, and some shooters handle them well. But for the longer, passing shots, the pistol grip configuration generally affords the shooter more control.

The comb — top of the buttstock — on sporting clays guns generally is flat, as opposed to an upsweeping Monte Carlo design or the tailing-off angle found on many Nineteenth Century side-by-sides.

For comparative purposes, the configuration commonly used in skeet is about right for most sporting clays shooters. This design helps the gun shoot where the shooter is looking. An unusually high comb causes the shooter to shoot high, and an abnormally low comb causes the shot to go low. In sporting clays, where a wide variety of angles are involved, it is better for the gun to shoot exactly where the shooter is looking. Some shooters call this a "flat-shooting" gun.

Any credible shotgunsmith can check a shooter to see whether a particular gun fits properly. For example, in addition to the factors mentioned above, a gun with a stock too long will shoot low, and one with too short a stock will shoot high. Also, if the stock is too long, the shooter will perceive more recoil. And, if the stock is too short, the recoil can force the thumb or fingers of the trigger hand to smack the face. This is not only uncomfortable, but often results in a cut, fat lip or even a bloody nose. Aside from these types of problems, the shooter will not be able to hit as many targets as consistently, and that is the really important subject here.

A credible gunsmith can either alter an existing stock for proper fit, or can fashion a custom one if needed. Stock bending is another option that can help custom-fit a stock to an individual shooter's body configuration. Bending can be really important for shooters who might have body measurements that are quite far from the norm, or who have some special physical requirements that could be addressed with a stock that is bent in a particular way or ways.

Finally, there is the butt. Yes, the butt of a sporting clays gun can win or lose a tournament. Since sporting clays is a low-gun event, the gun must be mounted, swung and shot, all in a fluid series of movements. Anything that impedes or interrupts this fluid movement costs targets. Hence, the top edge of a sporting clays butt needs to be radiused so it will not hang-up when the gun is mounted. In contrast, the butt of an American trap shotgun often is concave so it partially encircles the shoulder. This is fine when the gun is mounted before the target is launched. But the same type of butt on a sporting clays gun serves as a hook, ready to catch on a coat, vest or shirt as the gun is mounted. And a mismount is a missed target.

So, it is normal for field guns to need their butts altered for sporting clays. Usually, this is done by installing a radiused rubber recoil pad. Some shooters, however, prefer nothing but the wood butt on their guns. For them, it is a matter of radiusing the top edge of the wood butt itself.

These are the major forms of retro-fitting done to turn a field gun into a sporting gun. Many of these features are built into guns that are made specifically for sporting clays. Certainly, not every shooter needs to have all of the procedures done to have an effective sporting gun. However, each alteration does have a purpose, and it is up to the individual shooter to decide which kind of work, if any, is needed — and whether it is worth the time and money.

CHAPTER 8

THE TWO FACES OF SPORTING CLAYS

The British And International Styles Have Different Courses — And Demands!

Gas-operated autoloaders such as Beretta's Model A-303 are popular in the FITASC version of the sport. This sporting clays game allows two shots at a single target, just as in actual hunting.

N ITS simplest form, the concept of sporting clays pivots on simulated field shooting. This is what attracts hunters to the game and makes it more dynamic than skeet and trap shooting. The lifelike setting of targets streaking through tree crowns, skimming ponds, popping out of bushes, and bouncing along bumpy glades turns just plain clay target shooting into an entirely new experience. It is a most fascinating way of enjoying one's bird guns throughout the year.

But hunters aren't the only people who enjoy the scattergun. There are a lot of individuals out there who have competitive personalities. Give them a game of any sort, and sooner or later, they'll devise a set of rules and start running tournaments. Whether it's wrist wrestling, poker, chess, dog training or roping steers, the competitive side of human nature always has shown through. From the Super Bowl to the rodeo, from the local pool hall championship to retriever trials, we've always given our sports form and carried them to more sophisticated levels.

And so it is with sporting clays. Although a casual shooter may look upon this sport as just a fun game and a

way to have some light-hearted outings with his hunting buddies, the actual origins of sporting clays lies in competition. The first time this concept was tried, we are told by British sources, was when a British shotgunner set three trap machines afield to emulate the flights of driven pheasants, red grouse and gray partridge, then invited his friends to take ten shots from each trap to see who could hit the most overall. It is assumed they toasted the winner and teased those who missed, but the point is that clay target shooting is steeped in competition with a set of rules for tournaments.

There are, in fact, *two* sets of rules for "sporting clays" as the term actually is a generic title that fits a pair of different formats, which are known as (1) British Sporting Clays and (2) FITASC. There are considerable differences between them, so let's discuss them individually covering rules, equipment and course layout.

Outdoor writer Don Zutz has made a project of looking at both versions of the sporting clays game and has come up with thoughts on both styles and how they compare.

We figured we'd be foolish not to take advantage of his

input, so we asked him to give us a rundown on what he has learned:

BRITISH SPORTING CLAYS

The kind of sporting clays encountered at most American layouts is basically a version of British sporting clays, although there well may be a few minor corruptions or radical departures from the pure British structure because of an owner's lack of background. Essentially, British sporting clays features repeat pairs of doubles at each stand; there are few, if any, singles. A normal one hundred-target tournament shot under traditional British style would find each entrant firing at five pairs of doubles from ten different stands.

There are three different types of doubles thrown in British sporting clays: (1) the simultaneous pair, (2) the trailing pair and (3) the report pair. The simultaneous pair are two clays — not always of the same size or color —

thrown at the same time. They generally come from the same trap machine, but on occasion, may be released from two different traps.

In reality, the simultaneous pair in British sporting clays is much like that of American trapshooting with both targets being launched by one trap. The pairs can be spread widely or can fly quite close together. Those that spring out in close proximity tempt the shooter to try for both with one shot, the result often being a total miss! The reason why so many simultaneous doubles come from one trap is generally to ensure the proper timing on the release and to save labor costs.

The trailing pair is a double that finds two targets coming in rapid succession from the same trap machine. This is the type of field shooting one experiences on driven game and American-style dove shooting.

The trapper is the key here. The second bird comes as rapidly as he can recock the trap, set the next target and

The FITASC targets are more varied than those in British sporting clays, with several types on a single stand.

Numerous extemes are incorporated on a single stand in FITASC competition. One may shoot long crossers, loopers and climbers right off the gun's muzzle. There are big surprises on good courses.

release the spring. Some trappers are greased lightning at this, and the trailing clay is streaking past almost as the gunner triggers his first pattern.

A report pair is one that finds the second target being released on the muzzle blast as the shooter tries for the first bird. In many instances, the report pair utilizes two different trap machines, as timing isn't a problem as it is with the simultaneous pair. The second trapper can release using the report as his cue.

The nice thing about report pairs is that different target angles can be introduced, such as criss-crossing pairs or high-low tests rather than merely repeating the same angles from one trap. Of course, the use of two trap machines for report pairs increases an operator's expenses, as a second trapper must be in place for each shooter.

One prime example of the report pair of British sporting clays is the so-called "fur-and-feather" stand that is used widely Stateside. This has a rabbit target, plus a flyer coming from the same trap machine on which two throwing arms are mounted. One trapper can operate both rather easily. On many American sporting clays layouts, the fur-and-feather stand is the only one employing the report pair presentation, while the British often include report pairs and two traps in their tournament programs.

To repeat, then, British sporting clays traditionally has been a game of doubles at all stands. Some few singles may work their way into some programs, but mainly the doubles dominate. This is the form of sporting clays that has gained widespread popularity in the U.S., and it will no doubt remain the leading version, because it requires no more

Basic British sporting clays is a game of doubles. This pair has been launched from behind gunner.

than one trap and trapper per stand. But those who have experienced the second form of sporting clays — namely, the international format known as FITASC — find a dynamic new world of shotgunning there!

FITASC SPORTING

Pronounced "Fee'-task," FITASC stands for the name of the governing body of this organization, *Federation Internationale de Tir Aux Armes Sportives de Chasse*, which is headquartered in Paris, France. The organization is commonly known as International Sporting Clays, although that appellation is an informal one.

There is a significant difference between FITASC and traditional British sporting clays. Whereas the British version used the above-mentioned repeated pairs, FITASC tends to be far less repetitive. The goal in FITASC is to make *every shot different*, which obviously brings the game closer to actual field shooting. Indeed, how often in hunting does one get the same chance at a double? Thus, FITASC doesn't use the repeat-pair concept, but instead

blends all sorts of shots from each stand. And if a target angle is repeated in FITASC, the target size and/or color will be changed.

The use of multiple target angles from a FITASC stand implies the presence of more than one trap machine. Unlike the typical American sporting clays courses — which tend to have but one trap in action for each stand — there can be multiple traps in operation for FITASC. Seldom does a FITASC stand have fewer than three trap machines, and some major championships will find five or six traps at a single stand. This, of course, increases the cost of FITASC shooting and has caused club operators to balk at international sporting clays, but to a certain degree this can be handled by reducing the number of stands; rather than having ten British-type stands, one can have three to five FITASC stands.

Most readers probably have stood on a British-type sporting clays course and seen the repeated pairs spin up and out, so we need not spend time reviewing that. However, let's step onto an imaginary FITASC stand to illus-

A pair of targets race past shooter in this British sporting clays game. Speeds are a highly deceptive factor.

A high looper comes dropping in on the shooter. This is an easy target to hit, if one takes it at its apex.

trate how that differs from the British version.

We'll say that the stand is at a pond with tall timber on the right, cattail growth on the left and across the pond. The shooter takes his place in the blind-like stand and is shown the targets at which he'll be shooting. The referee points them out: a high single will cross from left to right, climbing steeply over the trees at high speed. The target's starting speed is explosive, and it'll take a fast swing to catch it before it tops the trees and is gone. Next is a battue that comes from the right, quartering and peeling off as it crosses the pond like a swift teal settling into the rushes. This one not only needs a fast swing, but the shooter also must get under it to handle the battue's dive. It's a tough shot at thirty-five yards.

As a third shot from the same stand, there's a lobbed incoming bird angled toward the blind, but slightly left to right. It seems to be coming to the blind, but the trap's spring has been backed off and the clay's speed is deceptive. As it reaches the edge of the cattails, it stalls and drops in like a mallard with its wings cupped. The problem here is getting the pattern below the bird far enough, as it's always difficult to go down with a shotgun. And the thirty-yard poke across the pond confuses the situation.

Finally, from behind comes a really high midi streaking like a spooky duck. The shot resembles the station 1 high-house shot in skeet, but the range and target speed are greatly extended. You can't spot shoot this one!

That's four singles to be taken, and in FITASC each

shooter will try those targets before doubles are explained. But here's another interesting difference between FITASC and British sporting clays: In the former, the shooter can take *two* shots at any single target! There is no penalty for hitting it with the second pattern; as in hunting, you still get the target. Many shotgunners find this part of FITASC to be especially attractive, as it is realistic. Most hunters use multiple-shot smoothbores, anyway, and they invariably take second shots afield. Why, then, not include the follow-up shot in sporting clays? FITASC does!

After each shooter in the FITASC squad — mandated at six, according to the rules — has taken his singles, the referee explains the doubles. No two pair will be identical. In the FITASC sport, each pair will be different regardless of the number of pairs. Some FITASC stands can have but one pair of doubles, while others may have three or four pairs. Whatever, none will be repeated.

Let's say our fictitious pond-side stand has a couple pairs. One includes a battue coming from the right as it did in singles, while the trap that lobbed the mallard-like target that dropped on the far side of the pond now slings an air-cutting midi that comes farther and angles downward in a long, shallow arc. This means the shooter again *must* swing briskly on the battue, while compensating for its fast dive, then swing back to the right on a swift midi making a shallower trajectory.

The second pair is higher. From the left comes the streaking target climbing over the trees, although this time it's a mini that makes the shot look deceptively long because of the target's size. On report, the trap behind the stand throws a standard-size clay overhead, again emulating a duck or dove that is sneaking in from behind and getting out while the getting's good.

In doubles, the shooter can fire his two shells at the first target, if he misses with the first. However, he must make an attempt to hit it, and cannot hold both shells for the second target in case that looks easier. No more than two shells can be loaded.

The point here is that the shooters each have fired at eight targets, most of them different angles or with different size clays or in different sequences. This is nothing resembling a steady repetition of the same pairs as in the British version.

Put together a tournament with eight to ten such FITASC stands, using totally different trap settings with variously sized and colored clays at each station, and a shooter feels like he's been wrung out as he steps from the last stand.

The significant departure between British and inter-

The Americanized versions of British sporting clays, with doubles being thrown, requires that the gun be held below the level of the arm pit until the target appears. FITASC rules demand lower gun level of 25 centimeters.

national sporting clays, then, is that the latter demands all-around sophistication with a scattergun to handle the myriad shots. One goes through a number of FITASC stands without being able to "groove" his moves, as is possible in the repeated pairs of British sporting, wherein one can overcome his mistakes on the first pair and score well thereafter on the remaining pairs. Of all shotgun games, FITASC is the tougher test of shotgunning skills.

If there is anything unfortunate about the trend of FITASC competitions, it is that the sophisticated shooters want continually more difficult courses. This isn't conducive to extensive growth, as beginners and casual shooters who can't handle the demands will quit. Ideally, a shooter will try to improve, but that desire isn't a part of every hunter's make-up. The hunter-type of casual shooter simply wants fun, not frustration. To an extent, observant sporting clays shooters already have seen some hunters leave the game due to heightened demands of skill as courses are made tougher. Sporting clays club owners and managers must walk a tight-rope, as they set up their courses, realizing that the difficulty level of an international FITASC layout is beyond the range of a typical hunter's skills and that, like international skeet and trap (bunker), a truly stiff FITASC course will appeal only to the most hearty — the most skilled shooters who dote on improvement and accomplishment.

ADDITIONAL DIFFERENCES

Besides the differences in target presentation, there are

The events shot under the FITASC rules attempt to offer a different angle, speed and target size on each shot.

Left: Both FITASC and British sporting present targets from the high tower, but the English-style is much more likely to throw challenging doubles than a single bird.

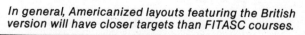

In general, Americanized layouts featuring the British version will have closer targets than FITASC courses.

Coming up from a low-gun start, this shooter is going after a bird that has been launched from the high tower.

A pair of rabbit targets bouncing between two obstacles is normal in British sporting clays.

International sporting clays uses a wide variety of clay target sizes and colors so no two shots are the same.

other departures between British-style sporting and FITASC. In actual competitions, for example, American sporting clays rules permit a maximum load of 1⅛ ounces of lead shot over the 3¼ drams equivalent powder charge (about 1255 feet per second) in the British-type events featuring doubles at all, or most, stations.

In FITASC tournaments, however, this is increased to a maximum allowable load of 1¼ ounces of lead shot — including nickel- or copper-plated shot — over a 3¼ drams equivalent powder charge. In effect, the old "live pigeon" 12-gauge round of 3¼-1¼ still is viable in FITASC gunning. More than a few shooters use it, as FITASC layouts don't hesitate to throw forty to fifty-yard crossers. The allowable shot sizes are Nos. 7½, 8, 8½ and 9.

It must be noted here that recently the British have rewritten their rules and have dropped the legal shot charge to the 28-gram level, meaning a few pellets less than an ounce. A 28-gram shot charge has 432 grains, while a full ounce has 437.5 grains. This has no effect on FITASC, of course, as the two games are governed by their own respective bodies, and the 1¼-ounce charge still exists in international events, regardless of where they are held. Whether the one-ounce load will become a part of Yankee sporting clays still is a moot question. To date, all American clay target games have balked at the thought of using less than 1⅛ ounces in 12 gauge.

Another definite difference between the games is the gun's starting position. In the Americanized version of British sporting clays, the U.S. rules mandate a low-gun starting position. The gun butt is supposed to be held below the armpit until the target appears, and most clubs demand that stance.

In FITASC, however, there is a relatively new (1991) rule in the book that requires that the gun be held twenty-five centimeters below the center of the top of the shoulder. This converts to 9⅞ inches and is commonly referred to as "nipple level" by judges. Why the lowered position? Because some shooters continually tried to sneak the gun higher from the former armpit hold position. Thus, the powers-that-be lowered the gun's starting location so "hunching" is less likely to go unnoticed.

Surprisingly, the original British sporting clays rules as shot in the United Kingdom permit a fully mounted gun. There has been a hassle in the U.K. to change the rules and require a lowered gun, but after some research, the findings are that those who hold a pre-mounted gun tend to score lower than those who do indeed lower their piece. For the present, then, British sporting clays rules will continue to allow the pre-mounted gun in the United Kingdom, something that one can only hope doesn't happen Stateside. How many hunters walk about the fields and woodlots with a solidly mounted gun waiting for a bird or rabbit to jump?

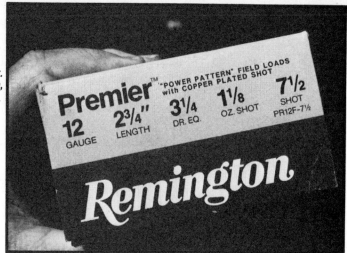

Americanized sporting clays still permits the 1⅛-oz. load with 3¼ drams equivalent charge. English, though, have gone to a 28-gram (1 oz.) load in their game.

Two targets fly through cover, a standard shot in British sporting clays which employs repeated pairs.

The 12 gauge is employed almost universally in FITASC, and most serious shooters select at least a twenty-eight-inch barrel for smoothness and a positive follow-through. The lesser gauges — 20, 28 and even .410 bore — can play a role in the closer ranges of Americanized British sporting clays, but they lose effectiveness in the longer distances and faster targets of FITASC competitions. The thirty-inch barrel isn't uncommon in FITASC, and although there was a certain fad involving the thirty-two-inch barrels, this hasn't caught on widely. Over/unders with twenty-eight to thirty-inch barrels are the common fare, with certain gas-operated autoloaders — such as the Beretta Model A-303 and some Remington Models 1100 and 11-87 — catching on. If the current trend continues, there will be more and more autoloaders in both FITASC and British-style events, for shooters will begin to appreciate their lower recoil levels which expedite recovery for the second shots so vital in both games.

COMBINE THE TWAIN!

Before some creative thinker beats us to it, we must ask: Why not combine British-type sporting clays as practiced Stateside with elements of FITASC? Why not, indeed? There is no rule in basic sporting clays to thwart singles, although there are rules against using a second shot on them. Only bona fide FITASC events allow the second shot on singles. However, a single or two per stand in basic Americanized sporting clays, perhaps thrown with a different sized or colored target than those used for doubles from the same trap, would spice up the procedure a bit by eliminating the repetitious pairs that are now so common in Yankee sporting clays.

However the future of sporting clays evolves, though, there are currently these two different forms of tournament competition — and shooters should know into which one they're stepping. Currently, the United States Sporting Clays Association (50 Briar Hollow, Suite 490 East, Houston, TX 77027) is the North American affiliate of *Federation Internationale de Tir Aux Armes Sportives de Chasse.* To be eligible for entry in a FITASC tournament anywhere, one must first be a member in good standing at USSCA. And for those who aspire to the highest level of shotgun competition, FITASC is a must!

CHAPTER 9

LAY OF THE LAND

Shooting stations usually feature some sort of enclosure that restricts the shooter's gun swing, keeping it within a safe arc. One or more sides may be covered, preventing the shooter from seeing target too soon.

SPORTING CLAYS affords a degree of creativity when it comes to course layout which is unparalleled in any of the other shooting sports. Not only is each course supposed to be different, but it is the vogue for operators to establish courses that reflect the geographic area in which they are located — and the personality of the owner/operator, as well.

When sporting clays is likened to "golf with a shotgun," the analogy is correct. In the same way that each golf course around the world is unique, so is each sporting clays layout. What makes the establishment of a sporting clays facility so exciting is the fact that it can be an exceedingly simple, basic set-up, or it can be as lavish as the imagination — and the bankroll — of the operator will allow.

As discussed elsewhere in this book, there are a number of basic types of shot presentations in sporting clays, and a credible course will include examples of at least the basic types of presentations. Or the course can include a number of variations of any or all, depending upon the size and complexity of the layout.

It is the manner in which those target presentations are fitted into the immediate terrain that makes courses interesting and exciting. For example, a really basic course can be as minimal as a temporary modification to an existing trap and/or skeet field, or it can ramble opulently over many acres of scenic real estate.

Foremost in any course design consideration is safety. Because sporting clays involves the shooting of aerial

Layouts For A Sporting Clays Course Are Governed By Terrain And Individual Imagination

targets at various angles and distances, and because shooters need to swing their guns through major and minor arcs, shotfall is a critical consideration if accidents are to be avoided. It is much easier to factor out any unnecessary safety risk than it is to rely upon the skill or abilities of the shooters to preclude problems. Simply put, if there can be a problem, there will be one.

One of the most notable safety devices on a sporting clays course is the so-called "cage" at each shooting station. Certainly, some of the courses feature stations that literally have cages from which the shooters shoot, but often the "cage" is an open-sided booth with vertical and/or horizontal bars or boards to prevent the shooter from swinging too far in a particular direction.

On some courses, the operators will close-in one or more sides of the cage to limit the shooter's visibility of targets. That way, the shooter cannot see the target until it is fully developed in flight — and until it reaches the hit zone intended by the operator. This technique is used as much to determine the desired degree of difficulty for a shot as it is to accomplish anything else.

SIMPLE, BASIC LAYOUTS

Starting with the most simple layout — which usually is the temporary conversion of a clay target field for sporting clays, the "terrain" features can be as basic as bales of hay or straw, stacked to block the shooter's view of the targets until they reach the intended area or "window" where they are to be broken.

This type of layout is illustrated well in the "Fur and Feather" configuration suggested by the National Skeet Shooting Association in a diagram showing how to convert a normal skeet field into a sporting station.

The diagram shows the use of a hedgerow and other foliage, which is ideal for aesthetics. However, the use of stacks of bales could accomplish the same tactical objective. Note that the walkway actually allows for three separate shooting stands. And even though the targets would be thrown the same — regardless of which of the stand locations is being shot — the actual presentation of the targets to the shooter would be different at each stand.

Note that there is a "fur" or rabbit thrower at the base of the high house and that there are barriers (like straw bales) just to the right of the high house, as well as at centerfield. If the shooting stand is located at position 1, the rabbit target would be thrown from the shooter's left, and bounce along the ground, visible only as it bounded through the "window" area between the bales next to the high house and the bales at centerfield.

Generally, the rabbit target would be thrown when the

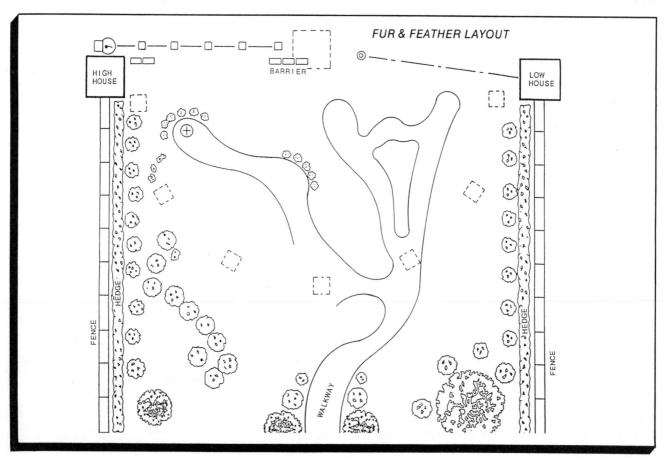

FUR & FEATHER LAYOUT

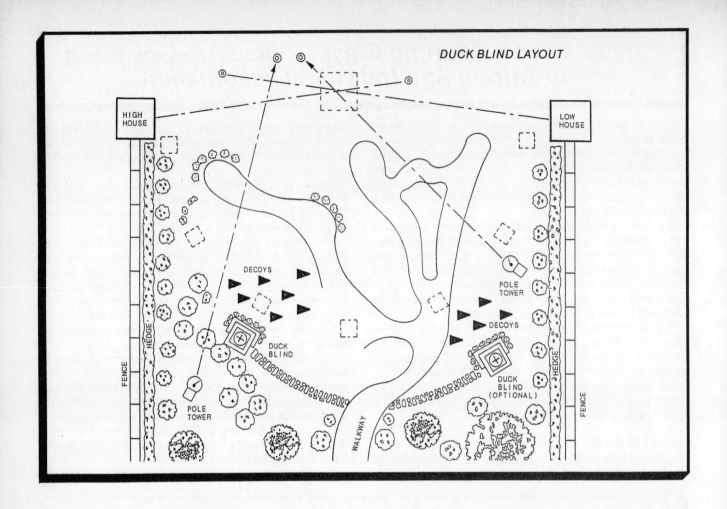

HIGH HOUSE

LOW HOUSE

DECOYS

POLE TOWER

DECOYS

DUCK BLIND

DUCK BLIND (OPTIONAL)

FENCE

HEDGE

POLE TOWER

WALKWAY

HEDGE

FENCE

shooter first calls for a target. Depending upon how the operator decided to structure the shoot, the "feather" or aerial target part of the fur-and-feather station would see a target launched from the skeet low house on the right. It would fly the exact same path as a normal low house skeet target. It could be launched simultaneously with the rabbit or on report when the shooter shoots at the rabbit.

To add still another dimension to this stand, it might be the trapper's option to launch the aerial target from either the high house or the low house, and to alternate which house, meaning the shooter would not know which of the skeet houses the second target might be coming from on a given call. That would force the shooter to be more reactive when taking the second shot, thus adding a higher degree of difficulty to the station.

Continuing with this same layout, the shooter might next walk to Station 2, as indicated on the diagram, and be presented only aerial targets. Again, the presentation could be singles, pairs or reporting pairs — or a random mix of all. The same scenario would follow at Station 3, with the major difference being the angle of the target flight with respect to the location of the shooter. A change so seemingly minor as this can, in fact, make the target presentation totally different and more or less challenging.

This particular configuration would require that shooters occupy only one of the three stations at a given moment. Otherwise, there would be the possibility of overswing or resulting safety problems.

The Duck Blind sketch shows a potentially more complex scheme of possible target presentations. As configured, there are two shooting stations, one on the left, the other on the right.

In addition to the skeet high house and low house, two pole tower launchers have been integrated into the plan. These pole tower launchers can be atop an actual pole or

The shooting station cage can be extremely basic. Just the PVC plastic pipe is enough to keep the shooter from overswinging, bringing the muzzle into a danger zone.

placed upon any other kind of elevating device, including scaffolding. Hence, the heights of the pole towers can vary and they need not be the same height.

As shown by the target flight directions, shooters are presented with going away and quartering targets, as well as right and left crossers. The order the various targets are launched and whether they are singles, doubles or reporting pairs is, of course, a matter to be determined by the shoot master. In fact, with four traps, the game can be expanded to include "poison" targets.

Using this example, orange-domed clays might be used as the "normal" target on this layout. When loading the traps, the operator might include a random number of black targets and designate those black targets as "poison." In a duck blind setting, they might be considered hen ducks, or some subspecie that cannot be bagged. The way this can work is if the shooter breaks a "poison" clay, a point is subtracted from his score.

Added degrees of difficulty can be injected with the use of specialty targets. This would be a logical layout for the use of battue targets, launched singly or in pairs from one or both of the pole towers, or for the use of midi or mini targets from any or all of the traps.

The Grouse Butt configuration shows the same skeet field base, with a single grouse stand. As indicated, there are four traps involved. One is behind and to the left of the stand, another slightly forward and to the right of the stand. The others are standard high house and low house traps of the skeet field.

As shown in the diagram, four different flight paths are available here, with the vertical angle of target flight one of the many potential variables. Again, the targets can be launched singly, in pairs or reporting pairs. Each time the routine is altered, the degree of difficulty is lessened or increased.

There are other possible configurations for skeet fields, as well as for trap fields, or fields that feature both traditional skeet and trap houses on the same field. These diagrams merely serve to suggest some of the ways the traditional clay target facilities can be altered for the shooting of sporting clays.

The plastic pipe used in the shooting cage is heavy-duty, as it will have to withstand elements as well as swings.

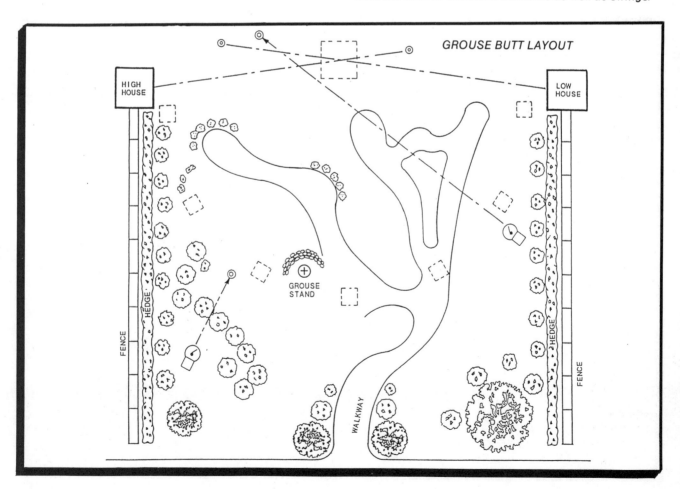

GROUSE BUTT LAYOUT

PERMANENT COURSE LAYOUTS

Terrain, ground cover and foliage are all elements to be considered when laying out a sporting clays course. Generally, the most restrictive factor is the amount of land available for the course. Since there needs to be at least a three hundred-yard shotfall safety zone from each shooting stand, a multiple-station course can require the use of several to many acres.

Generally, sporting clays courses feature five or ten stations. Regardless of how many stations there are, each shooting position should feature a different type of target presentation. A course should include incoming and going-away targets, crossing targets, quartering-in and quartering-away birds, as well as overhead clays. By presenting singles, pairs and reporting pairs, and by using specialty targets, those few basic types of shot presentations can be varied enough to provide any degree of difficulty the course designer cares to make.

For flat land areas, the accompanying Flighting Duck station layout shows how an extremely basic situation can be made into an extremely interesting station or even pair of stations. Note that there is only one target thrower needed for this station. By altering the target flight path only slightly — accomplished by either changing the position of the targets on the trap arm, by rotating the trap itself or both, the shooter in either of the "blinds" is presented with a classic passing duck-type shot.

Although the relationship of the two blinds on the target flight path may seem similar, the shot presented at each station is decidedly different. For example, at Station 1, the presentation would be either a quartering-away or a near-right-to-left going away shot. At Station 2, the shots could be quartering-in, if the shooter took the shots quickly, crossing if taken in front of the blind or going-away/quartering-away if taken late.

The diagram for the Duck Field layout is more complex, and takes advantage of a small pond on the course. There are two concealed throwers, one launching essentially incoming targets to the two blinds. The other offers either overhead crossers or quartering-away targets.

By using the traps in sequence, simultaneously, or variously with singles and/or pairs, the shot presentations at this station could be varied incredibly. Add to that situation the use of minis and midis, and the degree of difficulty could be changed at will. As is the case on many sporting clays courses, the operator at this station has the option of using either of the two blinds during a shoot, or both of them. The shot presentation to the shooter is different from each of the blinds, even though the actual target flight is the same.

The Goose Spread configuration is another relatively simple layout that offers maximum flexibility. From the hidden thrower, the targets fly from right to left over the decoys. From Station 1, this translates into a classic right-to-left crossing shot. Yet, the same flight pattern from Station 2 presents a more complex presentation which is

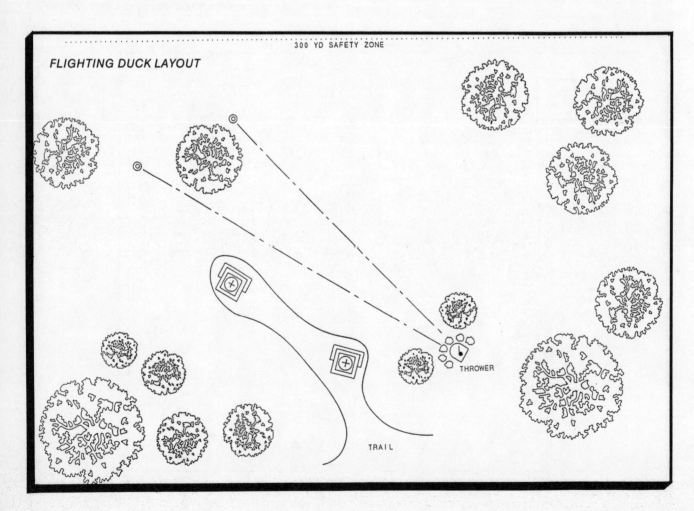

FLIGHTING DUCK LAYOUT

300 YD SAFETY ZONE

THROWER

TRAIL

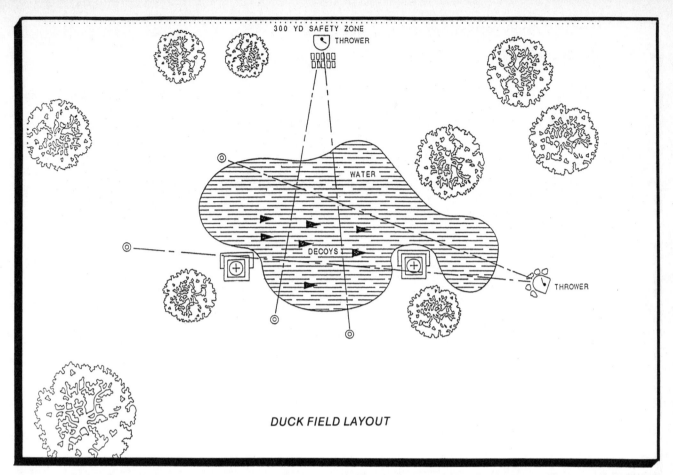

300 YD SAFETY ZONE

THROWER

WATER

DECOYS

THROWER

DUCK FIELD LAYOUT

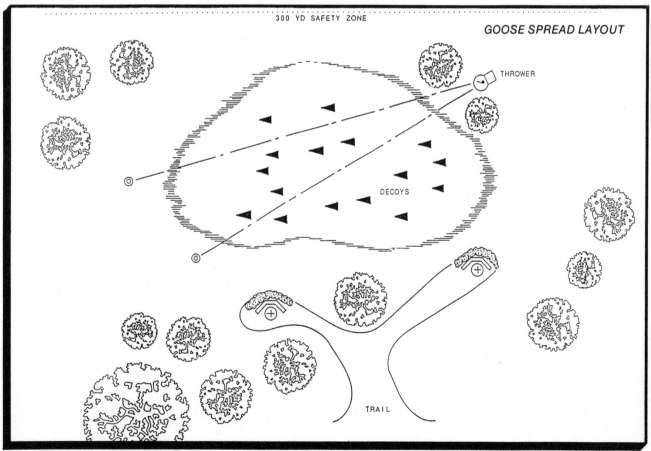

300 YD SAFETY ZONE

GOOSE SPREAD LAYOUT

THROWER

DECOYS

TRAIL

TOWER LAYOUT

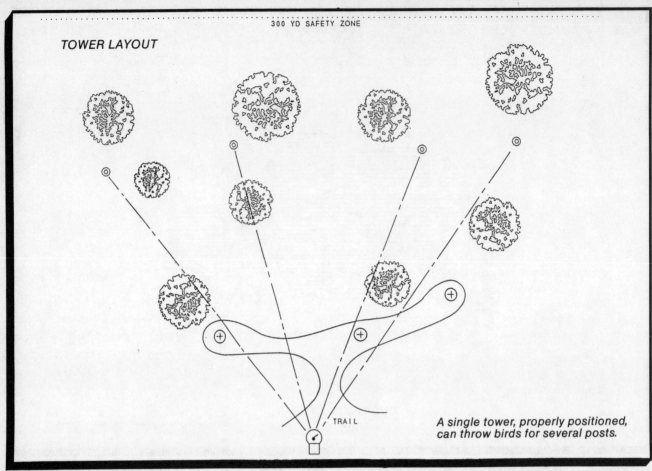

TRAIL

A single tower, properly positioned, can throw birds for several posts.

TOWER LAYOUT

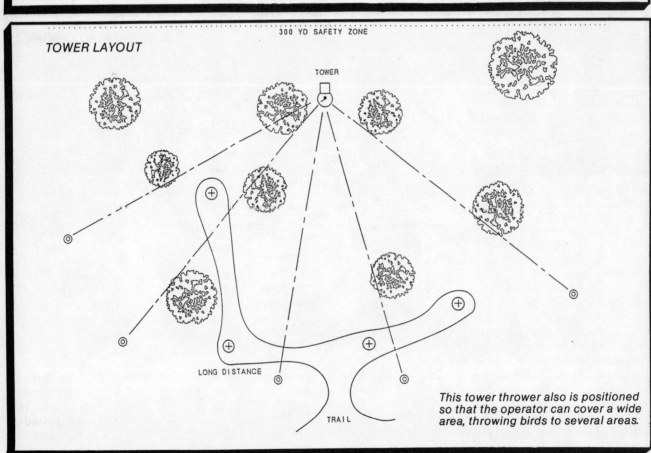

TOWER

LONG DISTANCE

TRAIL

This tower thrower also is positioned so that the operator can cover a wide area, throwing birds to several areas.

Use of natural vegetation can add both fun and challenge to a course. Shooter cannot see target until it "flushes" from the thick cover, just as a game bird might during an actual hunt. Such innovations make course even tougher.

either a quartering/crosser or a quartering-in situation. Again, there are two potential stations served by a single thrower. By mixing or matching single targets, the various pairs or different sizes of targets, the degree of difficulty can be changed markedly.

The Tower layout shows even more kinds of variables a course can offer, using a minimum number of throwers. From this single-tower thrower, the operator has the option of establishing four separate stations, or of using one, two or three stations, but altering the angle at which the target is launched.

For example, the shooter at Station 1 in the diagram would find the farthest left target presentation to be almost an overhead situation. Yet, that same shooter would see

the farthest right target as a high, left-to-right, long-distance crosser. Certainly, any of the angles between represent still other variations. And, as one goes from one of these stations to another, it is easy to see how the same target flight paths represent a tremendously different number of types of target presentations.

The Woodcock Pair diagram demonstrates how a course design can take advantage of foliage to establish shooting station presentations. For example, a shooter at Station 1 would not be able to see the target from the left thrower, until it had cleared the tree to the shooter's left. That shooter would not be able to hit the target after it passed the tree to the right of Station 2. That is called a "window," and the width of a shooting window can dictate how quickly the shooter must take the target. This establishes the degree of difficulty — the higher degree being at stations where the window is shortest and where the targets are launched the most quickly.

Similarly, the shooter at Station 1 would be unable to see the target from the right thrower, until it went past the tree to the right of Station 2. Nor could the shooter at Station 1 hit that target after it went past the tree to the left of Station 1. Hence, the same window exists for both targets. To that shooter, it is one thing to shoot a single from the left, then a single from the right. It is quite another thing to shoot a reporting pair or a simultaneous pair. Similar considerations apply to the shooter at Station 2, but because of the difference in the angle of the shots, shooting Station 2 is quite unlike shooting Station 1.

Sometimes, even a few feet in the location of a shooting station can change what had been a relatively easy target presentation into a really challenging event. This is evidenced in the Chukar Shoot diagram where two potential shooting stands are located relatively closely behind the butt at the end of the trail.

Although the angles of the targets relative to the shooters in either of the stations are quite similiar, the tiny difference in the shooting stand is enough to change not only the point in the flight of the target where the shooter would most likely elect to break the target, but the order in which the targets might best be broken.

For example, if shot from the right shooting position, a right-handed shooter logically would break the right-to-

left, close-in crosser first, then quickly follow through to break the quartering-away target by the time it was essentially directly in front of the station. However, that same shooter, if standing in the left shooting position, might opt to take the quartering-away target first, hitting it when it is approaching a straight-out position, then taking the right-to-left crosser as it approached the trees to the left.

A quick look at the Quail Rise explains how both target presentation and degree of difficulty can be altered, even though a single thrower is used. Note the windows of opportunity as they differ from the three shooting positions. Add to this station the use of singles, various kinds of pairs or different size targets, and it can be either a simple station or totally complex challenge.

The Springing Teal diagram also offers three totally different kinds of target presentations. Since the teal targets go almost straight into the air, throwing a single or a pair changes the complexion of the difficulty. Positioning the targets on the thrower arm so one target goes straight up and the other target goes up and out in an arc causes the layout to take on a whole new meaning. Similarly, by shooting this presentation from any of the three stations shown, the angle of the shot changes. As is the theme throughout, variety can be virtually endless.

If the course has hills or valleys, even more types of presentations can be included, with uphill and downhill shots interspersed with the more classic crossing targets. Downhill shots can be among the most challenging, since most shooters are more familiar with upward shots.

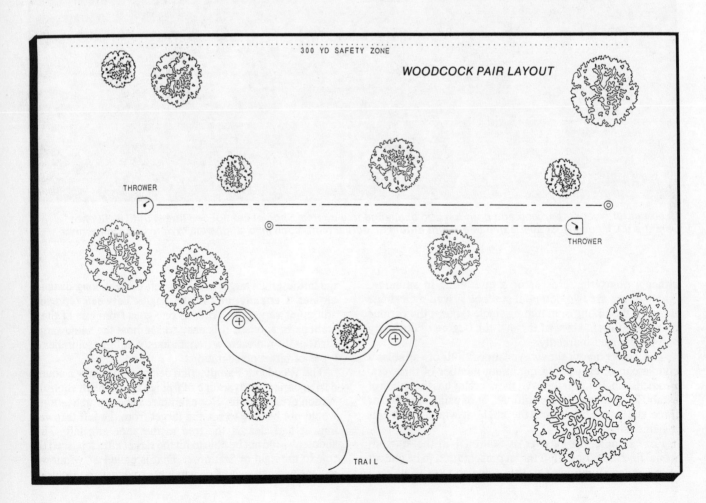

WOODCOCK PAIR LAYOUT

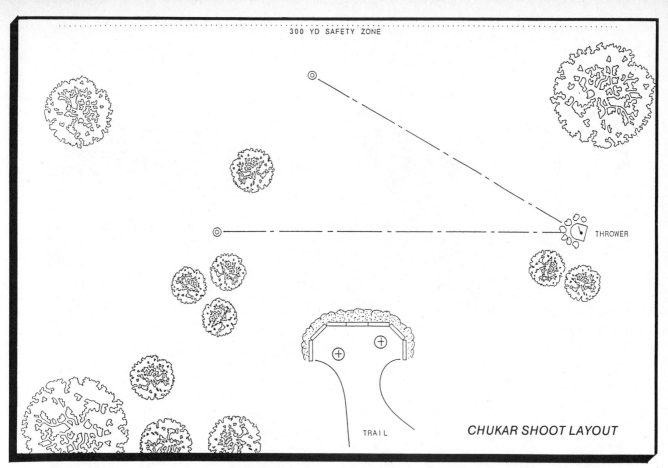

THROWER

TRAIL

CHUKAR SHOOT LAYOUT

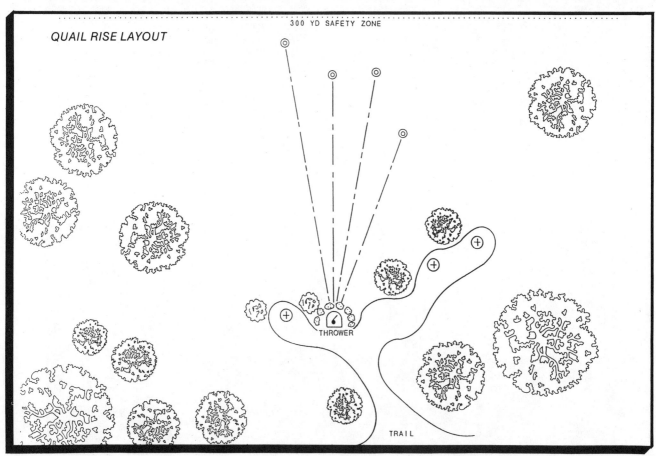

QUAIL RISE LAYOUT

THROWER

TRAIL

When a sporting clays course is laid out in heavy brush like this, the possibilites, challenges are great.

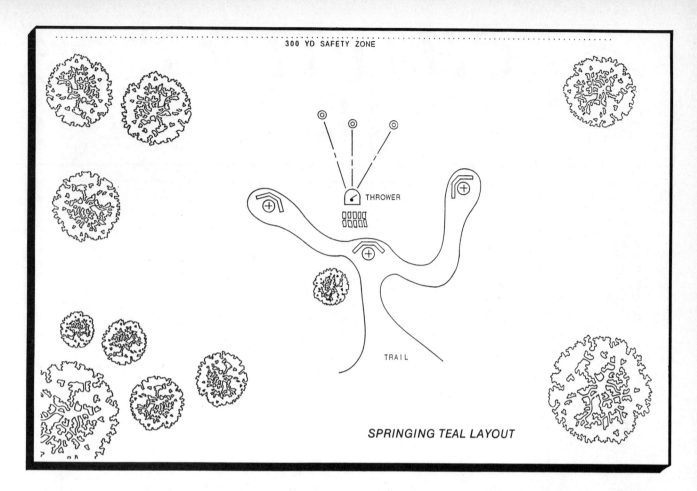

THROWER

TRAIL

SPRINGING TEAL LAYOUT

Any course layout, as discussed earlier, can be easy or difficult, depending upon subtle differences at any given time. In addition to the relocation of the shooting station by as much as only a few feet, or change in the angle the thrower is set, there are other ways to alter the course. It could be as simple as tightening or loosening the springs on the throwers. This results in faster or slower target presentations.

Not all difficult targets are fast targets. Sometimes, a really slow, arcing target can be the most difficult to hit — especially if the shooter has a long time to watch it before it is fully developed. In such instances, shooters often try to take the target too soon when it still is too far away.

When laying out a course for general shooting, there are some important things to keep in mind. No one wants to shoot a course that is so easy a credible shooter could break all the targets routinely. Nor would shooters want to keep coming back if the course was so difficult that a credible shooter might be able to break only a couple dozen out of every one hundred targets.

Generally, it is not a bad idea to configure a course so a good, general shooter could expect to break between sixty to seventy targets on a normal day. Such a course still will challenge the top shooters, but will not discourage others.

What this also should mean is that there are at least a couple of fairly easy stations — ones at which the better shooters will hit the targets and where the lesser shooters still will do well enough to keep interested.

Also, it is a good idea to alter the course from time to time, just to keep the regulars from becoming bored. As

shown in the accompanying diagrams, this doesn't have to represent a major course modification. By simply moving the shooting stations in, out or from one side to the other, the course can take on an entirely different complexion.

Tournament courses are entirely different from the standard configurations, even though any normal course can be transformed into a tournament-level facility fairly easily and quickly. Again, it is the use of different sizes and colors of targets and changing the shot presentations that turn a cream puff course into a real backbreaker.

Ambience plays a major role in sporting clays. A stark, basic course might offer exactly the same kinds of shot presentations as a posh, manicured facility, yet seem like a different shoot just because of the surroundings. Posh is nice, but not necessary. The degree of fancy, however, does have an effect on both the shooting and those who frequent a facility.

It is always a good idea for any course layout to take full advantage of any significant terrain feature that tends to make it unique. For example, if there is a tall cliff somewhere on the grounds, the layout should include at least one station where the shooters are at the base of the cliff, shooting targets thrown from the top. The layout should include at least one other station where the shooters are atop the cliff, shooting out and/or out and down from the high spot.

If nothing else, it is the intent of this chapter to show some of the kinds of layouts that are possible and to impress that courses need be limited only by the imagination and bankroll of the operator.

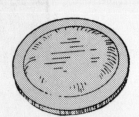

CHAPTER 10

Sporting clays courses are not designed to be easy. All of the problems of actual hunting are designed in them.

CLUES TO THE COURSE

Depending Upon Your Goal As A Sporting Clays Shooter, There Are Certain Facets To Seek

"I HATE driven grouse. Not real driven grouse like they shoot in Europe, though I've never done it, so I wouldn't know whether I liked it or not. I mean the driven grouse station at sporting clays. Virtually every course has it. And at virtually every course, I miss more than my share of targets at it.

"Technically, it's an easy shot. Overhead incomers are thrown directly at you. All you have to do is swing like hell, blot out the target and pull the trigger. In many ways, it's like station eight high house at skeet, and when I shot competitively as a sub-junior and junior back in the late Fifties and early Sixties — long before sporting clays ever made it across the Atlantic — high eight was a 'gimme'."

Those are the words of Barry G. Davis, the shooting sage of Merry Hill, North Carolina. He is first of all a game hunter, so he is interested in a sporting clays course that is going to help him be on target for the various species he'll be hunting.

We asked for his thoughts on his own attitude toward the sport. Here are his thoughts:

I can shoot the singles pretty well, but when it comes to doubles, that thirty yards between the shooting stand and the hidden trap looks like ten. In a hurry to get on the second target, I inevitably screw up the swing on the first bird, and poke and stab at the trailer. It's pathetic.

A course owner friend of mine is always trying to get me to wager a few bucks at the station, and gets an additional, perverse pleasure out of calling, loudly, "Lost a pair!" whenever I miss. However, when I try to get him to go double or nothing at the pheasant flush or quail field, he refuses.

"No way," he says. "With all of the hunting you do, I know you can eat those fields up. They're the kind of shots birdhunters take all the time. No, I've got to pick your pocket on something you rarely see."

Fifty percent is good for me at driven grouse. Other shooters have similar problems at other fields and stations. The key is that missing targets here and there isn't the end of the world. Everyone misses. What's really important is what a good sporting clays course can teach you.

When the game migrated form England a few years back, it took hold here in the States like a junkyard dog munching on the backside of a trespasser. Growing pains, however, were inevitable.

Because it was so new, the initial ranges, no matter what

their configuration, received almost universal support. It seemed that anything capable of replacing the near mechanical precision of skeet and trap was okay to the majority of hunters and shooters. Subsequent to the explosive growth rate during its infancy, however, the game's inherent phys-

Although the claybirds often are camouflaged by cover, each of them does offer a possible shot for competitor.

Stands of green timber offer the same challenges as in an actual hunt. Some of the trees carry a lot of lead!

ical limitations — large chunks of land and five to six figure plus start-up costs — have acted like a sea anchor on a boat with lots of power, but no rudder.

Shooters also have become more sophisticated. The guidelines today demand versatile, functional, attractive courses offering a wide variety of representative targets. They must be capable of challenging top shooters, yet not be so technically difficult they overpower and intimidate the average hunter. In short, the days of haphazardly sticking a handful of trap machines along a wooded, brushy windbreak and calling it sporting clays are long gone.

So, what is a solid sporting clays course? It all depends on your own perceptions and persective. For some, it's the ambiance; for others, it's the realism. And for still another group, it's the potential for an ever-increasing challenge. Let's examine it through three sets of eyes: a hunter who enjoys the game for what it can do for his field shooting, a tournament level shooter and the guy who has to put it all together in proper balance, the course designer. The input of each is fundamental to sporting clays' future.

In addition to owning and operating Beaver Dam Sporting Clays, one of the first ranges in the Southeast, Rick Spivey (Route 4, Box 97-M, Greenville, NC 27834) is also the architect of more than three dozen other courses.

The job seems simple on the surface: clear some shooting lanes, set up a few machines, pace off a fair distance to the shooting stands, then have at it. The more you get into it, however, the more complex it becomes.

Spivey says, "What I do is really hard to define in a single sentence. I guess you could say it's a mix of practical engineering and survey skills blended with an intuitive feeling for what the lay of the land itself will allow you to do."

In brief, the course designer has to wear multiple hats; from that of the owner making the investment all the way down to that of the once-in-a-while shooter. He has to consider projected long-term operating expenses as well as the initial building costs, then balance them against the need to make the course challenging and interesting enough to develop a consistent, repeat clientele. Like I said, it's more complex than it looks.

The course designer's first step is to conclude that the proposed site — including a nine hundred to a thousand-foot shot fall zone — is large enough. Next comes obtaining zoning clearance in writing. With those two items clear, cost limitations are set and the owner has to decide what type of course is expected, especially the visual impression and aesthetics, within those dollar constraints.

Birds going away from the shooter, headed into deep brush, require an instant reaction, shot.

Naturally, the bigger the budget, the more options the designer has. Only after all of these things are settled can he get down to real work.

Rick Spivey's first step is to spend hours studying topographical and survey maps of the property. Step two is to walk it at a snail's pace, looking for natural variations in elevation. They're difficult to find in some areas, like the Great Plains and certain areas of the Southeast, but their use makes for a more attractive and functional course design.

Following the walk-through, it's back to the maps where he decides if an outer or inner circle layout is most practical. Outer circle set-ups, where the shooters shoot to the center, are rare, because shot fall limitations would require property almost unrestricted in size. Inner circle layouts, where the shooters shoot out, are the norm.

Spivey's second walk-through is calculated to produce a practical route. Every possible field and station that exists, even if they conflict with one another, is flagged with fluorescent tape. "I put in every conceivable station I think

will work," he says, "and, as I go, draw maps as accurately and close to scale as possible."

Universal, established standards virtually necessitate that each course have a quail flush, springing teal, fur and feather, my nemesis, driven grouse and a tower field that presents high, crossing targets to flanking stations, plus outgoing targets thrown from above and below the shooter. The other fields are left to the designer's imagination, and most often focus on quartering and crossing, incoming and outgoing, left to rights and right to lefts. After noting every type of target presentation and shot possible, the difficult culling process begins.

"In most cases, budget limitations call for ten to fifteen fields," says Spivey. "It's my job to determine which of them is the most versatile, and which fits the lay of the land best. Some designers don't mind a lot of cutting and bulldozing. I don't like cutting anything. Using the natural cover as much as possible not only makes it more like real hunting, but cover also helps to muffle and minimize any potential problems with sound travel."

The better sporting clays courses are designed around the natural terrain and growth to provide a challenge.

The final, critical clue for a designer in creating a solid sporting clays course is to avoid repetition and monotony, plus find that oftentimes delicate balance between too easy and too hard. An easy course, with too many similar target presentations, leads to boredom. And a course that's miles beyond the skill level of the average shooter quickly becomes frustrating. Such frustration leads to giving up, and giving up on a course does not bode well for its long-term success. For anyone thinking about building a quality, sporting clays range, the investment in a professional designer is not a "maybe." It's an absolute necessity.

Although the name may sound like silver spoons and prep school, former two-time All-American John Dunn, III, also of Greenville, North Carolina, is far from being a member of the pedigreed Blue Book. Instead, he's an honest-to-goodness, hound-chasing, hard-hunting country boy who just happens to shoot sporting clays well enough to have lifted himself into the upper echelon of the sport.

Most sporting clays shooters visit a couple or three ranges during the course of a year. John Dunn, on the other hand, may do the same thing in a month when finances allow him to follow the tournament schedule. Because of the cumulative experience of having shot at a wide variety

of ranges, I asked him what he considered the clues to a good course.

"Safety is first and foremost," he replied. "I want to know for sure that everything possible has been done to prevent an accident. Even the distraction of being rained on by shot from another squad at a distant station is a clue that the course hasn't been well designed, or that it's being run carelessly. Most ranges are extremely safe. I've only been to a couple that made me think about it for more than a minute.

"As a shooter, I want to see a wide enough variety of shots so everyone's strengths and weaknesses are tested. Psychologically, variety also keeps a shooter's interest level at a peak. For example, a sequence where the tricky, near vertical shots of springing teal follow the long, high pass shots at a tower field keep you more interested and involved than, say, two quartering stations in a row. Each course should sequence its stations so the interest level stays high."

Two factors critical to success at any individual station are the size and speed of the targets, plus the background against which they are thrown. Even more important than determining how well you can see a target against its back-

This shooter powders a low flyer that has been thrown across his front. Such targets are difficult to see.

ground is calculating how long the target is visible within "killing" range. Target size can make it tricky. A ninety-millimeter midi at thirty yards, for example, appears identical to a full-size target at fifty. The optical illusion can screw-up your swing easily, especially if you think about it too much.

"You wouldn't believe how many shooters, particularly those who haven't hunted much and shot that many live birds, tend to overcomplicate everything when it comes to judging and studying speeds and target flight. By getting wrapped up in the technical stuff, they subconsciously talk themselves right out of the target," John Dunn said.

"It's far more natural to take a look at a sample target, let the brain absorb the obvious information, then shoot it. Most of the time, whatever adjustments you have to make will be slight."

Inexperienced and new shooters also have a tendency to overemphasize choke selection. They see experienced shooters changing tubes frequently, and believe it's necessary for them to do the same thing to minimize their disadvantage. It's not true in non-tournament situations, at least. In tournaments, target difficulty and sometimes absurd distances often necessitate tighter chokes. Non-tournament

set-ups, however, are pretty much designed around improved cylinder. Going to modified or full is often self-defeating. According to John Dunn, "You can adjust for the handful of longer distance targets by switching to tighter patterning loads of #7½s. In fact, if I had to choose a single load for any course — sight unseen — it would be light target #7½s."

Dunn offers one basic tip for new shooters dealing with simultaneous doubles. "On doubles, both going away, rising targets and straight incomers, a right-handed shooter should train himself to always visually find and take the left bird first. The recoil of the first shot will push the muzzle to the right, making it far easier to get on the right side target. Taking the right-side bird first forces you to work against the recoil, and on really fast moving targets, that split second can easily cost you the bird."

His final comment makes sense for everyone. "I think the real clue to success at sporting clays is that it genuinely relates to hunting. Naturally, there are some tricks, because the conditions are controlled. But here the tricks don't come into play until you get to tournament grade course set-ups. Up 'til then, the body positioning and movements, the pure, natural rhythm of the swing are the

It's not exactly the Jane Fonda workout routine, but swinging on targets from the various required angles can do much to stretch muscles that aren't used in the ordinary course of one's normal, day-to-day activities.

same as they are in the field. Everyone, experienced or inexperienced, whether realizing it or not, has his own style. Shooting sporting clays at a well designed, hunter-oriented range is, by far, the best way to develop and make the most of it."

Increasing the difficulty factor on a course generally requires simple mechanical changes. Changing target types and sizes, adjusting the angle of delivery and increasing or decreasing target speed are easy tasks. Therefore, a good

clays course should be set up not for the tournament pros, but for the average guy. And that's where I come in.

I don't shoot registered targets, and I don't shoot tournaments. And it's not because I don't shoot reasonably well. Granted, I wouldn't be even an ultra-long shot to make the bottom of the scoreboard in high overall, but I wouldn't be totally humiliated, either. At this point, what I care about isn't the narrow breadth of competition, but what I can apply to my days in the field.

For real difficult shots, a bit of coaching or the help of a professional is sure to help one's scores.

From a hunter's perspective, the first clue to a course is the amount and type of natural cover. If a course is laden with wide-open shots, even if they offer tricky angles and speeds, to me it's not realistic. Except for huns, sharptails and sage grouse in limited areas of the far West, where the land stretches like a table top clear to the horizon, I've never seen real hunting situations where all of the shots are open and clear. Hunters are forced to deal with a myriad of obstructions and shadows in the field, and a well planned clays course incorporates those factors.

I don't expect a perfect simulation of quail along a swamp edge or grouse in second growth poplars, but a course that's as antiseptic as an operating room just doesn't cut it.

Like John Dunn and Rick Spivey, I look for variety. An overdose of the same thing, even though you're mounting the gun, pulling the trigger and steadily breaking targets that wear fluorescent orange paint jobs can turn you into a robot. A hunter who expects to put weight in his game pouch can't afford that. The end result will be a lot of misses on birds that wear real feathers.

Not being concerned with the competitive aspects of sporting clays leaves me a lot of leeway. During the long off-season, I'll shoot a full course no matter what fields and stations are being used. However, prior to the different hunting seasons, I'll focus on those that best serve a practical purpose.

For doves or pass shooting geese, I'll work on high crossers at the tower field. For pheasant, it'll be the flush station where targets rocket out from under your feet down a hedgerow. For woodcock and grouse, it'll be a wood's station where targets are thrown through openings in the trees. For ducks, it'll be everything and anything that rises or settles or slips through timber. You get the picture. And a clays course that not only offers but permits this kind of specific emphasis, even if it's between, after, or before other shooters completing a regulation round, is a good one.

Finally, the one thing that, to me, carries as much weight as all of the other factors combined is a range that's run by hunters and caters to hunters. That's not a knock at the tournament guys. The fact is, most of them are hunters, too. I simply want to break targets and miss targets and just have a damn good time with folks who feel the same pleasures, pains and passions I do. And that's the one clue to a course meticulous design and deep pockets can't buy.

CHAPTER 11

THE ORGANIZATIONS

SPORTING CLAYS has grown in England to be one of the dominant shooting activities, with nearly 2000 tournaments a year and more than 5000 participants.

There are various reasons given for why the game began. Certainly, one of the major factors in making it so popular has been the fact that it is a less expensive alternative to game bird shooting. Also, such a clay target game afforded gunmakers to better fit their creations to their customers, because the controlled environment allowed them to con-

centrate on the specific measurements needed for each individual's body configuration. This would be much more difficult with live birds, because there is no real control over their flight patterns.

Regardless of the initial reasons for the game becoming a fact of life, it is the fun factor involved in shooting it that has made it big, and which has resulted in it being a premier type of activity in its own right.

Duck tower shoots were popular long before any Americans ever heard of sporting clays. So, too, were other

Shooters Have A Choice Of Styles And Rules;
Just Choose Your Association

shooting games practiced in the U.S. before sporting clays became part of the shooting vocabulary. Some of those games were given names like crazy quail, quail walk or pheasant flush. Most of these games were impromptu at best, and there was no evidence of even the slightest interest in taking them beyond something to do on a Sunday afternoon among shooting buddies.

Both trap and skeet dominated the American clay target shooting scene so completely that there seemed to be no room for anything else. There were more practical reasons. For example, traditional trap and skeet fields are relatively easily built and maintained. They require a minimum of investment, and can be established just about anywhere there is adequate open space.

Some might argue this is a chicken-and-egg situation — which came first — but an historic look at shooting in the United States shows clearly the types of guns Americans preferred to shoot throughout the first half of this century, and perhaps a decade or so longer, were totally in tune with games such as trap and skeet.

For example, American trap and the Model 12 Winchester shotgun were virtually synonymous in concept

through the 1950s, at least. The single-shot Ithaca trap gun was legend back then, but there were comparatively few of them around. During the same period, skeet was shot commonly and routinely with guns like the Model 12 or Ithaca Model 37 — both pump guns. Slide-action shotguns, after all, are an American phenomenon.

But all that was destined to change as the world began to shrink in the Jet Age. Americans were ready for something new — more challenges — and the shooting sports were no exception. Variants of what now are called sporting clays fields began to pop up here and there. There was a such a course, for example, at Remington Farms, on Maryland's Chesapeake Bay. And, visitors to Winchester's Nilo (Olin spelled backwards) Facility in Illinois were treated to a variation of sporting clays before that particular name was known generally in the United States. Specifically at Nilo, the game was a quail walk. And, there were others. Certainly by the late 1970s, some of America's shooters were trying different games, but they were more curiosities than serious attempts to accomplish anything.

The Orvis Company generally is credited with sponsoring the first sporting clays event in the United States. That

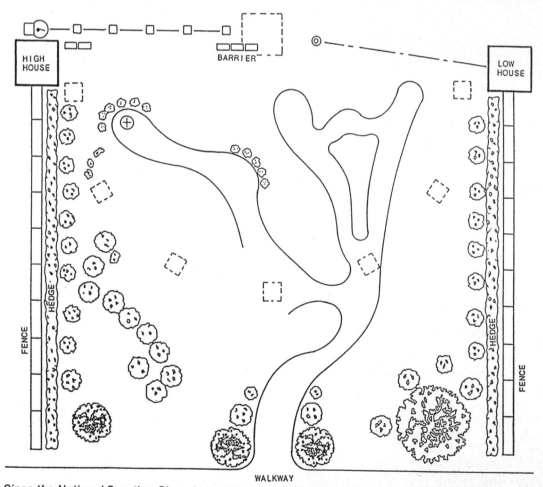

Since the National Sporting Clays Association is an offshoot of the National Skeet Shooting Association, it is not surprising, perhaps, that early course layouts were on existing fields.

Limitations on guns is governed mostly by needs of the shooter, although no black powder arms are allowed in competition. Ron Baisden uses his Browning Model B-25 over/under in various phases of serious contesting.

was in 1983. By 1985, the first sporting clays group was formed — The United States Sporting Clays Association.

As the governing body for sporting clays in the United States, the USSCA was responsible for rules and regulations governing the sport and for adopting those rules to the changing needs of the participants. The USSCA provided its members with a national handicap system that classified members according to shooting ability. The group has sanctioned tournaments held at USSCA affiliated sporting clays ranges throughout the year, including a national tournament each year.

For more information about the USSCA, contact the United States Sporting Clays Association, 50 Briar Hollow, Suite 490 East, Houston, TX 77027, or phone (713) 622-8043.

In April, 1989, the National Sporting Clays Association, a division of the National Skeet Shooting Association, was formed in San Antonio, Texas, to promote sporting clays in the United States and Canada.

"The National Sporting Clays Association (NSCA) is a non-profit organization owned and operated by and for its members," the NSCA states. "The primary objective of the NSCA is to promote the growth of sporting clays in a way which is beneficial to all who enjoy and participate in the game. The division of NSCA is guided by an advisory council comprised of range owners, both competitive and recreational shooters, and the shooting industry."

For more information about the NSCA, contact the National Sporting Clays Association, P.O. Box 680007, San Antonio, TX 78268, or call (800) 877-5338.

Among registered sporting clays shooters, some are affiliated with one or the other governing bodies, while still others are members of both. The same is true of sporting clays facilities. Some are affiliated with one or the other group, while others are tied to both groups.

Although there are some differences in specific rules and regulations between the two governing bodies, most of the rules are either the same, or quite similar when it comes to conducting shoots and how shooters perform during them. Shooters are classified according to ability in both groups.

Under the USSCA classification system, the classes are based on shooting percentages. They are:

AA: 78 percent and above.

A: 70-77.9 percent.

B: 60-69.9 percent.

C: 50-59.9 percent.

D: 49.9 percent and below.

The NSCA also bases its classifications on shooting percentages. They are:

AA: 75 percent and above.

A: 65-74.99 percent.

B: 55-64.99 percent.

C: 54.99 percent and below.

Regular registered shooters are classified by what is called the "average method." These shooters are unclassified until they have registered their first three hundred targets in a calendar year. Their class designation is whatever their percentage average is for those three hundred targets. During the year, shooters may be reclassified after every added three hundred targets. However, they are reclassified only upward during the year. At the beginning of the next year, they may be reclassified downward, if their scores reflect a lower level of shooting ability.

At the various shoots and tournaments around the country, there are obviously many shooters who want to participate who are not already classified. To classify them for the purposes of the specific shoot, range operators use a number of different systems. One is called the Lewis Class method.

This system is based on the final scores at the shoots and gives every contestant an equal chance to win, regardless of shooting ability.

The NSCA explains how the Lewis system works:

"When all the shooting has been completed, the scores are listed in numerical order from the highest to the lowest. They then are divided into as many groups as there are classes. For example, if there were sixty entries and four classes, there would be fifteen scores in each class. The highest score in each class would be the winner."

To accommodate those situations in which there are tie scores on the dividing line between classes and odd numbers of entries, there are specific formulae followed in the Lewis system. For example, if there is an odd number of entries, there would have to be more shooters in one class than another. In such cases, the short class or classes are at the top.

If the dividing line between classes falls where there are tie scores, those shooters with that score are classified in whichever class would contain the most of the tie scores. Where that break sees an equal number of shooters with tie scores above and below, all with that score are put at the top of the lower class.

The serious, big-money competitions have led to a new design approach, including Browning's GTI Sporting Clays.

Another form of classification at some shoots is called the "blind draw."

In this system, the range management decides which fields are to be used. Generally, half of the fields which are being shot on the course for that event are used. The total score from those chosen fields — or stations — is added together and multiplied by two. That number then is used on a classification table to determine the shooter's class for that day.

Still another shoot classification method is called the "stencil system." This system also uses half the targets shot. A stencil or overlay is made to be placed over the shooters' score cards. All of the "hit" targets showing through the holes in the overlay are counted, then multiplied by two. That number becomes the base upon which that day's shooter average is computed.

Although used infrequently, there is another method which is somewhat less objective. It is called the "known ability" system, and it merely classifies shooters as they are known to the management. For example, if the range operator knows a shooter is of AA ability, but the shooter is not currently classified by one of the governing groups, that range operator under the "known ability" system would classify that shooter as AA for a specific shoot.

There are procedures to help guard against that activity called "sandbagging." This is when a shooter might try to compete in a lower class than he or she should just to be able to win that class. For example, an AA shooter competing as a B or C shooter probably could win that class just about every time, and it would be unfair to the legitimate B or C class competitors. Sandbagging also might occur at a shoot where, for example, there were only a couple of AA shooters and a large number of A shooters. When it comes to things like option money, unscrupulous AA shooters might be tempted to try to compete as A shooters in order to win more money. This, of course, is unsportsmanlike and frowned upon.

Both governing organizations require that guns used in competitions be 12-gauge or smaller bore. The USSCA addresses the gauge question even more extensively. Shooters may be classified to an extent by gauge in that organization.

"Any USSCA member who has not shot registered targets, must establish what gauge shotshell in which they will be classified, on the first one hundred targets," the USSCA states. "All additional USSCA tournament targets must be shot with this gauge or a smaller gauge. Persons wishing to change their established gauge to a larger

Bill Houston of The Shotgun Shop uses a Browning B-25 Superposed shotgun which he retrofitted for his needs.

Richard Kumferman uses a side-by-side for sporting clays. The stock must be positioned below the armpit at the time the target is called. Actually, the side-by-side is a bit of an oddity on sporting clays courses, but does serve well.

gauge shotshell will automatically be reclassified to the next highest class. Persons found in violation of this rule will be disqualified from the tournament without refund of entry fees. Shooters desiring to shoot a smaller gauge shotshell may do so, but must remain in their established class."

Rules governing protests, low gun position, calling for targets and mounting the gun are similar and, in some instances, identical between the two governing organizations. There are other slight differences, however. For example, the USSCA makes provision for ill-prepared competitors:

"It is the responsibility of the shooter to begin any event, station and/or field with sufficient equipment and ammunition. Failure to do so, which in the opinion of the field judge will delay the shoot, will result in the loss of all targets as required to keep the shoot proceeding in an orderly and timely manner. Make-up targets will be provided only at the discretion of the field judge."

There are other quite general rules when it comes to shooting sporting clays. For example, shooters may use guns with multiple barrels and/or interchangeable chokes. Any barrel or choke changes, however, must be done between stations or fields, and not while the shooter is in the

stand. Or the shooters may change guns during a shoot, but again, the change has to take place between stands.

Ammunition is restricted somewhat. Even though both organizations have general rules with respect to ammo, officials at individual shoots may opt to further restrict the type or types of ammunition allowed at that shoot. Using 12-gauge as an example, generally the heaviest shot charge allowed is 1⅛ ounces, and shot size generally is limited to No. 7½ (U.S. designation) or smaller.

When shooting, competitors must start with what is called the "low gun" position. This means the stock must be visible below the shooter's armpit.

When the shooter calls for a target, it may be launched immediately, or there can be up to a three-second delay, and the shooter is not permitted to mount the gun until the target is visible.

Violations of these rules generally result in the designation of "no target" at first. However, after three such violations during a day's shoot, the shooter may be penalized.

Target scoring really is quite simple. If a visible piece of the target is broken, it is "hit." If no visible piece is broken, it is "lost" or a "miss."

During tournaments, the field judge or scorer announces

Television celebrities such as Steve Kanaly enjoy this sport. Many shooters belong to both of the associations.

aloud whether a target is hit or lost. Any protest must be made immediately. Also any other shooter protest must be made as soon after the alleged problem as possible — either before the shooter goes to the next stand, or by the end of the shoot, depending upon the specific situation.

Protests generally are considered by what is called a "jury." This group normally is established before the shoot begins, and is comprised of selected field judges or shooters who are familiar with the rules and regulations of the game. When in doubt, however, the ruling of the field judge stands.

Malfunctions of both guns and ammo can be a factor. Generally, a shooter is allowed a maximum of two malfunctions per day which are attributed to the shooter's gun or ammo. There are specific sequences of activities required whenever a malfunction is claimed. It is up to the field judge to determine whether the malfunction will be allowed, or whether there will be lost targets.

For example, if the shooter fails to load the gun, it is not considered a malfunction. Or if the shooter fails to take the gun off "safe" when attempting the targets, it is not considered a malfunction. Rather, a malfunction in NSCA events might be called if the gun failed to strike the primer,

or if the shell failed to fire when the primer is dented. The USSCA is more restrictive:

"If there is a gun malfunction which prevents the shooter from attempting a target, that target will be scored as 'lost.' If the bird would have been lost in the shooting field, then it is lost in sporting clays."

However, if a shooter has a gun malfunction at a station, that shooter may be allowed to replace the gun to shoot subsequent targets, if the field judge determines it can be done without delaying the shoot.

Similar provisions are made for ammo malfunctions at USSCA shoots. In fact, the USSCA sums up its feeling about malfunctions quite succinctly: "Targets shall be scored as lost if the shooter is unable to fire for any reason."

Safety is foremost at all sporting clays facilities. In addition to all of the normal gun safety procedures, there are other specific safety-related requirements. For example, guns must be unloaded when shooters go from one station to another. They may be loaded when the shooter is in the stand, ready to shoot.

Further, both shooters and range officials are quick to point out any safety violations, and such violations can dis-

Veteran character actor Dub Taylor is an avid shooter who has come to enjoy the challenge of sporting clays.

qualify a shooter instantly from an event, and even cause that shooter to be ejected from the course. Simply put, no sporting clays organization or facility will tolerate unsafe practices.

As Americans become more involved in sporting clays shooting, many are entering the various international events. When this happens, another organization comes into the picture. Headquartered in Paris, France, it is the *Federation Internationale de Tir aux Armes Sportives de Chasses (FITASC)* which is one of two world bodies governing all international shotgunning events. The other world body is the International Shooting Union (ISU) which governs the Olympic shooting sports.

In the United States, for sporting clays purposes, FITASC is represented by the USSCA. In addition to sporting clays, FITASC also internationally regulates the disciplines of universal trench, ZZ clays and live pigeon competition. Increasingly in the United States, there are FITASC-style shoots being held, and they are somewhat different from the English style of sporting clays which is shot at most American sporting clays facilities. The USSCA explains how FITASC and English-style shoots differ:

"A traditional English sporting field is laid out with a series of stands, often five to ten. Frequently, ten targets per stand are shot, mostly in pairs, whether simultaneous, on report, or following. Either one or two different traps are used at each stand.

"The traditional FITASC sporting layout is composed of several stands around an oval, all stands often utilizing the same several traps. Since each stand is in a different location, the targets are viewed at different angles, trajectories and speeds."

And there are some other differences. For example, a full FITASC course usually has several of these layouts,

Top competitor Dan Reeves gives his wife, Mern, tips on how to shoot the game.

The two associations place slightly different emphasis on segments of competition, but with the same intent. The purpose of sporting clays is to offer a challenge that is not found in current trap and skeet competition.

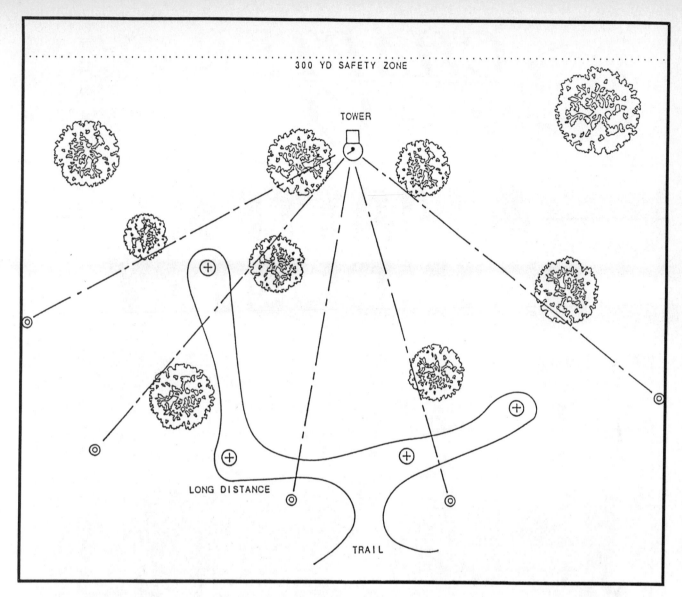

TOWER

LONG DISTANCE

TRAIL

A properly placed tower can be used to launch clay birds in a number of patterns even on a skeet or trap field, but natural growth and terrain features add to challenge.

with twenty-five shots taken per layout. Also different is the way targets are shot. In FITASC, there are single- and double-target presentations. The singles usually are shot by each member of a squad, then the doubles are shot by each shooter. Two shots are permitted at the singles. There are more specialty targets launched in FITASC events than in most of the English-style shoots. These include targets like 90mm midis, 60mm minis, rabbits, rockets and battues.

In 1988, a new style of FITASC was presented at the world championships in Australia. And now, this form is being encountered rather frequently. Instead of being laid out in ovals, the fields are established in a straight line with each stand having its several traps.

"This permitted competitors to shoot each stand simultaneously versus the more traditional system physcially permitting only one competitor to be shooting in a layout (at one time)," the USSCA reported.

The number of facilities offering FITASC-style shoots is growing in the United States, as are the number of major FITASC shoots. George P. Van, the U.S. representative for FITASC, is affiliated with the Grinders Switch Club in Tennessee. For more information about FITASC, contact the USSCA, or Van at Grinders Switch Club, 1608 Chickering Road, Nashville, TN 37215.

Even though U.S. shooters have been competing in the world sporting clays events for a relatively short time, they are making a name for themselves, and are becoming major factors at the international level. Sporting clays not only is growing rapidly in the United States, but the United States is growing rapidly in sporting clays.

CHAPTER 12

A MATTER OF INDUSTRY

When the sporting clays semi co-sponsored by Red Wing and the National Sporting Clays Association is unloaded, it reveals all of the requirements for setting up a full-scale shooting course, even including the shotguns!

DID YOU ever try to explain to someone just what sporting clays is all about? Chances are you mumbled something about it being "a little like trap or skeet, but a lot different." Or, "try to think of it as 'golf with a shotgun.'" Or, something about "simulated hunting." In most instances, your explanation was greeted with blank stares.

That was the problem faced by the National Sporting Clays Association (NSCA) when trying to get hunters, casual shooters, women and youngsters interested in the growing game of sporting clays. Word-of-mouth from a core of sporting clays enthusiasts was helping to expand the sport, but it wasn't growing fast enough outside of the ranks of converted trap and skeet shooters. Hunters, seeking a chal-

Outdoor-Oriented Businesses
Recognize The Lure Of Sporting Clays!

For the past year-plus, the customized truck-trailer has been criss-crossing the country to visit tournament shoots, gun clubs and sporting events, demonstrating what the sporting clays game is all about, in the available space. (Below) Jon Kruger, winner of national and world titles in the sport, travels with the trailer doing his show.

lenging shooting sport to replace their dwindling hunting opportunities, were not going to be interested in a sport that was just like trap or skeet; that much became apparent.

In this country, the National Shooting Sports Foundation was the first organization to start promoting the sport, issuing press releases and brochures. Perhaps the first firearms manufacturer to become involved was Remington, which set up a sporting clays course at Remington Farms in Maryland. This layout was used to introduce the press and influential shooters to the sport.

A bit at a time, other arms and ammo makers began to realize that sporting clays could mean loot in the corporate coffers and they, too, began to support the sport.

Magazine articles and videos all have helped to enlighten people about sporting clays, but until someone actually goes out and tries the sport, they really don't understand how exciting, challenging and educational it can be. Not only is there virtually endless variety in the kind of courses and shooting stations, but there are almost never any perfect scores. And, for hunters, the variety of shots and degree of difficulty makes anyone a better shooter in the field almost immediately. That has only been partially true with trap and skeet.

The best way to build the sport, the National Sporting Clays Association reasoned, was to give as many people as possible a chance to try the sport in as many places across the country as possible.

"We wanted to give people a chance to sample the fun, excitement and challenge of sporting clays at minimal

expense, in a low-pressure atmosphere," says Mike Hampton, executive director of the NSCA.

The result of that goal was the Red Wing Irish Setter Sport Boots/NSCA Sporting Clays Demonstration Unit, a joint venture of Red Wing Shoes, Incorporated and NSCA to promote the new sport. The unit is a truck and thirty-six-foot trailer that contains everything one needs to set up a challenging sporting clays course anywhere shotguns can be safely discharged.

With initial funding for the unit from Red Wing Shoes, and support from other manufacturers such as Beretta, Winchester, Remington, Browning, Federal, Laporte, White Flyer, 10-X and others, the unit has been extremely popular wherever it has appeared across the country.

During its first seven months of operation in 1989, the truck appeared at nineteen shooting events in twelve states from California to New York and from Minnesota to Texas. At major shooting competitions, game fairs, shopping centers and at demonstrations put on by Red Wing shoe stores, more than six thousand shooters participated in events put on by the unit that first year. More than 385,000 shotgun shells were fired and more than 400,000 targets were used.

Dave Armstrong (left) and Pete Marsh, both employees of NSCA, are in charge of the mobile demonstration unit.

Although the unit and its equipment are valued at more than $250,000, event organizers are able to have the unit appear at their event for $2500. That includes all the equipment, setup, takedown, guns, ammunition, targets and the technical expertise of two NSCA employees who travel with the truck. The best part is that the cost to participants averages only about fifty cents per shot — a price which includes the course, the use of a high-quality Beretta, Remington or Browning shotgun, 12-gauge ammunition, clay targets and lots of fun.

"People are much more willing to try something new if you make it easy and inexpensive," says Hampton. "If you force people to make a commitment first, like buy a shotgun, get some ammunition, find a shooting club with sporting clays, find somebody to shoot with — the growth of this activity is going to be a lot slower than it could be. On the other hand, if you let them experience how much fun it is, many of them will come back for more as they develop a commitment."

It seems that philosophy is working for the NSCA. During 1989, membership more than doubled to three thousand members. The number of member gun clubs also increased to two hundred.

Another goal of the Red Wing/NSCA mobile unit has been to improve the quality of sporting clays competition in America. Whereas most sanctioning organizations simply write rules to guide tournament organizers, the Red Wing/NSCA mobile demonstration unit has been invited to major tournaments to augment courses and improve the quality of competition for all participants.

Along with the state-of-the-art automatic traps and computerized sporting clays games, champion shooter Jon Kruger often travels with the unit to offer his expertise on course design for major tournaments. Kruger also appears widely for Red Wing Irish Setter Sport Boots, putting on his Shotgun Magic shooting demonstrations.

As a part of a sporting clays demonstration, Jon Kruger performs shooting magic for onlookers attending any gathering of shotgunners. Sponsors are noted on banner.

After suffering the loss of most of his right hand in an accident two years ago, Kruger has come back to top form. By wearing a specially made shooting glove that sticks to the gun stock with hook-and-loop fasteners, he is able to hold the gun and pull the trigger with his little finger. With quiet determination, Kruger has redeveloped his skills to the point that he is winning ninety percent of all the tournaments he enters.

For the past three years, the Chevy Sportsman Team Challenge has been a major shooting event carried by ESPN and features some of North America's top rifle, pistol and shotgun shooters. The Red Wing/NSCA mobile demonstration unit has been responsible for setting up the shotgun events for this.

Teams of three compete in a three-part pistol event, a small-bore rifle event and two shotgun events. The shotgun events consist of a three-man Flurry and a three-man Flush. The Flurry is a three-station sporting clays game with fifty crossing and outgoing targets being thrown at random in sixty seconds. Each shooter is permitted to load only two shots at a time, but each must shoot and reload as quickly as he can. Teamwork and coordination are musts, for if all the shooters are reloading at the same time, two or three targets can fly unmolested and cost you the game. Perfect scores are more rare than quail lips.

The Flush is a similar three-man game with fifty randomly thrown incoming targets in sixty seconds. Once again, teamwork, nimble hands and fingers, plus concentration are just as important as target-dusting accuracy.

NSCA furnished a tent for registration during annual conference of the Outdoor Writers Assn. of America.

Although incoming targets tend to be easier to hit, the shooters have less time to track and hit the targets than in the Flurry. Out of fifty teams in the 1989 competition, only one team shot a perfect score in the Flush.

At other sporting clays competitions, the Red Wing/NSCA mobile demonstration unit has set up automated shooting games similar to the Flush and Flurry to help competitors warm up and stay sharp while waiting for a shooting time on the course. One particular game featured with the unit has been the Bird Brain, a five-stand, computer-controlled shotgun game developed by Raymond Forman. It features eight automated traps that throw overheads, fast and slow crossers, incomings, springing teals and rabbits. The traps are controlled by a computer to provide a number of interesting target variations.

With Bird Brain, five people can shoot at once for the fun of it or for serious competition. At the end of a game, the computer prints out a permanent record of each individual's hits and misses. It's great for beginners to get a tangible record of their shooting performance — or lack thereof — and for advanced shooters, it's helpful to see which type of targets caused problems.

As the sole representative of this new game in the United States, the NSCA — through the Red Wing/NSCA mobile unit — has been the major channel for exposing shooters to this particular form of sporting clays.

Bird Brain is ideal for existing shooting preserves or trap and skeet clubs which do not have enough room to install a full-blown sporting clays course, yet want to give members the fun and challenge of this sport.

The purpose of the demonstration unit is to promote and introduce sporting clays shooting throughout the United States. The unit is designed to get people involved in improving their hunting skills as well as introducing shotgun hunters to the sporting game. Gun safety is taught and stressed in all events and the unit also attracts the general public to this new shotgun clay target sport.

The unit comes complete with everything needed to set up a sporting clays course, to enhance an existing range or to set up games and/or practice fields. Space permitting, a sporting clays course can be set up wherever desired. It is equipped with twenty fully automatic trap machines, including specialty targets, twenty-five loaner guns, ammunition, generators, electrical cords, shooting stands and a large tent for registration purposes. Two full-time employees pilot this unit across the country. The majority of the trap machines are the Beomat, but also included are Universal, Laporte and Winchester machines.

As the major sponsor of the demonstration unit, Red Wing Shoes, makers of Irish Setter sport boots, has taken a keen interest in sporting clays and the footwear requirements of shooters. Each time the unit appears, there is a display of various kinds of Irish Setter boots and a Red Wing expert to discuss proper outdoor footwear. Although no

Red Wing Shoes, a major sponsor of sporting clays, puts its team where its mouth is. The Red Wing team shoots in numerous competitions around the nation during the year.

Sponsor's flags are flown each year at the San Antonio club when national sporting clays competition is held.

sales are made at these appearances, shooters are educated on the importance of proper footwear for good shooting form and safety.

Besides appearing at major shooting competitions, the Red Wing demonstration unit has been used in a variety of other ways to spread the news about sporting clays.

For the past two years, the unit has attended the national conference of the Outdoor Writers Association of America (OWAA), a group of fifteen hundred national outdoor writers. At conferences in Salt Lake City, Utah, and Niagara Falls, New York, the unit allowed more than two hundred writers to shoot a round of sporting clays at each event. Many of these writers, who write for some of the top national outdoor publications, were shooting sporting clays for the first or second time in their lives.

"This points up the tremendous job still ahead to bring sporting clays even to those strongly associated with the outdoors," NSCA officials admit.

In Europe, clay target shooting is a big spectator sport. Here, it is a participation sport for a relatively small but growing group of enthusiasts. One of the primary goals of the Red Wing/NSCA demonstration unit is to educate and involve the general public in the sport, either as spectators or recreational participants.

Numerous appearances by the unit over the past two years have been aimed specifically at a general audience. At local game fairs, shopping center displays and special public demonstrations, the unit has appeared just to expose the public to the sport in a fun, non-competitive atmosphere. Hunters or one-time hunters and their families who never would enter a local sporting clays competition were drawn to the unit, because it offered a low-risk opportunity to sample the sport without the fear of humiliation in a serious competition.

A Red Wing shoe store in northern Arkansas decided to put on a day-long demonstration of sporting clays for the local residents. The truck set up two sporting games for people to try and Jon Kruger put on his entertaining Shotgun Magic demonstration several times during the day. Even in this relatively remote area, more than two hundred people showed up on a Sunday to watch, learn, shoot and have fun.

In Minnesota, the Anoka Game Fair held each year just outside of Minneapolis/St. Paul attracts more than twenty thousand people over two weekends. For the past two years, the demonstration unit has set up a Flurry and a Flush sporting game that attracts hundreds of shooters and thousands of spectators.

A game fair held in Omaha, Nebraska, saw sporting clays introduced to those who attended outdoor event.

In each case, hundreds of people are given a chance to sample this fast, fun and challenging sport in a highly supportive environment. Most of the people at these events are not from the ranks of serious trap and skeet shooters or even average league shooters. Nearly all are people interested in the outdoors, people who participate in hunting sports to a greater or lesser degree, those who may have heard something about this new game of sporting clays, but have not made the effort to seek it out.

But it is from these ranks that the sport will grow. If growth depends on merely attracting disenchanted trap and skeet shooters, it will continue as a minor shooting sport. By aggressively educating people from outside the serious shooting community, this sport has the potential to someday rival its European counterpart and become an' important component of American outdoor recreation.

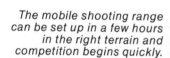

The mobile shooting range can be set up in a few hours in the right terrain and competition begins quickly.

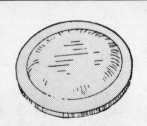

CHAPTER 13

THE COST FACTOR

SPORTING CLAYS represents one of the better values of any of the shooting sports. However, it does cost money to play the game. How much money is needed depends largely upon the needs and desires of individual shooters. Like any sport, there can be a lot of cost. But shooting sporting clays need not strain the budgets of most working shooters.

Two things contribute to the seemingly higher price tag on the shooting of sporting clays, when compared to some other shooting games like traditional trap or skeet. Foremost is the way a "round" of sporting clays is defined as compared to the more traditional disciplines. For example, a typical round of trap or skeet is twenty-five targets. A

typical round of sporting clays is fifty or one hundred targets. When considered on a per-target basis, sporting clays shooting generally compares equally or just slightly more than trap or skeet.

There is a broad range of prices at the various sporting clays facilities. Some courses are established as adjuncts to existing shooting facilities and the prices at these locations tend to be fairly close per target with the other shooting sports. Some sporting clays facilities, however, are located at exclusive clubs or hunting preserves and the cost of a round of clays there can be on the pricey side.

Depending upon how a sporting clays course is set up, there can be a significantly higher cost per target for the

Is Sporting Clays An Expensive Pastime? Check It Against Golf!

Steve Comus shoots from a goose pit on a sporting clays course. Side-by-side 12-gauge is a Bernardelli Model 12. (Right) Installing interchangeable choke systems is one of the more common gunsmithing costs encountered by the new sporting clays shooter. Reamer prepares a barrel.

facility operator. This is especially true when the course features traps that have to be operated by a human — a trapper. It is much more labor intensive to operate such a course, compared to one that features automatic traps that can be activated by the push of a button by the scorer or even other shooters in a squad.

Another determining factor present in many of the tournaments is whether any or many of the so-called "specialty" targets are thrown. These targets are more expensive than the standard clays and when a higher percentage of the total number of targets is made up with specialty targets, the costs go up. These specialty targets are the rabbit, midi, mini, battue and rocket.

Sporting clays often is likened to playing golf with a shotgun. This usually means that no two sporting clays courses are the same, just as no two golf courses are identical. The general participation sport aspects found in golf are also present in the sporting clays ethic. Not surprisingly, the range of costs to participate also are generally parallel.

The cost of sporting clays can be substantial when it comes to rebuilding guns for the purpose, but it also can be relatively casual. It depends upon how involved the individual shooter wants to become in the sport.

Trigger work is another common job on sporting clays shotguns. The sear at left has been touched up by Bill Houston of The Shotgun Shop in City of Industry, Calif. Sear at right is fresh from factory; note uneven top.

At left is the trigger mechanism from a Citori as it came from the factory. Note milling marks on the side and the top. At right is part touched up by a gunsmith.

For example, shooting a round of sporting clays generally ranges from $24 to $38 per one hundred targets. Determining factors include everything from the poshness of the course to its location relative to population centers. At most courses, there are reduced member prices for those who shoot the course frequently. Such rates may be $35 to $45 per one hundred targets and that pricing often includes a lunch.

If there is any significant purse connected with the shoot, tournament fees can be in the $85 to $100 range, with a percentage of return as well as trophies to winners. For higher level shoots like state, regional or national competitions, the prices can get into the $250-or-more league quickly.

Ammunition is a major expense in sporting clays simply because shooters go through a lot of shells. The rules have been lightened in sporting clays quite a bit and, in most

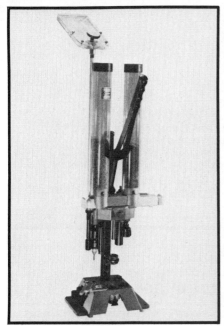 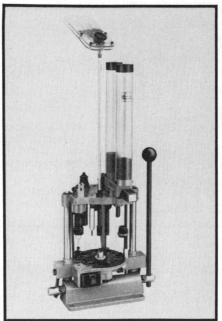 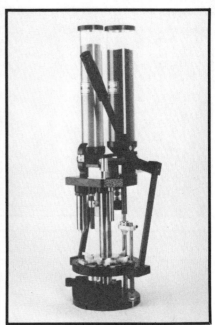

There is no doubt that one can save considerable amounts of money by reloading. These shotshell reloaders all are made by Hornady, but some are faster than others. From left are a Model 155, the 366 auto type and Model 91.

Winchester's new Super-Lite powder is outstanding choice for sporting clays reloads. The powder burns cleanly meaning that it will work well in gas-operated guns.

instances, reloads now can be used. However, some of the major events still require the use of factory-loaded shells.

Factory target loads usually can be purchased at the sporting clays ranges for $6 to $8 per box of twenty-five. When shooters buy ammo by the case, costs drop to $4 to $5 per box. Ammunition companies also market what is called promotional ammo, often dubbed "field" grade or something like that. This is the kind of ammunition often put on sale by mass merchants and it typically goes over the counter for somewhere in the $3.49 to $4.49 price range. Hence, it is easy to see that the more one shoots, the more this part of the financial equation comes into play.

Travel also is a factor for sporting clays shooters who opt to go beyond the infrequent, recreational level. Obviously, the only real travel expense for shooting a home course or any other nearby installation comes in the form of gas money for the car or pickup. But for tournaments across the state, elsewhere in the region, around the country or overseas, the travel factor becomes increasingly considerable.

In addition to mileage and/or airfare, there are costs for things like hotel/motel, food and incidentals. Lodging typically ranges from $29 to $79 per night. That cost can be reduced, of course, if two or more shooting buddies share quarters.

The guns themselves represent some degree of initial expense, whether they already are owned as hunting guns or not. Although virtually any shotgun can be used in sporting clays, credible models generally are in the $500 to $1200 range at full retail. For over/unders, the general retail range usually is $1000 to $2000. Used guns, of course, can substantially lower the entry level cost.

Sporting clays shooters who go beyond the purely recreational level also find themselves joining one or both of the major sanctioning organizations in the United States.

Steve Comus feels that if you're going to haul costly gun around the country, it deserves proper protection. (Below) Lockable hard gun cases are a must for airlines. Browning model, called the Travel Vault, serves well.

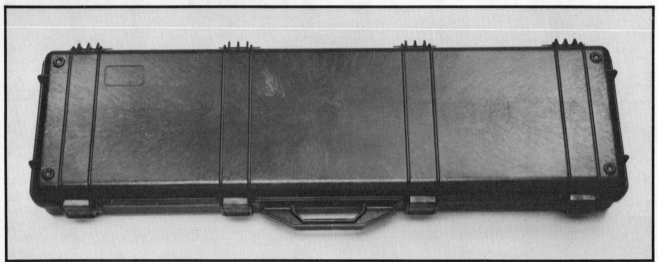

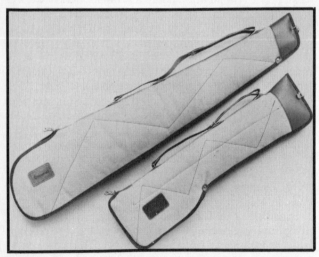

For transporting sporting clays guns to the local range, soft cases such as these from Browning will do the job.

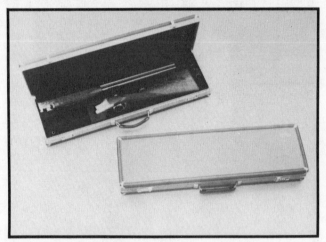

If you favor an over/under, Browning's European Collector series is made for the gun and will handle hard abuse.

They are the United States Sporting Clays Association and the National Sporting Clays Association. Annual membership fees are $35 for the NSCA and $45 for the USSCA.

In order to be classified in either organization, a shooter has to shoot at least three hundred registered targets in a one-year period. The NSCA operates on a calendar year schedule from January 1 through December 31, while the USSCA bases the year from the date of membership.

Membership fees include a subscription to the organization's official magazine publication. For the USSCA, that is *Shotgun Sports* magazine and for the NSCA it is *Sporting Clays* magazine. Also included are membership credentials and patches.

Gunsmithing costs are a factor in sporting clays for those who become avid participants. Most of the gunsmithing involves gun modifications for competition.

These are such things as removing the forcing cones in the barrels just forward of the chambers, installation of interchangeable choke tube systems, backboring — enlarging the diameter of the main bore in the barrel — porting to reduce muzzle jump, stock work to fit the gun to the individual shooter, action work to slick up the mechanism or improve the feel and performance of the trigger system, installation of recoil pads contoured specifically for the sport and similar types of modifications.

There are a number of supplies that sporting clays shooters find themselves purchasing specifically for the sport. For example, if commercial airline travel is in the cards, the shooter needs to have a lockable, hard case. Special shooting glasses are in order and at least one vest with the right kind of padding for sporting clays can make the difference of a target broken here or there that might have been missed otherwise.

Above: Ammo makes a difference. Remington's Premier Light Target loading is a good choice at most stations. (Left) Federal markets a load that is designed just for the sporting clays shooter; it works quite well.

For specific courses, shooters might find themselves buying extra choke tubes with a little different degree of restriction, to say nothing of the many special gadgets — some of them battery-powered — that are available to help the shooter change chokes quickly and easily. Then there are all the lubricants, cleaners and solvents needed for routine gun maintenance.

Although relatively few shooters travel internationally on the sporting clays circuit, some do — and many more are interested in knowing just how expensive such a prospect might be. Actually, it isn't all that much more expensive than simple travel itself.

For example, for a one-week trip to Europe to shoot in an event there, the shooter could get away for $2000 to $2500, assuming he or she didn't go crazy on some shopping spree or other high-ticket activity while on the Continent. Closer to home, the nationals are certainly within striking range for most shooters.

Based on an assumed airfare of $300 round trip, $50 per night lodging and $250 entry fee, a shooter can do the nationals for about $1200, which also would include prac-

Good shooting glasses not only protect the eyes, but different colored lenses can help shooters see targets better against various types of backgrounds on course.

Federal also is marketing a target load called Top Gun.
This particular shotshell has found favor for sport.

Not all of the expense of sporting clays
is borne by the shooter. The cost of land
for such courses is an escalating plane.

Crossing birds that emerge from bushes
makes use of terrain and demands a good
gun even in the hands of expert shooter.

tice rounds and other small, incidental expenses.

Back on the home front, there are some typical daily
costs for sporting clays. Starting with what would be considered a full day of sporting clays — two hundred targets
— the shooter could expect to spend about $100 total.
That would include both ammo and targets.

To put this into proper perspective, it takes generally
about two hours or slightly more for a squad to complete a
one-hundred-target round of sporting clays. That means
that, on a full-day schedule, the shooter would go through
the course once in the morning, break for lunch, then go
through it again in the afternoon for the two-hundred-target
full day.

Most shooters, though, would rarely, if ever, shoot such
a "full day." Rather, a day at the course probably would
consist of shooting fifty or a hundred targets. Costs would
be proportionately less, meaning $25 to $50 for both targets
and ammo.

This level of cost compares favorably with other rec-

Walls and other static restraints keep a shooter from over-swinging in a dangerous direction — or obscures the view of the target until it is well on the way. (Left) Sometimes a shooter is made to feel his performance has been flushed down the toilet, using this psychological aid.

reational activities. For example, a parent and child could spend an entire day at a sporting clays facility and each shoot one hundred targets for a total of $100 or less. That is about the same total amount that could be spent at any of the country's major amusement parks. It is all relative.

In a real sense, sporting clays can cost comparatively little for those who merely want to shoot it occasionally and recreationally with the same equipment they use for hunting or back-forty, hand-thrown clay busting.

Sporting clays can become a major form of entertainment and enjoyment and reflect whatever level of commitment the individual shooter has or can afford. Unlike some recreational activities, sporting clays does not require a special vehicle, like a four-wheel-drive pickup, nor does it require an additional vehicle, like a bass boat.

There is only one major initial expense and that is the shotgun. Beyond that, the costs are related directly to the amount and frequency of shooting the person desires to do. Yes, sporting clays costs money. But it doesn't have to be a budget buster.

One warning here, however: Sporting clays can be addictive!

CHAPTER 14
TRAVELS & THE SHOOTER

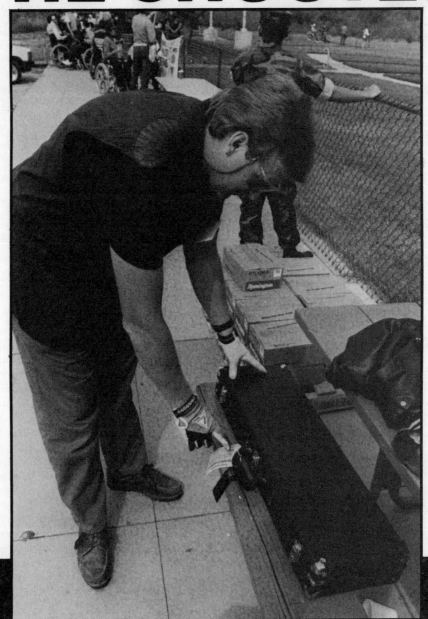

Browning markets a series of Travel Vaults that fit virtually any type of gun. A special seal keeps out water, dust, sand. They are available in black, orange.

THE SHOOTING of sporting clays requires some degree of travel for virtually everyone. About the only way to shoot the game and not to travel would be to live on a course. In reality, anyone who shoots sporting clays more than just casually at a single, local course does find himself or herself confronting many situations that can be routine or nightmares, depending upon how certain requirements are addressed.

"For most shooters, the travel involved in sporting clays is limited to putting the gun and other gear into the car or truck, driving to a nearby course and shooting. Basic requirements in these situations are simple," according to Steve Comus, who speaks from experience.

"The shooter needs to have some sort of gun case to keep the shotgun from being dinged or scratched in transit. Traditional, soft gun cases can do the trick nicely. Ammunition can be carried in anything from a cardboard box to a sports bag, and things like shooting glasses, ear plugs and shooting vest can be thrown on the seat or in the trunk and everything is fine."

But for even the most casual shooter, there are realities in the 1990s that should be considered. For example, it does not pay to "advertise" when it comes to transporting any type of firearm — even the most pure-bred sporting models. Theft is always a possibility, regardless of what part of the country one calls home.

Hence, it is a good idea to transport any firearm out of sight. Automobile trunks are good for this, as are campers on pickups, or spots out of view in vans. There is simply no good reason to invite attention to a shotgun when in transit.

Another good idea for traveling shooters is to separate the gun from the ammunition. This can be accomplished in a number of ways. It can be as simple as carrying the shotgun in the trunk and the ammo elsewhere. Or the ammo can be carried separately in the trunk itself. Best of all combinations is to carry the shotgun in a locked case and carry the ammo in a second locked case.

Many states are enacting laws that dictate more stringent rules when it comes to transporting and/or storing firearms and ammo. It is the responsibility of the shooter to understand what laws are in effect wherever that shooter happens to be and to comply with them.

Some of these laws — which may be less than brilliant in their wording — have been passed in attempts to avoid accidents with firearms. Non-compliance generally does not become a factor until there is an accident, and at that point it is simply too late to do anything about it. So it is always a good idea to be overly cautious if for no other reason than to avoid the kinds of problems that can result otherwise.

Entering out-of-town events like quasi-local tournaments, state and regional shoots — or even the nationals — results in another major type of travel for sporting clays shooters. If these trips are via the shooter's own vehicle, the only significant concern would be those times when the trip would include staying overnight in a motel or hotel. It is always a good idea to keep guns and ammo locked in the trunk of an auto, or secured in some similar type of obscure compartment in a truck or camper.

Taking guns into hotel or motel rooms may be necessary

for things like maintenance or cleaning. To a greater or lesser degree, this exposes the shooter to some risk. It is never a good idea to flash guns around, either in or out of cases. First, it invites the attention of those elements in society that might steal them. Second, it can be a form of inadvertent intimidation to other citizens who are not avid shooters. Both of these are negatives.

When guns do need to be taken to a room, keep the number of times to a minimum and keep the room locked at all times. It may not be a particularly good idea to take the cased gun back to the vehicle, lock it up, then go back to the room or elsewhere, leaving the vehicle parked in the same spot. By doing so, the shooter has presented a target of opportunity to would-be thieves.

On any occasion when travel with a gun involves transit on a commercial airline, a whole new set of requirements goes into effect. First, there are basic Federal Aviation Administration rules regarding the transportation of firearms and ammunition on commercial airliners.

The gun must be unloaded and in a hard case (as opposed to a soft, sleeve-type case). The case should be lockable. Ammunition must be carried in a separate container and both must be handled as "checked" baggage. They cannot be taken into the main passenger section of the airplane.

However, individual airlines have the authority to impose

Americase used by All-American Rick Kennernecht features partitions to keep the guns apart, undamaged in transit.

further requirements, and those requirements vary from airline to airline. In fact, experience has shown that the requirements can vary from one airline employee to another, and from one airport to another, even when the same airline is involved.

The FAA and the airlines all encourage anyone who is going to transport a firearm and ammunition to check with the airline involved prior to the trip — well before showing up at the airport. This can help avert procedural problems. Certainly, arrive at the airport somewhat earlier than normal, because without exception, firearms must be checked individually at the counter.

It is common practice for the ticket agent at the airline counter to ask that the shooter open the gun case so the firearm can be checked. The reason is that many airlines require their employees to verify that the firearm is not loaded. Whether the employee personally checks the gun or not, the shooter must fill out and sign a bright orange/red tag that establishes the gun is not loaded.

Some airlines require that this bright tag be attached to the outside of the case. Others allow it to be stowed inside. The former demand, of course, is an invitation to thieves.

Ammunition is not supposed to be carried loose in any kind of container. It should be boxed and must not be carried in the same container as the gun. Increasingly, airlines are requiring that the ammunition, too, be carried in a locked, hard case. This has become common enough that some firms like Americase market special ammo cases with locks.

There is no need for the check-in procedure to be stressful for the shooter, even though there are times when other passengers, or even airline employees, voice a personal dislike of firearms. The object of the procedure is to check the baggage, get on the plane and go to the destination as smoothly and efficiently as possible.

Making any kind of a scene when a firearm is involved is not a good idea. Security forces at airports may or may not overreact in such situations. Certainly, any problems at the counter will be larger problems for the shooter than for anyone else. There are other ways and other times to argue any concerns about rights and procedures.

Added insurance is available for checked baggage. Some traveling shooters buy it and it can be arranged at the ticket counter when the baggage is checked. However, frequent travelers generally do not purchase the added coverage, simply because if they did they would buy their own gun again about every year, just in insurance fees. Shooters who do not carry sufficient insurance, though, face the loss

Hard, lockable cases are best for travel, whether in a private vehicle or a commercial airliner. Shotguns usually break down so a lengthy case is unnecessary.

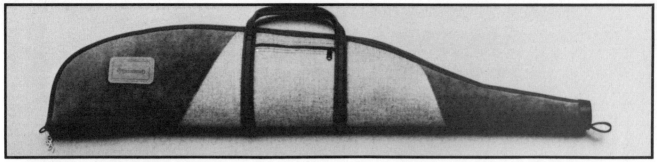

For trips to the local range, Browning produces several soft cases to protect a gun, including the Silver Suede.

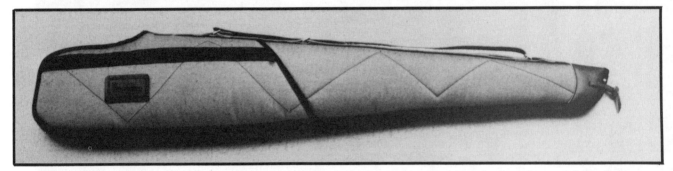

Another flexible case being marketed by Browning is the International Sporter, which features heavy reinforcing.

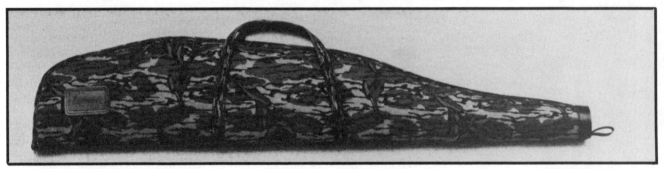

The Mossy Oak green leaf pattern featured on this case is more to meet demand than for practical utilization.

if the gun comes up missing in action. And guns do disappear. It is an individual choice.

For shooters taking their sporting clays guns out of the country to some kind of international shoot, there are other considerations. First, the shooter should take the gun to the U.S. Customs office at the airport where the international flight originates, or to any similar customs facility, and have a personal property inventory form completed with serial number or numbers.

This is necessary so that when the shooter comes back into the United States, the customs employees can see that the gun was taken on the trip and not acquired outside the country. Other foreign-made items also should be listed on the customs form. It makes everything so much slicker when returning. Without such documentation, the shooter could be faced with a number of problems.

For example, if when returning, the customs officials suspect the gun had been purchased abroad, the shooter might be required to pay an import tax on the gun. Should this sort of scenario develop, there are attendant headaches, as well.

Americase also makes an ammunition carrier that meets government and airline requirements and safety rulings.

Separate, lockable containers for guns and ammo are the best bet for the traveling sporting clays competitor. This Americase ammo carrier is dimensioned to carry standard shotshells without room for rattling around.

Not only would the tax matter be at issue, but there would need to be a Federal Firearms License involved. What would be happening in such a case would be a technical import. And then there would be the import license and any fees — and this list goes on.

In real world terms, this likely would mean that the gun would be impounded by the officials until the whole matter could be resolved. Such resolutions invariably take a lot of time — like months. And, such situations also increase any possibility that the gun will turn up missing in action. Simply put, it is not worth the potential hassle that can evolve when the proper documentation is missing.

Also before leaving on the trip, check with the embassy or consulate of whatever country or countries are involved in the trip. Each nation has its own set of rules and regulations involving firearms and ammunition. Some are extremely rigid and restrictive. Some require entire sets of documents that must be completed and approved before the trip. Some

even require photos as forms of identification on the various documents.

Generally speaking, when shooters have their guns and ammo encased properly and have all of the necessary documentation, traveling with firearms is more or less totally routine. But failing to follow all of the proper procedures only invites problems.

Beyond bureaucratic requirements and common sense, there is the added concern of protecting the gun from abuse in transit, whether it is in the family car or a commercial airliner. Travel cases need to be built well so they can handle incidental banging around. The interiors need to be padded.

Among hard cases, there are generally two types of interiors. One type involves foam padding which not only protects the exterior of the gun from banging around, but also holds it firmly when the case is closed. The other form of case involves internal sectioning which keeps gun parts

Lockable hard cases for guns and ammo are necessary for air travel. At left, the gun case sports a black fabric cover. This helps in keeping it from becoming scratched; it also helps to disguise the contents against theft.

Sporting clays All-American Rick Kennernecht carries his hard cases in his car if going only a short way for a practice shoot. He also uses it for all airline travel.

or entire guns themselves from banging around and scratching themselves. Both work fine. It is critical that, whatever design is used, the gun and/or gun parts are not able to flop around inside the case. This averts damage to the gun in transit.

Some shooters even wrap the guns or gun component parts in special soft "socks," then place them in the padded case, just as an added precaution.

And, there should be space in the case for gun-related gear like extra choke tubes, shooting glasses, cleaning materials, hearing protection devices and the like. Although that sort of gear could be carried elsewhere, experienced travelers prefer to keep everything together for many reasons. The most important reason is that they are less likely to forget and leave some piece or pieces of important gear behind at home if their case is not set up for everything.

Also, once at the shooting destination, it is easier to keep track of all the gear and not lose it if it is all stowed in the same case. Obviously, however, if everything is in one single case and the case is lost, all is lost. But so go the rigors of travel.

Whether traveling to the local range or around the world, there is one overwhelmingly important concept the shooter should accept totally: Never travel with a gun you cannot afford to lose.

With the proper precautions and preparations, though, the risk is minimized.

CHAPTER 15

COACHES & INSTRUCTORS

Just Where Do They Fit Into The Scheme Of This Sport?

Actor Erik Estrada of the television series, CHiPs, gets pointers from coach and two-time world champ, A.J. Smith.

A.J. "Smoker" Smith has been one of the better coaches for rising young shooting stars in England and here. His credentials speak for themselves.

ONE THING becomes apparent immediately whenever anyone shoots sporting clays for the first time: The game can be, and usually is, humbling. Hunters who rank high in field shooting find themselves walking away from sporting clays stations mumbling to themselves and wondering what had just happened. How could they have missed so many of those targets? The clays didn't look all that difficult when they watched someone else shoot at them — and miss.

Then there are the accomplished trap shooters who can powder targets by the hundred on trap fields, but who have done all they can do to break half of the clays on a sporting range. Skeet shooters, too, find themselves challenged beyond imagination.

Perfect scores are routine in skeet. In sporting clays, they are all but non-existent. And no one is a natural, "born" sporting clays champion. Courses are designed to preclude perfect scores. In sporting clays, missing a target not only is okay, it is predictable.

But there are different levels of shooters, and with practice and exposure, just about any shooter can improve his or her game — but only to a point. Depending upon the individual shooter, that point can come quite early. In fact, for shooters who want to improve their sporting game more

quickly — whether for enjoyment or competition — consideration should be given to instruction from a "pro."

Just as there are shooters, then there are shooters, there are instructors — and there are instructors. A.J. "Smoker" Smith of Great Britain is one of the world's leading sporting clays shooters. He was twice the world champion, and over the past two decades, has won just about every title worth having in the sport. He heartily recommends instruction for shooters, but warns a person needs to be careful when choosing an instructor, because relatively few are totally qualified for such a position.

"By having someone who has shot sporting clays instructing you, not only are you learning the technique of shooting, but you learn the technique of how to make a lot of successful shots at the birds easier," Smith explains. "Usually, the instructor who has shot a lot will teach not only how to shoot it, but *where* to shoot it. He will explain why you're shooting it there and why it makes it easier."

Smith allows that even shooters such as himself could take some instruction from time to time when it comes to some new or drastically different presentation.

"I'm sure people like myself, who've had a vast amount of experience, having shot birds all over the world at almost every conceivable angle, always can learn something," he

Smith explains shotgunning technique during one of the many sporting clays clinics he conducts in this country.

explains. "I sometimes come across a bird that I haven't shot, but nowadays that I have shot so much, it is pretty rare."

So where does that leave everyone else, especially those new or fairly new to the sport?

"I would say the good, average hunter who comes into sporting clays will immediately go into about the B Class," Smith says. "Now, to elevate yourself out of that, I think it comes down to fine-tuning on birds. Certain birds will be defeating a shooter. Obviously, you've got to be keen to want to shoot competition. If you're not keen to actually do well in competition, your scores will not go up. You will only stay at your own ability.

"Once you've got that, and you're missing particular birds, that's when you can draw on someone like myself — people who've got experience and can tell you why you are missing a particular bird, and how to overcome it," he continues. "It's not just: 'Oh, you're behind' or 'you're in front,' but for a reason. And if someone who knows a bit about shooting can tell you why you're missing, it's far better, and actually can show you how to hit it.

"There are not a great many shooting instructors who can actually put into practice what they're talking about," Smith observes. "A lot of them don't know, themselves, which is fact. There are extremely few shooting instructors who cannot shoot. Are there any good shooting instructors who cannot shoot? I would say definitely not."

Smith compares the situation in sporting clays to that faced by golfers the world over.

"Take a golf professional. Now, a golf professional is a person who can earn his living through playing the game. Every club professional is better than any of his club players. Now, you wouldn't go to a golf instructor and take a lesson from him if you said: 'Look, show me how to hit this ball down the fairway,' then he took a swing and missed it. You'd say: 'Well, I can do that. I want to see how to do it properly.'

"I feel quite strongly that to get over and above your average shooting, you've got to have someone who actually understands and can show you how to hit the more difficult, challenging targets," Smith notes. "If you want to get beyond the point of being an average shooter, you've got to listen to someone who actually understands and can show you how to hit top flight competition targets."

So what separates great shooters from the rest? Not a lot, really, according to Smith. Consistency is the key.

"If we set up a difficult pair and you hit that pair once, and I hit it five times in succession, I am not shooting any better than you shot," Smith explains. "All I'm doing is shooting more consistently. And to become more consistent, you've got to learn why you're hitting the target, and make yourself do it every time. Good shooting is consistency.

"Once anyone has hit one target of a really difficult nature, if he knew why he hit it, how he hit it and knew how to read the pieces — interpret the hits — he'd be as good as the best shooter," Smith insists. "It's just knowing what to do and becoming consistent. It comes with someone telling you, then actually practicing and doing it."

Smoker Smith — so named because when he hits targets, they often are reduced to a smoky dust — should know. In addition to holding every level of title in the sport, he travels the world, helping other shooters become their best — even though he admits he'd rather play than work anytime. He visits the United States at least annually, and offers both individual and group lessons at courses throughout the land. He's one of the best in the game.

MICHAEL LEE FINGER

At age 15, Mike Finger has already made a name for himself in sporting clays circles, most recently becoming the 1991 USSCA junior champion. Also in 1991, Finger became a member of the USSCA All-American team and was a member of Team USA which resulted in his com-

peting in the FITASC world championships in Andorra.

Finger insists that, without an instructor, he would not have gone as far in the game as he has — and that is a long way, considering that he began shooting competitively in 1989.

"I think a coach is important, because he helps you with fine detailing in your shooting," Finger explains. "Coaches help with your stances and all of the other basic parts of shooting, such as gun mount, swings, places to pickup (see) targets and pass-through techniques. Coaches definitely are an important asset if you want to become a good shooter and maintain a good average.

"When I started," Finger adds, "everyone told me I had good judgment, and that I had a natural instinct for it, but I could never be consistent. My coach — I started with Neal Etherton — got me to where I am today. He helped me in all kinds of different ways. For example, if I would break the back sides of targets, he taught me how to tell that I was hitting almost behind them, and that if I didn't get ahead of them a little more, chances were good I would shoot totally behind the next target. I then would swing a little faster, pull through a little bit faster so I could hit the targets right in the center."

Even though Finger's coach helped the young shooter

Youthful Mike Finger (right) gets some shooting tips from his coach, Neal Etherton. He recognizes need for coaching.

Mike Finger, the USSCA's top junior shooter in 1991, uses Beretta shotguns exclusively. (Right) Finger clowns by hitting a clay with the gun upside-down and above his head. This trick the shooter learned from John Cloherty.

reach the world level, it was not time for the teen shooter to stop learning.

"He still helps me, even today," Finger notes. "You never become too good for a coach, I think, because even though you might be good, you find the better you do, the more you tend to slack off and play around a little bit. It's like you are not as smooth as you were — you are not as focused. The coach can show you exactly what you are doing wrong, and can help you fix it. He can help you find those spots that have changed in your technique — you might have changed your stance a little, you might be jerking the gun or you might be taking your head off the stock. He can help you see those things when you don't notice them yourself."

Champion Mike Finger (center) discusses sporting clays with (left) Zachary Ewing, 14, and Zachary Morse, 11. Both of the latter are champions in their own right and will advance to the senior rankings.

John Cloherty is a top competitor, a trick shooter and a shooting instructor. He won the first side-by-side title for sporting clays competition in California, using this Bernardelli model. Most shooters favor over/under guns.

JOHN CLOHERTY

John Cloherty is an AA sporting clays shooter whenever he competes, but at other times, he splits his efforts between exhibition shooting and instructing. Cloherty is a good teacher in his own right, which means it is easier for him to be effective, regardless of how much experience or ability a student might have. He is quick to explain some of the things both the instructor and student should be addressing when it comes to sporting clays instruction.

"I think one of the most important things about being an instructor is an ability to deal with the wide variety of people you will meet in the different shooting disciplines," Cloherty explains. "In the lessons I've been giving, I've taught construction workers, bankers, art dealers, Hollywood movie personalities — and everything in between!

"One of the secrets to really getting through to these people is to approach the subject on their level and try to take something out of the context of their lives, compare it to something I'm trying to get them to do now and draw a parallel," Cloherty notes. "An example is, if I know a guy also spends a lot of time golfing, I'll use different moves and maneuvers — the way he looks at the ball, addresses the ball — and I'll just kind of form that image by using

words and draw him a mental picture of what I want him to do."

Does Cloherty have trouble determining whether he is getting through to his students?

"I can look at their faces and absolutely instantly tell when they have no clue," Cloherty insists. "It's so obvious by watching the looks on their faces. It takes a little work to be an instructor. You just can't stand behind the guy and tell him: 'You're behind.' You have to be observing not only what he's doing with the gun, but you also have to observe the expressions on his face, the way his eyes are moving, the way his body is moving. Just by watching the individual's actions and reactions to a shot, you can tell whether he is on the level or not. You can tell if he is understanding where you are going.

"I have a policy," Cloherty said in discussing how he begins sessions with shooters. "I always start with each shooter at ground zero, even if he is advanced or has been shooting for forty years. I start with checking their eyes and the way they mount the gun, plus their eye position on the gun, checking to see if they're using both eyes or are trying to close an eye.

"Even if somebody has been shooting for thirty years, it

doesn't mean he or she has been doing it right. So I start from square one and start working up. Sometimes that process goes quickly with people who are familiar with shooting and do everything right. But it's an embarrassing situation for an instructor to be half-way through a lesson, after somebody's paying you good money to teach him, then realize this individual has cross-dominant eyes, and you didn't check it."

For beginners, Cloherty feels it doesn't have to take a long time to get into the swing of things with shotgunning. The basics can be taught fairly quickly to students who want to learn.

"Generally, when people have no fear of what they are doing, and are willing to listen to what you say, it's really a pretty quick process," he contends. "What I find in teaching, even the people who have been shooting for thirty years know what they are supposed to do, but have one key missing — it is technique. They know they have to lead the target, they know they have to shoot in front of it and they know they have to get the gun up there. Giving them a step-by-step, mechanical method of making the gun do what they want it to do is what they lack. So, the gun may be coming at the target from any odd angle. They may be mounting the gun in a highly erratic fashion. What I teach them, almost to a man, is slow down.

"You have more time to get to that target by taking your time in mounting the gun and moving to the target, because you don't make physical mistakes on the way up on your approach to the target," Cloherty confides. "For every mistake you make — every time you go past the bird — it takes you three times that length of time to correct the mistake. So, by moving slowly and deliberately, and being

When instructing students, John Cloherty uses a 12-gauge Beretta over/under, also competes with the same gun.

John Cloherty, second from left, is a most enthusiastic instructor. Here he gives tips to novices in the sport.

poised in your maneuvers to approach the target, you actually get there in a much shorter period of time than you otherwise would."

Cloherty said there are some typical situations he has seen when instructing shooters who have been shooting for a long time, but who never have developed proper technique.

"Most of them end up by just throwing the gun to the shoulder, putting the gun out in front of the target and squeezing the trigger. And maybe, maybe not, they're going to hit the target," Cloherty stresses. "By building them a technique, which really only takes maybe four hours of lessons, they develop that technique so that, when they do miss a target, they have an idea why they missed it. And, when they hit it, they know it — they feel it. 'Oh, that was pretty. I felt that one,' is one of the things I hear all the time. 'Oh, that felt good,' they'll say. That's what happens when they hit the targets really, really well, because they

execute a proper technique to arrive at the position to pull the trigger and break a target."

Cloherty explains that even accomplished shooters need some tips from someone else — like a coach — from time to time.

"If I could step back behind myself, I probably would be correcting myself left and right," Cloherty chuckles. "Unfortunately, I can't do that. I think anybody and everybody has times when they will start making little physical changes in their approach, in their stance, in the way they hold or move the gun. They would change themselves if they were able to see it, but when you're behind the barrel, you can't. You really need somebody to stand behind you and just clue you in on those little things. There are only so many things you can do wrong with a shotgun.

"Sometimes you have to be behind the shooter in order to see the things that are going wrong," Cloherty continues. "Otherwise, you run through the process of elimination. You try a bunch of things. You say, okay, I can see I'm doing this, I can see I'm doing that. Everything looks good here, but I can't figure out what my problem is. Then you ask somebody behind you, and he'll tell you right off the bat, because it is quite obvious to the guy standing behind you what you are doing right, as well as what you are doing wrong."

Hence, there are places and times when just about every shooter needs the help of an instructor or a coach, if he or she is to shoot sporting clays better. For beginners, a coach can get them "kick started" and on the right path. For intermediate shooters, an instructor can show proper technique, and get them shooting better. Even for advanced shooters, a coach can help the shooter get back on track when that shooter begins forming bad habits, but is unable to figure out what is happening while he or she is shooting.

Cloherty's big smile and personality make him an ideal type to serve as a coach for beginners in the sport.

CHAPTER 16

CLAYS & STEEL

INCREASINGLY, DISCUSSIONS around sporting clays facilities are focusing on questions about whether — or when — non-toxic steel shot might be required for clay busting, as it now is for waterfowling in many areas.

Even though there is no real reason why lead shot should ever be phased out, shooters are aware of social and political situations which could force such a change. What would it be like to use steel on clays?

The very mention of steel shot is guaranteed to elicit a response among shooters. Good or bad, there will be a response. Suggest that steel might be used to shoot sporting clays, and all kinds of things are likely to happen.

Suffice it to say that sporting clays *can* be shot with steel pellets, but it is bound to be some time before anything which approaches an effective sporting clays load is generally available.

Since its inception, steel shot has received widely mixed reviews among most hunters and shooters. It is lighter, harder and ballistically inferior to lead. But it also is considered non-toxic and as such, has been required to replace lead shot for waterfowling in all but two of the fifty United States — as well as in a number of other countries around the world.

Increasingly, there are areas of the country where, on a zone basis, non-toxic shot is required for any shooting — and that includes forms of target shotgunning. Some feel that eventually, steel shot, or at least non-toxic shot, will be the norm for target shotgunning, including sporting clays. Currently, steel is the only generally available non-toxic alternative.

Although there is increasing experience in the creation of steel waterfowl hunting loads, any such application in the target arena remains in its infancy.

The earliest form of factory-loaded steel shot for target work has just come onto the scene in Great Britain. It is a light target load by the Gamebore Cartridge Company. In 12-gauge, this load features seven-eighths-ounce of No. 7 (.100-inch diameter) shot. Although preliminary testing in England indicated that such a load was okay for some purposes, it was recognized to leave quite a bit wanting for any overall application.

So, too, is the experience in the United States, where the only available factory loaded steel ammunition is designed for hunting purposes. The smallest shot here is No. 6. For

For loading steel shot, presses must be retrofitted. MEC has a kit to make transition easy and effective.

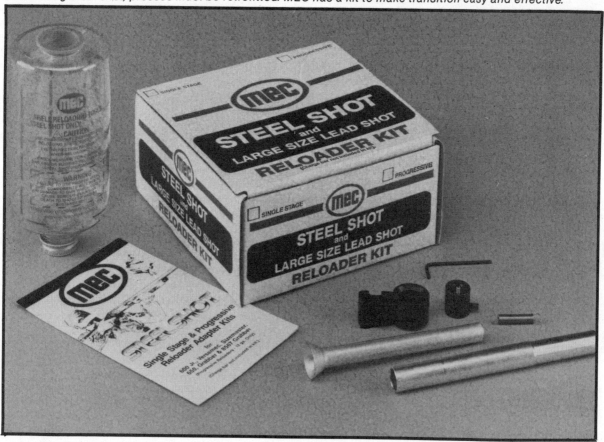

Steel shot components are becoming readily available. MEC markets both shot and wads for loading up steel.

this writing, Remington's 1⅛-ounce loading of steel No. 6 shot, Winchester's one-ounce loading of No. 6 steel and Federal's 1⅛-ounce loading of No. 6 steel were used.

Guns included a Remington Model 870 pump with interchangeable Rem Chokes, Perazzi's MX3 Special Sporting Clays over/under with that company's updated interchangeable chokes which will handle steel shot and a Winchester Super X Model 1 semi-auto with .004-inch choke restriction.

Also shot in an effort to establish overall performance characteristics were a Marlin Model 120 pump with modified choke, Browning's Auto-5 with a true cylinder bore and a Winchester Model 12 with a Hastings barrel and interchangeable choke tubes. The only side-by-side double gun used was a Bernardelli Model 112 with interchangeable choke tubes.

Since pattern performance is a four-dimensional phenomenon, field use included patterning boards as well as target shooting at ranges of fifteen to fifty yards — the normal span of distances at which sporting clays targets are shot.

The Rem Choke restrictions from the .727-inch bore diameter were minus .006 (marked skeet), plus .002 (improved skeet), plus .007 (improved cylinder), plus .018 (modified) and plus .038-inch (full).

Choke restrictions for the Perazzi were true cylinder, plus .008, .016 and .024-inch, while the restrictions for the Super X were plus .002 and .004-inch.

Quicky, certain things became apparent which precluded the need to do any degree of testing with restrictions of each thousandth of an inch. For example, until the restriction was .007 to .008-inch, the pattern never really formed with steel shot. In other words, the pellets were merely spewed out of the end of the barrel in what appeared to be totally random sprays.

Although the first indications of the phenomenon were apparent at distances as close as fifteen yards, they really were pronounced when shot at thirty-five and forty yards. These random non-patterns featured all of the bad characteristics one would expect. There were tight concentrations of shot at some points in the "pattern," with varying degrees of open holes and swaths at random spots elsewhere on the paper.

When used on actual clay targets, restrictions of less than .007/.008-inch produced predictable breaks only on extremely close (fifteen yards) going away targets. Crossers shot with these open bores were broken inconsistently. Those which were broken came apart in two or several large chunks. Many were broken into two pieces, hinting that perhaps only one pellet connected.

At the .007/.008-inch restriction level, rather erratic patterns began to form. On paper, distances beyond fifteen yards indicated that the continued large holes in the pattern would grow even bigger. When shot on clay targets with those restrictions, performance was consistent with expectations.

Breaks were predictable, but still rather chunky. At distances of twenty to twenty-five yards, breaks were still predictable, but the prevalence of large target chunks indicated that one — or very few — pellets actually connected with any degree of regularity. Occasionally, however, a target would be broken decisively, also confirming the glomping together of pellets as had been shown on the patterning board.

When the restriction of .016/.018-inch was used, everything improved. On the patterning board at distances from fifteen to forty yards, the pellet distribution was more uniform and there definitely was a predictable pattern. However, there remained noticeable holes in the pattern, as well as several small concentration areas of pellets.

When used on targets at ranges of fifteen to fifty yards, this level of restriction proved best overall, even though it was somewhat tighter at the close targets than some shooters might prefer.

However, for the longer targets — especially those from thirty-five to fifty yards — this level of constriction proved to be the minimal acceptable amount. At all of the various distances, breaks were decisive and complete. In fact, it wasn't until this degree of restriction was used that any of the close targets were "smoked."

Yet, even the fifty-yard crossing targets were well broken, indicating that the smaller holes in the pattern shown in the patterning board were telling the proper story.

When the restriction was increased to .024, performance remained about the same. Good, solid breaks at all distances from fifteen to fifty yards. There was no noticeable difference in the ability to make repeated hits with the tighter .024-inch choking.

Best patterns of all were achieved with the .038 restriction. However, those patterns were also incredibly small in diameter. At distances of fifteen to fifty yards, all targets hit were broken decisively. But, the shooter needed to be absolutely on the mark in order to hit the targets, due to the almost rifle-like size of the pattern. For example, at thirty-five yards the entire pattern was thirty-six inches in diameter.

When tried at sixteen-yard American trap, the .038 restriction and steel shot totally obliterated targets in ways that didn't leave even an "ink ball" in the air. The targets merely ceased to exist.

When used to shoot sporting clays, in addition to the patterning performance, there were four extremely noticeable characteristics of both the one-ounce and 1⅛-ounce steel loads. Those factors were muzzle jump, speed of the shot, recoil and heat.

Compared gun-for-gun, shooter-for-shooter on the same target presentations, muzzle jump from the steel loads was significantly greater than with Winchester's AA lead target loads, Remington's Premier lead target loads and Federal's Champion lead target loads — all 1⅛-ounce No. 7½ shot offerings.

Certainly, the speed of the steel shot compared to the speed of the lead shot contributed significantly, if not totally, to the increased muzzle jump experienced. Lower velocity steel loads, like those being tried in England, would likely take care of that problem. The steel loads used ranged between 1300 and 1400 feet per second. The lead target loads were 1200 fps.

The speed of the steel shot was not a significant factor while shooting the closer sporting clays targets. Gun speed, swing and all of the other movements were the same to hit targets.

However, when the distances went from thirty-five to fifty yards, there was a significant difference in the amount of "lead" needed in order to hit the targets. At those distances, the amount of lead needed was almost exactly half — which means it dropped from a perceived four feet to two feet of sustained lead!

Recoil, like muzzle jump, could be attributed easily to the velocity of the steel shot loads when compared to lead. And that recoil was not only perceived as heavier, but also as significantly and unpleasantly sharper.

Although these factors were predicted, the heat problem experienced when shooting sporting clays with steel shot came as a total surprise. It is logical, but was a surprise just the same.

Barrels quickly became too hot to touch and they did not cool off nearly so quickly as they did while using lead on the same day on the same range. As few as five shots would heat the barrels to the point they could not be touched without burning a finger. This was when the ambient temperature was 70 degrees F.

Although the maximum powder charge used in the steel loads would logically contribute to somewhat hotter barrels,

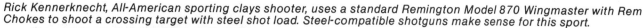

Rick Kennerknecht, All-American sporting clays shooter, uses a standard Remington Model 870 Wingmaster with Rem Chokes to shoot a crossing target with steel shot load. Steel-compatible shotguns make sense for this sport.

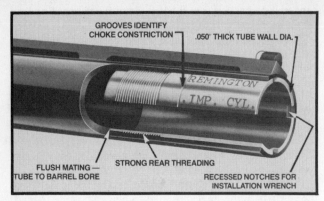

GROOVES IDENTIFY
CHOKE CONSTRICTION — — .050" THICK TUBE WALL DIA.

REMINGTON
IMP. CYL.

FLUSH MATING — — STRONG REAR THREADING
TUBE TO BARREL BORE — RECESSED NOTCHES FOR
INSTALLATION WRENCH

Remington's Rem Choke system is designed to handle lead and steel shot. This shows how the system works.

that degree of fast heat buildup was not experienced when the hottest, heaviest lead shot hunting loads were used. Obviously, there is a friction factor associated with the use of steel shot which has not been addressed before.

Certainly, there would be no apparent need to get into that subject when discussing waterfowling, because waterfowlers would not find themselves shooting more than three quick, successive shots. However, for target shooting, strings of five to ten rapid shots are routine. Certainly, when ten-shot strings were fired with the steel, the barrels were so hot that the guns had to be put into the rack to allow them to cool off.

During these cooling-off periods, screw-in chokes were

changed; this procedure required the use of gloves, because the tubes were far too hot to handle. This type of nearly instant heat buildup would have to be addressed and solved before steel loads could be considered seriously for any kind of shotgun target work.

From a tactical performance standpoint, shooting steel shot for sporting clays would typically see the shooter opting for a fully open bore only on the extremely close target presentations.

Improved cylinder (.008-inch level restriction) would be the logical choice for targets out to twenty or twenty-five yards maximum. From there on, restrictions of .016 to .024 (modified) would be most logical. There appears to be no reason for the use of greater restrictions for shooting sporting clays with steel.

Some of the greatest criticism steel shot has received among hunters is that it doesn't dispatch the birds as well as lead — that more birds are hit, wounded and escape the bag, only to die uncollected elsewhere.

Those field experiences are obviously the result of a combination of factors, including the ballistic inferiority of steel when compared to lead.

Such a lethality factor does not exist in clay target shooting, since the inanimate target merely needs to be hit to be broken. But, there were some characteristics encountered when shooting sporting clays with steel shot which should be considered by anyone hunting with steel shot.

In fact, these characteristics were so noticeable that waterfowlers who do find themselves required to use steel shot should seriously consider shooting sporting clays with their hunting guns and loads as a form of both educational

Rick Kennerknecht uses a field bench to pattern the performance of various choke tubes on Model 870 Remington pump-action 12 gauge. Steel loads being used are from Federal, Remington, Winchester.

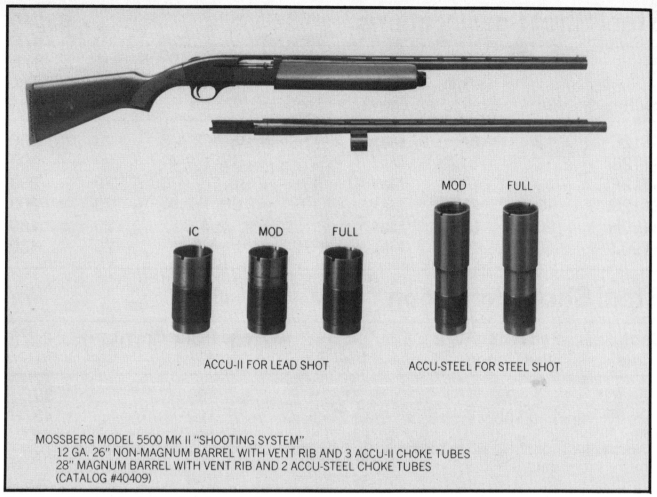

MOD   FULL

IC   MOD   FULL

ACCU-II FOR LEAD SHOT   ACCU-STEEL FOR STEEL SHOT

MOSSBERG MODEL 5500 MK II "SHOOTING SYSTEM"
12 GA. 26" NON-MAGNUM BARREL WITH VENT RIB AND 3 ACCU-II CHOKE TUBES
28" MAGNUM BARREL WITH VENT RIB AND 2 ACCU-STEEL CHOKE TUBES
(CATALOG #40409)

Some interchangeable choke tubes do not indicate whether they were designed to handle steel shot. Mossberg has made the system easier to judge. Lead tubes screw in flush with muzzle; the longer tubes are for steel shot.

and humane practice.

Although the bulk of the loads used for this effort were the No. 6 steel shot variations, when the patterning inconsistencies became apparent, some other hunting loads also were tried. These were No. 3 and No. 2 steel. At distances of thirty-five yards and more — when restrictions of less than .007/.008-inch were used — there were gaping holes in the patterns through which geese could fly. At distances as close as fifteen yards, there were holes through which teal could go untouched.

Within the area of inconsistency, there were really only two noticeable consistencies. First, none of the steel shot loads patterned well when compared to target quality lead loads through the same barrels at the same distances. Second, it didn't matter which manufacturer's loads were used, they all patterned equally erratically. Yet, each of the company's lead shot loads patterned with predictable uniformity at the various distances and through the same range of barrels and chokings.

When the sporting clays experiences are interpreted in hunting terms — and especially when the distances go beyond twenty-five yards — there is no question that the most acceptable degree of choke restriction is the range from .016 to .024 (modified).

Also of critical importance is the difference in perceived lead needed at the thirty-five to forty-yard distance. Targets were missed easily by shooting in front of them with the steel and a significant number of those which were hit were hit on the front side when a more or less standard lead was used.

When that lead was reduced, hits were more predictable and more even. As of note, when the long crossing shots were made with steel, the lighting conditions were such that observers working with the shooters could visually see the shot going to the target.

This significantly aided efforts to understand not only what was happening, but to quickly compensate so the performance information could be developed more comprehensively.

During the test sessions, a variety of shooters were enlisted, ranging from casual shooters who had never fired a steel shot round to world class competitors.

The casual shooters noticed little difference when shooting most sporting clays target presentations with steel, compared to lead shot. However, even the most casual of them did notice quickly the need to cut back on lead when shooting the long crossing targets. All shooters noted the increased recoil, muzzle jump and heat.

Steel Shot Specifications

Model	Ga.	Length (in.)	Dram Equiv.	Ounces Shot	Standard Shot Sizes	Rnds. Per Box	Rnds. Per Case
ST12E	12	3	Max	1⅜	BB, 1, 2, 4, 6	20	200
ST123F	12	3	Max	1¼	BB, 1, 2, 4	20	200
ST12F	12	2¾	Max	1¼	BB, 1, 2, 4, 6	20	200
ST12G	12	2¾	Max	1⅛	BB, 1, 2, 4	20	200
ST20H	20	3	Max	1	2, 4, 6	20	480
ST20J	20	2¾	Max	¾	4, 6	20	480

Steel Shot Information

Shot Sizes	Pellet Count Per Ounce	Average Pellet Count		
		1⅛	1¼	1⅜
BB	72	81	90	99
#1	103	116	129	142
#2	125	140	156	172
#4	192	216	240	264
#6	312	351	390	429

Steel Shot Ballistics

ACTIV Loads	Average Pressure	Average Velocity	SAAMI Spec. Max. Dram
12 gauge – 1⅜ oz.	11.000	1280	1210
12 gauge – 1¼ oz.	10.800	1390	1375
12 gauge – 1⅛ oz.	11.000	1420	1365

The ballistic information listed above is drawn from information furnished by ACTIV Industries.
The firm makes not only finished ammunition but has a line of reloading equipment to handle steel shot, as well.

The top-level competitors were able to provide more detailed input when it came to matters like amount of lead or degree of target break. However, all of them were quick to note that, for the most part, the comparisons were somewhat skewed in that steel waterfowl hunting loads were being compared to target lead loads.

Although reports from England indicate that some of the early steel target loads there offer "acceptable" patterning characteristics, those same reports insist that much more study is needed before anything which might approach a definitive statement is in order.

Hence, there remains a mantel of mystery surrounding any supposed use of steel shot for sporting clays use. Much of that situation could change should there be further development of target loadings for steel shot. Yet, spokesmen for the major ammunition manufacturers have stated that there were no major development programs underway to that end.

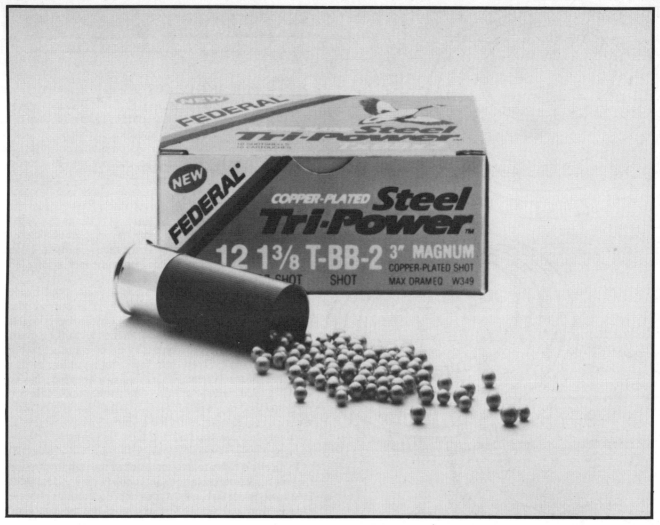

To date, all steel shot loads have been designed for use on waterfowl, not sporting clays. Ammo manufacturers load shot sizes larger than optimal for clays. Powder charges also tend to be a bit overdone for target work.

So at this point in the development of steel shot, it is impossible to say authoritatively whether steel is valid for serious clay target shooting, due in large part to the absence of anything approaching a serious clay target loading. It has taken decades for the industry to develop lead shot loadings to the high levels of performance now available. The development of steel shot hunting loads has come a long way in a relatively short period of time.

Regardless of what requirements might be put upon the use of lead or steel for target shooting, the availability of a truly viable factory load with steel shot is not likely to happen in the immediate future.

Although some of the patterning, recoil and muzzle jump problems associated with the factory hunting loads could be addressed by selective handloading for those who want to use steel shot for clay target shooting, steel cannot be considered a serious option until factory loadings are readily available. This is specifically true for widespread sporting clays applications, especially if the steel is to be used for high-level competitions.

There is another consideration which needs to be included in any discussion about using steel shot for clay target shooting. It is the way in which steel shot bounces and ricochets.

Anyone who has spent much time around a skeet range, for example, knows well that pellets can bounce and ricochet off clay targets. Although there is no reason to suspect it would happen any more frequently with steel than with lead, the steel shot does not absorb as much energy on the initial hit and it tends to bounce at a higher speed. Safety is at issue here.

Certainly, course design can preclude significant problems for sporting clays in this concern, but it is a factor which would have to be taken into account should steel be used widely for clay target shooting.

Perhaps steel shot will be used widely for sporting clays someday, but it's not likely during the remainder of this century.

PORTING CLAYS is the most complex of clay target shotgun games, and it is diversity in targets and their presentation to the shooter that makes this form of shooting so much fun. There is literally an infinite number of combinations of targets and flight angles which can be encountered in sporting clays.

The differences between sporting clays and the more traditional American clay target disciplines — like trap and skeet — begin with something as basic as the targets themselves. For example, in both trap and skeet, shooters are challenged to hit only one size target — a round, inverted saucer which is 4¼ inches (110mm) in diameter, 1¼ inches high at the peak of the dome.

When these "standard" targets are launched from a thrower or "trap" as the launching mechanism is called, they fly through the air, giving a side profile that is slightly more than an inch high and four inches wide. The reason clay target launchers are typically called traps is that clay target shooting evolved from the shooting of live birds in the last century. When live birds were or are used, they are held in a small cage — or trap — until the shooter calls for a bird, and then they are released from the trap. Hence, when a clay target shooter calls for a "bird," as the targets are routinely termed, the target is launched from a "trap." launched from a "trap."

In an effort to try to explain some of the infinite possibilities of target presentations in sporting clays, it might be best to consider first what types of presentations shooters face in trap and skeet. For example, the most straightforward situation is encountered in trap shooting where all the targets are launched from a single trap which is centrally located in front of five different shooting positions.

When shooting trap, the shotgunner fires five rounds from each of the five positions, and the targets are all launched at a slightly rising angle away from the shooter. The trap oscillates somewhat, and throws the targets within a determined lateral arc with respect to the shooter. However, all targets are rising and going away when the shooter sees them and takes them.

Skeet shooting is only somewhat more complex in its target presentations. For skeet, there are two traps; one is located in a "high" house on the left side of the field, and the other in a "low" house on the right side of the field. High and low here mean exactly what they suggest. The trap in the high house is located over the shooter's head when the shooter is at the first of eight positions on the field, and the trap in the low house is located about belt high when the shooter is at the seventh of the eight positions on the field.

The traps for skeet are rigidly set, and the targets always fly in exactly the same path — crossing at mid-field — to the front of all eight shooting positions. Again, the shooter sees targets which are essentially side-on when they are shot. There is one other slight difference in the relative positions of targets to shooters in skeet when compared to trap. In trap, the targets are launched within an arc, while

CHAPTER 17

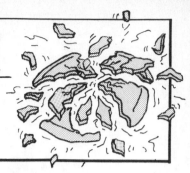

OF TARGETS & TRAPS

Understanding The Tools Involved In The Game Can Help Your Scores

Automatic traps like this model use a carousel-type magazine from which clays are fed to the throwing arm.

As one clay is launched to right, the thrower arm rotates under the target magazine and another clay is fed onto the arm, making the machine ready to throw still another target quickly and automatically, to keep the game moving.

in skeet, the shooting positions are located at points around an arc in relation to the targets when they are in flight.

Certainly, all of the kinds of target presentations encountered in trap and skeet are seen in sporting clays, but there are many, many more variables. And yes, standard targets of the type encountered in trap and skeet also are seen in sporting clays. However, they are seen in many varied ways.

For example, in sporting clays, these same targets also may be presented as incomers which means the shooter likely will see much more than just a modified side view. In fact, at times they are shot directly overhead, which means the shooter sees the entire bottom or belly of the target. In addition to being presented at any angle relative to the shooter, the targets might be presented at any distance from the shooter.

Again, this is different from normal trap and skeet. For example, in trap, the recreational distance from the shooting positions to the trap is sixteen yards. To challenge the better shooters, that distance is increased as a form of handicap, and typically goes back to twenty-seven yards. In sporting clays, similar presentations might range from literally under the shooter's feet to thirty yards — or slightly more.

In skeet, the shooter is always a known distance from the targets at a given station, since the shooting stations are pre-determined by the course layout; the target flight paths are pre-determined by the setting of the machines or traps.

In sporting clays, these same target presentations might be seen, but from any distance within forty yards of the shooting station. Even on a single course, the target presentations in sporting clays can be, and usually are, changed from day to day by the operator.

Shooting both singles and doubles or pairs is common to trap, skeet and sporting clays. However, sporting clays again varies the game significantly. For example, in trap and skeet, doubles are thrown simultaneously. In sporting clays, they may be thrown simultaneously, or they may be thrown in two other ways: as following pairs, or as report pairs. For a following pair of targets, a single clay is thrown when the shooter calls for a bird, then a second target is launched as quickly as it can be from the same trap. When shooting a report pair of targets, the shooter calls for the first bird, and the second target is not launched until the report of the shot at the first target is heard.

One's imagination could concoct literally thousands of combinations, but to this point, all of the targets under consideration have been of the same size and shape. It gets more complex, but before going further, it would be helpful to note that the flight characteristics of standard targets are quite simple and straight-forward. Since they are domed "flying saucers," they tend to fly in a straight line from the trap, and if rising when launched, will continue to go upward and outward until they slow enough to begin a downward path as gravity takes over. About the only time standard targets do any kind of dancing in the air is when Mother Nature lends a hand via strong winds, which can make the target go up or down erratically.

MIDI TARGETS

A second type of target seen in sporting clays is commonly called a "midi," because it is an in-between size clay. For example, the standard target, in metric terms, is 110mm in diameter. The midi is 90mm in diameter, but is configured the same as a standard target. This means it is merely a scaled-down version of the standard target, and its flight characteristics are the same as the full size targets. However, even with the same flight characteristics, the midi can be one of the more difficult targets for sporting clays shooters to master, because of the ways in which it usually is presented.

Determining the distance to a target is one of the inherent challenges for sporting clays shooters. This is difficult when only the standard target size is used. However, on a single course, it is common for both standard and midi targets to be used. This means shooters can easily think that a midi is a standard target, but is farther away. That can make a difference on the perceived lead needed to hit the target, and cause a miss if the shooter calculates wrongly.

To help offset some of the costs at sporting clays ranges, automatic traps like this old Winchester model can be employed at some of the stations, but it does take overseeing.

Everyone is familiar with the standard clay target used in trap and skeet. It plays a part in sporting clays, with other types.

But that's not the most difficult challenge normally encountered with midis.

Midis are rarely thrown alone, or even as pairs. Rather, it is common for a midi to be one of a pair of targets, the other target being a different size or shape. For example, it is quite common for a midi and a standard target to be thrown as a pair. In such instances, the shooter not only needs to judge the distances to the targets, but needs to judge their speeds as well. After all, the midi is not only smaller than the standard target, but it also is lighter in weight. This means it usually leaves the trap faster. What this can mean, for example, is that when the shooter first sees the targets, if they are thrown from different traps, or even the same trap, one of the targets will be in front of the other for a while, then the rear target will overtake the lead bird at a point as they both fly on non-converging paths.

So, the challenge of the midi for the shooter is to be able to identify it for what it is – and adjust shooting technique accordingly.

MINI TARGETS

The "mini" clay in sporting clays is the smallest target normally encountered, and is 60mm in diameter. The mini has the same general configuration as the standard and midi targets. It is simply a scaled-down version of the stan-dard. For shooters, the mini usually is not misidentified as is the midi. There is no question when one of these tiny "aspirin" targets is thrown.

However, there are some characteristics of minis which present their own kind of special challenge. Although some standard targets are all black, most thrown in sporting clays have colored domes — usually white, orange or green. The midis almost always have orange domes. Minis, however, are almost always totally black. That means that, in addition to being so small, they can and do blend into the background quickly and become virtually invisible in many instances, once they have been backgrounded by such terrain features as trees or bushes.

This means the shooter has a short visual "window" of time in which to shoot the tiny minis. Because they are so small and light, they leave the trap exceedingly fast. But by the time they have gone about forty yards, they have begun to slow significantly. This would make them easier targets, except that on most courses, the shooter can see them for only the first half of their flight. This requires spotting them instantly, and taking them quickly.

However, like the midi, the mini is rarely thrown alone. It is almost always one of a pair of targets. The other target might be another mini; it might be a midi; it might be a standard. At a single station, one pair might be a combination of two of the three different types of targets, and the next pair might be an entirely different combination. Again, the possibilities are endless.

The mini target is a real challenge, as it is small and appears to be much more distant than it really is from shooter.

The battue is tough to hit, because it is thin in profile and doesn't allow a shooter much image at which to shoot.

BATTUE TARGETS

The battue is an entirely different kind of target than the standard, midi or mini. These three all are configured similarly, relative size being the major difference. That means they all fly similarly through the air when launched. The battue is different.

A battue is 110mm (standard size) in diameter, but is only three-eighths-inch high, that thickness achieved by a slight "dome" in the center. It is an unnatural kind of target to shoot, and does not imitate any kind of game a shooter might encounter while hunting. It is among the more technically challenging targets to hit, as its design causes it to change attitude while in flight.

Battues generally are launched in pairs, going either from right to left or left to right with respect to the shooting stand. When launched, they are edge-on or flat, which means they present almost no vertical profile to the shooter. Some shooters refer to them as flying razor blades.

At about mid-flight, things change. The target begins to turn on its lateral axis, presenting more and more of its top or round profile to the shooter. This phenomenon is called "development." As the target develops, and the shooter sees more and more of it, he or she prepares to take it.

But the shot is not simple, because at this point in the target's flight, the angles become extremely complex. For example, at the point where the target develops, it also is falling and picking up speed as it falls. This means the shooter sees a target which is falling as it is going from right to left — or left to right. Depending upon how the station is set up, the targets also might be slightly coming toward or slightly going away from the shooter. This presentation is totally complex.

Sporting clays is more labor-intensive than some of the other clay target games because of the use of hand-set traps. Note that two trap heads are used in this set-up.

It is this required discipline — wait until the target develops — that frustrates many shooters when they first encounter the battue. Add to that the fact that they almost always are thrown as pairs, and the amount of time the shooter has to take the second target of a pair before it hits the ground or falls out of sight is typically brief.

RABBIT TARGETS

Since sporting clays evolved from upland game shooting, it is common for a course to include one station at which a "rabbit" target is thrown. Such stations typically are called something like "fur and feather." Again, rabbit targets rarely are thrown as singles. They are usually one of a pair of targets, and it is rare to see a pair of rabbits thrown.

Rather, the pair usually consists of a rabbit and a flier or aerial target. The aerial target is usually either a crosser or a rising, going-away presentation. The reason is simple. This presentation was intended initially to imitate a running rabbit which causes an upland bird like a pheasant or quail to flush from cover.

Rabbit targets, like standard targets, are 110mm in diameter. However, they have much thicker walls, and instead of a dome, feature a heavy, thick edge and flat center. This is because the rabbit target is launched so that it bounds along the ground like a jumping rabbit. Its thick edge helps keep the target from breaking as it bounces on the ground.

The rabbit presentation usually is quite close to the shooter — sometimes only a few yards from the muzzle of the gun. Because the bounce of the target changes whenever it hits any irregularity on the surface of the ground — a small pebble or a rut — it is seen not only as a crosser or quartering away target, but also one which might be rolling right along the ground, or bouncing up as high as several feet at some places.

When thrown as part of a pair, the rabbit target is usually the first. The second "feather" or aerial target in the presentation may be launched as a simultaneous pair, or may be thrown on report — when the shooter shoots at the rabbit. Generally, the aerial target thrown in conjunction with the rabbit is a standard size.

ROCKET TARGET

Another target thrown in sporting clays is called a "rocket." This target is more common in England and elsewhere in the world, but is encountered from time to time in the United States. A rocket is 110mm in diameter, but differs from a standard target in that it has a grossly reinforced edge. This means the rocket is relatively difficult to break when hit edge-on.

But the challenging aspect of rocket targets is that their configuration causes them to leave the trap extremely fast, then slow down quickly once in flight. This change in velocity causes problems for many shooters. The flight pattern is rather straight-forward, so the only real challenge is

The rabbit target is specially made of tough materials so that it will bounce along the ground and not break. Because of its purposely tough construction, it takes a direct hit in most instances to break it and thus score.

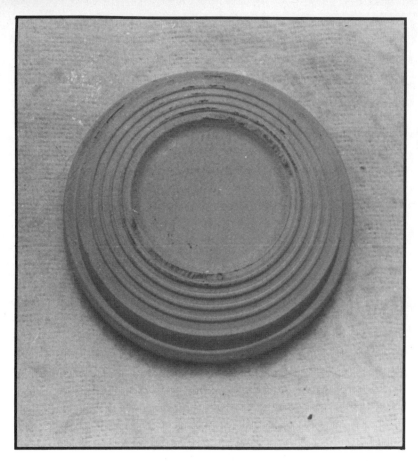

The midi target is smaller than standard size used in trap and skeet and has its own set of demands when it's fired upon.

Impromptu, transportable set-ups can be employed to add variety to the course or to throw special challenges.

To help obscure the trap from sight of the shooter and to protect the trapper, walls often are constructed on the course. In this instance, Chuck Stapel is the trapper.

to be able to "read" the target properly — to understand what it is doing.

It usually is better to allow the rocket to develop slightly more than a standard target. That way, it is going slower and giving the shooter a more consistent presentation. However, depending upon how the course is laid out, this waiting may be impossible, because by the time the target slows significantly, it may be out of sight.

OTHER TARGETS

Although the targets listed comprise most of those ever encountered in sporting clays, some slight variations are beginning to pop up in shoots around the world.

These variations are not radical departures from any of the more standard or specialty targets seen in sporting clays, but they do represent configurations designed for some specific application.

For example, LaPorte now makes a combination rising teal/rabbit target that is quite flat and heavily reinforced. The strength of the target makes it hold up well when bounced along the ground as a rabbit, and also makes it tougher to break when presented as a rising teal.

Typically, a rising teal presentation is a simultaneous pair of targets thrown from a trap in front of the shooter. The challenge when those teal targets happen to be the new La Porte design is that they are quite difficult to break when the distance to the target is around forty yards.

This can be one of those situations in which the difference in striking power between No. 8 and No. 7½ shot can make the difference between a break or a "miss." No. 8

shot on that target at that distance can result in the shot merely bouncing off the target and not breaking it.

TRAPS

The actual launchers — or traps — used in sporting clays often vary tremendously from station to station or from course to course. In the United States, more and more automatic traps are being used on many courses, primarily because of financial considerations. Sporting clays is much more labor-intensive than are other clay target disciplines like trap and skeet.

When automatic traps are used, they may be designs configured specifically for sporting clays, or they may be automatic models which have been used on a trap or skeet range. On some courses, most, if not all, of the traps are automatic. On other courses, only some of the traps may be automatic. And, on still other courses, all traps may be manually operated.

A trap is really nothing more than a spring-powered device which features an "arm" which flips the target into the air. Depending upon what effect the course designer wants, a trap may have what is called a single arm or a double arm. Two targets can be thrown simultaneously from either type of arm, but when simultaneous pairs are thrown, they usually are launched from a double arm, because two targets from a single arm, placed onto the flipper in tandem, fly away at radically diverging angles from each other.

However, two targets thrown from a double arm fly

Some of the newer automatic traps are complicated pieces of machinery such as this Laporte model sold by Winchester.

This is a manual rabbit trap with the regular manual aerial trap on a seated-tripod. It's also portable.

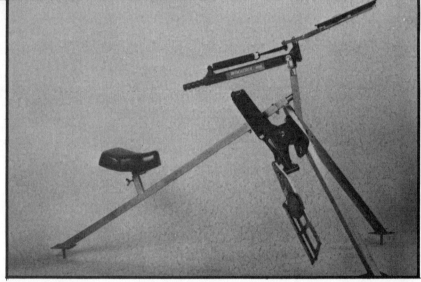

more like a pair of real birds going through the air. A double arm on a trap is merely one in which there are two launching platforms, one above the other.

When it comes to launching the non-standard "specialty" targets like midis, minis or battues, hand-set traps which require a person to serve as trapper usually are employed. There is some development of traps to throw the specialty targets, but since such targets routinely are thrown as mixed pairs, there is a limit to the degree of automation which can be employed.

Hand-set traps of all designs are used at the various sporting clays ranges, but they all are generally substantial in construction, because of the number of targets thrown. A busy sporting clays range routinely throws millions of targets a year.

It is necessary for sporting clays traps to be adjustable in a number of ways. First, the spring tension must be adjustable so target speed can be altered to fit the plan of the course designer, and so the speeds can be regulated when targets of different sizes and weights are thrown.

Also, the trap needs to be adjustable both vertically and horizontally so the flight pattern of the various targets can be altered to suit the needs of the designer when determining the target presentations to the shooters. It is because there are so many different possible combinations of targets and presentations that there are so many different kinds of traps used in sporting clays.

Without question, sporting clays represents the ultimate in variety when it comes to targets, presentations — and the machines to throw the targets.

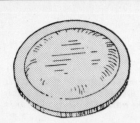

CHAPTER 18

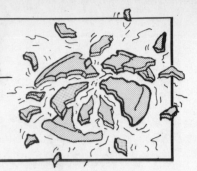

THE EXTRA-BIRD TECHNIQUE

Tom Forbes of Beretta takes a brief break before he tries another difficult pair. When the pressure is on, try breaking the gun, then clearing the mind before attempting to concentrate on any more targets.

CONSISTENCY IS the essence of good shooting, whether the game is sporting clays or any of the disciplines. Given enough opportunity, virtually anyone could hit a particular target presentation. The difference between that kind of random "luck" and good shooting is the ability to hit that same presentation repeatedly.

Technique is the keystone to consistent shooting. It enables a top shooter to register consistently good scores, because it enables him or her to repeat success. However, the same combination of factors which enable good technique to result in repeated success also make it possible for a shooter to miss consistently when the basic technique is not employed. This is the secret to picking up that one extra target, or couple of extra targets, at a particular stand in sporting clays.

The moment a shooter goes from a pure recreationalist who is shooting sporting clays only for the momentary fun of doing something, to a serious competitor, hits and misses take on meaning. Hence, the more serious the shooter becomes, the more meaning a hit or a miss has to that individual.

Depending upon the source of the information, good hunting field shooters can reasonably expect to hit between fifty and sixty percent of the targets on a regular sporting clays range and about half of the targets on a tournament course. Similarly, an AA sporting clays shooter should expect to hit between eighty and ninety percent of the targets on a regular layout, and at least eighty percent on a typical tournament course.

What does all this mean? It means that, based on a ten-stand, one hundred-target course, a solid hunter/shooter would average about three fewer targets per stand than would an AA champion-level shooter. That doesn't sound like a lot, but in many ways it is a quantum difference. By the same token, it does show exactly how important it is to pick up one extra target here, another there. Generally speaking, if a shooter can pick up one extra target per station, he or she will move up one whole classification in sporting clays.

Okay, this may sound all fine and dandy, but just what is

By watching other shooters who are hitting targets at a particular stand, it sometimes is easy to learn what needs to be done to be successful when you are in the cage. Downhill presentation is difficult.

the shooter supposed to do when he or she walks into a particular station to pick up that extra target? One trick is to pay close attention to other shooters as they shoot the stand. When a shooter is doing well at that station, really pay close attention. After all, whatever that shooter is doing, it is working.

Watch the shooter's foot placement, for example, and how he or she holds the body in the stand relative to where the target presentation is appearing. There is a term for all of those things — they are called addressing the target. So, if a shooter watches the way another successful shooter is addressing the target, something has been learned.

Look at the way that shooter is holding the gun. Some of these things are especially subtle, but they all count. For example, if the shooter is holding the gun farther in front of the body on this station than on others, that tells a person something important. Or if the successful shooter's feet are pointing a particular direction, it means such a stance is allowing the right kind of body movement to make the shots.

Watch where the successful shooter is breaking the targets. At most stands in sporting clays, there is an area shooters refer to as a "sweet spot." That is the area where the targets are broken easily and repeatedly. Sometimes, that spot is early in the target flight, which means the bird must be shot quickly. Other times, it is in the middle of the

flight pattern, or even late in the flight when the target has fully developed. Wherever it is, obviously someone who is shooting the station well has figured it out.

It might be important to notice which target of a pair at that station that the successful shooter is breaking first. Is it the lead target or the one following? Often, the sequence in which a pair of targets is shot will determine whether the shooter is successful or not.

What about those times when a shooter walks up to a particular stand, looks at the target presentation and knows that it is a tricky proposition? Is the target rising? Is it going flat? Is it going straight? This is when it pays to shoot smart rather than to shoot hard.

Walk around behind the stand, and view the presentation from several different angles. If possible, even go to an adjoining stand or area and look at the target's flight path. The whole idea is to figure out exactly how that target is flying relative to the shooting station. For example, a target that actually is rising may look like it is going flat. If the shooter then would just walk up to the station and shoot, thinking the target was going flat when it actually was rising, he or she would shoot under the target and miss it.

If the same shooter had figured out the flight path before shooting, he or she would have saved that target — and that alone is a pick-up of one. On some of the trickier stations,

Point of view is important to pick up one or more targets. Shooter in the pit sees target presentation differently from scorer at right.

though, it could represent a much larger gain, because it could mean the shooter would hit all of the targets rather than none or only a couple.

There simply is no way for a shooter to register good scores if he or she has to try to hit the targets on a trial-and-error basis. The shooter must know what the target is doing and how to hit it properly. That way, the only reason for a miss will be faulty execution of a particular shot, and the shooter can recover from that kind of problem easily. There is no easy recovery, however, if there is any doubt about what the target is doing.

Another key to picking up targets here and there has to do with what other shooters may be saying about a particular shot. It is important not to listen to what they say, but to understand what they mean. These two concepts are about the same if the other shooters say a particular target needs to be shot high or low. The reason is simple. A shooter's mental computer will help make up whatever that higher or lower difference might be on most targets.

However, on rapidly rising or falling targets, there may need to be some more radical adjustments.

Most shooters get themselves into trouble by listening to other shooters regarding lead — how much should a particular target be led in order to be hit? There are simply too many variables involved for there to be any single good answer.

For example, there is actual lead versus perceived lead, there is gun speed and its relationship to lead or all of the above. Logically, different shooters see and perceive the situation differently. One shooter telling another that a particular target takes four feet of lead means nothing. In fact, it can even hurt, because what looks like four feet to one shooter may appear as only a foot to another, ten feet to still another.

The important factor to keep in mind when someone says a target needs a certain amount of lead is to put it into context. For example, if on one station, that shooter says he or she feels a target needs two feet of lead, and on another station, that same shooter feels the target needs four feet of lead, what that shooter actually is saying is that the second station calls for twice as much lead as the first.

Given that situation, the second shooter, who noticed on the first station that it looked like the target needed a foot of lead for it to be hit, is in a good position to be able to figure how to hit the target on the second station. After all, the other shooter said he or she had to increase the lead from two to four feet. That means the second shooter need only increase the perceived lead from one to two feet, and keep all other factors equal in order to hit the target.

There are all kinds of variations of the watch-and-listen techniques which work. The important factors are to pay extremely close attention to details involved when a particular target is hit. Then work diligently to repeat that process each and every time on that target.

There are other ways to pick up an extra target at a given stand. One is to maintain focus right from the beginning. At the moment a shooter is ready to call for a target, he or she should be focused and concentrating on shooting the upcoming single or pair. It is easy to become cavalier about shooting a stand. Maybe it looks like an easy stand, or maybe it looks so hard there isn't much hope anyway. Or maybe it's the sort of stand where the shooter starts thinking about subsequent targets and stands rather than facing the immediate situation.

In order to be a good shooter or to become a better shooter, a person must know where the shot is going when targets are hit, as well as where the shot is going when they are missed. Without this basic understanding, there is no way consistency ever will be achieved.

Suppose, then, that the shooter is well focused and concentrating when the first pair of targets appears. Two shots are taken — and the targets are missed. This is not a disaster, because when considering that an AA shooter can afford to miss an average of two targets per stand, this stand still can be salvaged. But it can be salvaged only if the shooter, in missing the pair, understands exactly why the targets were missed, knows what has to be done to correct the errors — and is able to execute the corrections. That is a lot easier said than done, but it is precisely what is necessary.

Assuming the shooter maintains focus and concentration, has properly judged the problem and has corrected the errors, when the next pair of targets appears and the shots ring out, clays will break. The shooter then need only repeat that successful ritual three more times to finish out that station with eight of ten targets broken. This does not happen often, however.

More likely is the situation in which the shooter figures out what went wrong on the first pair, pops the next pair, maybe even the following pair, then drops a bird in the fourth pair and another target in the fifth pair. Wham! Bam!

When not competing, have a buddy watch as you shoot a particularly challenging stand. The other person can see much more easily what the shooter is doing wrong and what needs to be done to correct problem.

Heavy cover and other terrain features can make an otherwise simple presentation seem difficult. It is critical for the shooter to know what the target is actually doing, not be fooled by optical illusion.

The shooter just scored a six on that station — and is solidly back in the C class.

So what is to be done? (A) Stop shooting. (B) Get another gun. (C) Give up sporting clays and take up golf. The correct answer is none of the above. If the shooter did hit the six of ten, chances are that shooter is a C shooter. There is nothing wrong with being a C shooter. But, being a B, A or AA shooter can be better. So, rather than trying to go from C to AA, the shooter should try to go from C to B. How? Simple.

Looking back at the scenario, missing the first pair of targets at that station really is not what hurt the shooter the most. What hurt was missing one of two targets in each of the fourth and fifth pair. But rather than trying to bring everything up to speed instantly, it is better to consider how to bring the shooter up in a reasonable way.

The first step is to decide what it would have taken, for example, for the shooter to have missed the one target on the fourth pair, but finish the station by hitting the fifth pair. Keep in mind that the shooter already has broken the second and third pair. By missing one of the targets in the fourth pair, the shooter has taken off any of that building pressure which occurs when targets are hit in lengthy succession.

Before calling for the final pair of targets, the shooter should have broken whatever routine he or she had established, taken a deep breath and convinced himself or her-

self that the targets can be broken; that they *will* be broken. The shooter need only step up to the line, get ready, call for the targets and break them. This really does happen in the real world of sporting clays.

Or one might prefer to look back at that same scenario and consider how that same shooter might have averted missing the one target in the fourth set of birds. This one is a bit tougher, because there was probably one of two reasons why that target was missed. Most likely, it was missed because of bad execution. Why?

The shooter has just broken two similar pairs in a row, so obviously the shooter knows what to do and how to do it. But no shooter is a machine. Absolute consistency is impossible, and only top champions are usually disciplined enough to put long strings of hits together.

But there is another possibility. Perhaps the shooter missed that target in the fourth set of doubles because he or she choked-up. It felt good when, after missing the first pair, the shooter picked up the second pair. Then, when the third pair was hit, the pressure began to mount. The shooter begins to wonder whether there was just a little luck involved in those two pairs breaking. Doubt sets in. The fourth pair is called for, and the shooter's mind melts down. The first target is hit, but the second escapes untouched. Or the first is hit, and the pressure peaks, causing the shooter to think his or her way right out of hitting the second target.

There is no substitute for success, and this phenomenon

can play an extremely important role for a shooter who wants to pick up an extra target here and there. This situation, however, needs to be created during practice sessions. It might well be called the confidence factor. Here is how it works.

The shooter goes to a sporting clays facility on a normal day or evening, and arranges with the operator to shoot a specified number of targets for a specified price. But, rather than shoot all of the targets at all of the different stations, he picks out one of the types of presentations which has been bothersome. If all presentations have been bothersome, pick one of the more straight-forward presentations and concentrate on it.

It helps to have someone watching who can tell where the targets are being missed. Once the shooter determines how to hit that particular target presentation, repeat it. Keep repeating until the hits are consistent. This experience can be extremely important to the shooter when the pressure is on during a shoot.

First, this repeating of the same target presentation and the same shot teaches the shooter how to shoot that presentation. By purposely repeating the shot hit after hit, after hit, the shooter builds confidence he or she not only can make the shot, but that the shot can be made every time — or at least almost every time.

It is equally important during these practice sessions for the shooter to do some experimenting. Once the shot has been figured out, the shooter needs to determine whether the target is being hit in the center of the shot pattern, or whether it is being struck by one of the sides of the pattern. It is simple to determine this. For example, if a target is hit in a certain way, on the next, shoot a little more in front. Keep doing that until the clay is missed in front. Then, do the opposite. When hitting the target, purposely shoot a little bit behind. Repeat this until the target is missed from behind. Repeat the same process, going progressively higher and lower from when a target is hit until it is missed high or low.

By paying close attention to what is happening, the shooter can determine exactly how to hit that target right in the center of the pattern, and still know subconsciously how much "play" is involved, but which still will result in hits. This not only builds confidence, but can help one get on track when shooting similar, but not identical, presentations at other times.

It is well worth all of the practice time and effort needed to master just one troublesome presentation. Chances are good that in the course of shooting a competition, that individual will encounter either that same shot presentation, or something close to it. So how important was that practice session? Assume the C shooter would have averaged half of the targets at that station initially. Obviously, if the practice session was totally successful, if the shooter retained all of the knowledge and was able to execute flawlessly, the score on that station would go from five to ten.

But that's not the way things work out, because the C shooter by definition doesn't have the discipline it takes to do that — and that's not bad. More likely, what would happen is that the shooter would pick up one or two targets on that station. What does that mean? The score on the station would go from five to six or seven. Multiply that by ten different stations, and the overall score jumps from fifty or sixty to seventy or more. Not bad.

There still is another way to pick up an extra target here and there. It is perhaps the simplest of all, but one of the

These competitors are picking up tips on how to shoot a particular station by watching fellow shooter.

most difficult to execute. The shooter merely needs to refuse to let the station "get" him or her. This method comes into play primarily on those elusive stations where the shooter on that particular day doesn't have a clue about why the targets are being missed, or what should be done to correct the problem. Often in such situations, shooters tend to write-off that station mentally, and more or less give up. Wrong move! However, it is handy to be able to know when the mind wants to give up. This is when that extra target is hit.

Okay, the shooter goes to a station, misses the first pair of targets, but has no idea why. The second pair of targets is called, and they are missed, as well.

Here is where some shooters begin to shut themselves off. Certainly, by the time the third pair is missed, it's melt-down time. In gun safety terms, when in doubt, don't. Or, when in doubt, stop. The same thing holds true for sporting clays shooters who find themselves lost at a stand.

Open up the gun, take a step back and blank out the mind. Regain whatever semblance of composure might be possible under the circumstances, and make a mental vow: On the next pair, I'm going to hit just one of the targets. Then, when the next pair of targets is launched, visually lock onto just one of them, go after it and stay on it for both shots, if necessary. There are two important concepts to keep in mind here.

First, chances are pretty good that, by concentrating totally on just one of the pair of targets, it will be hit. Oddly, from observations on ranges, it also seems that when a shooter does that, the frequency with which the second target also is hit is higher than might be expected. But the more important aspect here is the decision to stay with the initial target for the second shot, if the first shot misses.

There are many shooters who insist that, if a target is missed on the first shot, the shooter should stay on that target and try to break it rather than going for the other

When the terrain goes up and down, it can make a target presentation confusing. What may look like a flat flight pattern might be a falling target. Here, shooters check out what the targets really are doing before shooting challenging station.

target as one would do naturally were the first target broken with the first shot. The arguments in favor of this approach have merit in situations where the target can be seen long enough for two shots.

For openers, the shooter already is swinging the gun on the first target, so it takes less effort to keep up the action and make whatever correction it takes to hit it. Secondly, most shooters don't miss the same target twice in a row. At least, statistically they will hit more missed targets with a second shot than they will miss with the second shot. That's one reason why so many apparently great wingshots are not so great on a sporting clays range. With real ducks, pheasants, quail, or whatever, they will bag birds repeatedly, but will have taken more than one shot per bird average.

The mere determination to pick out a single target and make a total commitment to hitting it also helps. It may be subconscious, but with such commitment comes a higher degree of focus, and as was discussed earlier, focus and concentration make for consistency.

Assuming the shooter who missed, say, the first three pairs of targets at a particular station decides to hit just one of the fourth pair, what does that really mean? After all, the shooter is already down six targets at that station, right? Yes, but at that point the shooter is not down ten targets at that station, and the subject here is picking up one or two targets here and there.

Put another way, if shooting an eighty sounds okay for a tournament, it means that twenty targets will have been lost somewhere. Missing the first six targets at one particular stand only means the shooter is down those six targets. It's time to recover. After all, if that shooter is ever going to hit another target in a lifetime, recovery is a must.

At this station, where lesser shooters may simply have given up, the determined shooter picks up, say, that one single he or she vowed mentally to hit from the fourth pair. The shooter repeats the vow for the fifth pair, and hits one of the two targets. At that point, the score is two from a

Even where a shooter stands within a station can make a difference in the degree of difficulty in a particular target presentation. This shooter is slightly to one side, enabling him to pick up a pair of crossers for a maximum amount of their flight.

possible ten at that station. Granted, if that situation were repeated at each stand, the overall score would be low. But, if rather than giving up on that station, the shooter got tough and hit the two, then there are two targets the shooter likely would not have gotten otherwise.

The point here is that the real difference between a C shooter and an AA shooter is repeatability. And, repeatability assumes the ability to rebound from adversity. To do that, the process is simple, but not easy. The first order of business is to stop whatever is wrong. The next thing to do is to correct what is wrong, and do it right.

Since there is almost never a perfect score in sporting clays, everybody misses targets. How one ranks depends upon the regularity with which that shooter hits targets, or upon what regularity that shooter misses targets. Rarely can a shooter "pick up" a lot of targets at a shoot. It should be considered a happy moment when one, or maybe two, can be picked up.

It doesn't take long when a shooter is picking up a target here, and another there, for the scores to begin to climb enough to be meaningful. Too often, C shooters might recognize the critical importance of an AA shooter being able to pick up just one more target. After all, tournaments are won and lost by a single target. In fact, it is more important for the C shooter to be concerned about picking up that extra target than it is for the AA shooter.

Why? Simple. The AA shooter is already good, knows how to shoot the game, knows how to recover from failure and has the confidence it takes to shoot consistently. That shooter's own discipline will put things back in order, if the shooter allows his or her mind to do it. The C shooter, though, has not developed all of these abilities and experience. Hence, the act of picking up just one more target for the C shooter has much more significance, because it is the only way that shooter ever will improve.

Again, virtually no one ever shoots a perfect score in sporting clays. Hence, all shooters can benefit from picking up just one more target.

On some courses, a duck station has a boat suspended on springs. Note how national champ Dan Carlisle is bracing himself. This allows him to break his targets much more easily. It is a detail that can mean points.

CHAPTER 19

THE
\\\\\ MENTAL GAME \\\\\

...Or What To Do, When You Start To Choke Up!

N ANY of the shooting sports, everything is new at first. New shooters have to learn so much just to be credible. They have so many things to think about that, for them, there is not much of a mental game involved. Rather, they can consider themselves as doing okay, if they simply figure out the basic coordinations needed to hit the target.

However, a shooter need not become advanced before the mental aspects of the game begin to become a factor, and the better a shooter becomes, the more relative impor-tance the mind makes in the score. For the top shooters, there comes a point at which the difference between win-ning and being lost in the pack is totally mental.

This also is true of most other sports, and should not be surprising. After all, by the time a person has attained top status, there is no question that he or she is able to perform. Hence, maintaining that extremely high level of consis-tency means keeping the mind clear at all times. Sounds easy? It isn't — for all the logical reasons.

First, a top shooter really must *want* to win and to break

Being totally focused and absolutely ready for a target presentation is what the mind game is really all about in sporting clays. Shooters know they can hit the the target with vigilance.

Among top sporting clays competitors, name of the game is concentration and being ready for surprise targets.

targets. That means the person is driven to succeed. Sec-ond, as the level of performance increases, so does the personal expectation. This means a self-inflicted pressure. Third, as the shooter performs increasingly better, he or she is entered in higher and higher levels of competition where the incentives for winning are greater and greater.

That is bad enough, but for those who have achieved top status, there still are more sources of pressure that can cause mental anguish. Often, for example, top shooters are sponsored by one or more companies. A shooter might receive sponsorship from an ammunition company in the form of free ammo or that which is drastically reduced in price. And top competitors shoot a whale of a lot of ammo. That same shooter likely is using a particular kind of gun which often is supplied by the manufacturer. Add to that other forms of sponsorship which range from cash to cover-ing travel and hotel expenses, and there can be a real need to perform well — not just to stay at the top, but to retain and/or expand the sponsorships. At this point, shooting no longer is a game; it is a business.

When the pressure is on, a moment of relaxation can be one means of helping the shooter keep his head straight.

tal and physical maneuvers may differ from one shooter to the other, but there will be an established routine initiated when it's time to set the mind straight.

The first thing any shooter does is to stop everything — even if only for the briefest of moments. It is totally necessary to halt whatever it is that is causing the shooter to miss targets. There is time to worry about doing the right thing, but the first order is to stop doing the wrong thing.

When the pressure is on, and a shooter is on the station, watch closely. Often, even before calling for the first set of targets, the shooter will take one or more deep breaths and exhale. If the shooter is already on the stand, and has just missed a target or a pair, watch again. Typically, the gun will be opened, the shooter will take a step back from the line, breathe in through the nose deeply and exhale through the mouth. This sends more oxygen to the brain, and helps the shooter clear the mind and think more clearly.

What is not outwardly visible in such situations, however, is the fact that the shooter is doing more than just clearing the mind. The shooter is clearing away anything negative. Negatives must be eliminated before positive results can be achieved. Once that is achieved, the shooter forces himself to go back to basics, and not make too much out of the missed target; not to read too much into the miss. This is the time when the shooter must center all of the focus on the targets still to be shot.

This looks like a prayer session, but actually, this shooter is building his sense of concentration for shot.

The reason this segment of the sport is mentioned here is that it is the level at which the mental aspects of shooting can be examined most easily. After all, it is at this level that the mental aspects are in their purest form. When a top shooter hits fewer than half the targets at a given station, it is a safe bet the problem is mental, because a top shooter is capable of doing much better than that, even on a bad day.

Although the stakes may be higher for the top shooter, the frustration of being "off the game" is no greater for a champion AA shooter than for anyone else. Hence, the proven techniques that top shooters use to put the mental game in order also are valid for any other shooter who cares about hitting targets.

For starters, whenever a shooter begins to miss targets he or she feels should not be missed — those which normally would be broken by that shooter — chances are good the remedy is in the mental department. There is one nice thing here. A mis-diagnosis is not a problem. It never hurts for any shooter to concentrate on his state of mind while shooting.

Rather than letting the frustration of missing a target or two get the best of them, top shooters have developed the discipline to put themselves back on track. It is not automatic, but it is a known procedure. The exact series of men-

What about those occasions when the shooter has a lot of time to think about things between shots? An example might be late in a competition. The shooter has been neck-and-neck with one or more other shooters throughout the day. At the ninth stand, the shooter drops a couple of targets. That means this competitor must finish well at the tenth stand in order to do well in the final standings. Yet, the shooter has a ten-minute wait between finishing the ninth stand and beginning to shoot the last stand. This time can help or hurt, depending upon what one does mentally.

That is the time for the shooter to instill confidence from within. It's time for the shooter to convince himself or herself that those kinds of targets to be encountered on the last stand have been shot successfully before; that it can be done now. The mind must impress upon itself that the shooter has the ability to break the targets. Really, what happens is that the shooter gives himself a little pep talk during the break. The thought pattern is that, yes, these targets are no different than they were in practice; yes, they can be broken; and there is no reason they shouldn't be broken.

One thing the shooter does not want to do is tell himself those targets have *got to be broken.* Such a thought pattern assumes that perhaps they may not be broken. That is negative. The positive response is: Yes, I can break them.

Assuming this scenario, the shotgunner enters the final stand. To win the tournament, he must do well at that stand, but what does it seem like to this shooter? If there are all kinds of crazy things going through this individual's mind, he — or she — is in big trouble. More properly, very little will be going through the shooter's mind, in fact. If the concentration is strong enough, it may seem to the shooter like nothing is going on in the mind.

The shooter has gone through the routine so many times that entering the stand goes unnoticed. There is no conscious awareness of loading the gun, because that also is rote. Assuming the proper stance is as automatic as just standing there, the shooter doesn't even notice it when the target is called. All he notices is the targets appearing and breaking. It is as though this person is in a self-hypnotic trance. Lest there be any misunderstanding, none of this is unsafe. This level of shooter under these circumstances is in a form of auto-pilot in which all of the normal safety practices are as much a part of the total picture as when that shooter is explaining safety procedures to a beginner.

The only real difference to the shooter at this point of the procedure is that all of the "normal" thoughts are in the auto mode. The conscious mind is beamed like a laser right at the target. It is at such moments that champions shoot their best. Top shooters can establish some of their longest strings of hits when this type of concentration can be continued. That is why some appear so strange when something breaks their concentration. Sometimes, it is difficult to regain that level of focus immediately if something breaks the thought.

However, some interesting things can happen to these shooters when they are in such a trance. For example, they don't seem to keep track of hits and misses. So, in the scenario above, a shooter going into the final stand, and needing to do well there likely would not be able to tell a bystander the final score when this stand is completed.

Shooters in such a mental state might shoot the first four pairs of the station, and start to walk out, only to be reminded by the scorer that there still remained a final pair of targets

Breaking the shotgun and taking a moment to reflect is another ritual practiced by experienced competitors.

With a gallery of onlookers and other competititors, it can be difficult to give the targets proper attention.

The trap operator has a part in how tough a target can be, since he governs the delayed launch of claybirds.

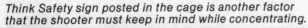

to be shot. Oddly, even though conversation with the scorer must have had some effect on the shooter's concentration, those who have been observed doing that most often return to the stand, appearing almost relaxed, and usually break both of the final targets with ease.

Sometimes, these shooters will break all five pairs at the final station, and start to reload — only to be reminded by the scorer that all targets have been shot.

What is actually going on inside the shooter's mind at such moments? A logical, methodic series of thoughts, actually. Rather than concerning themselves with how many more targets are left to be shot, or how many targets have been shot, they are focused totally on the upcoming pair of targets. They are thinking constantly about breaking the next pair — and that concentration is so well zeroed that the individual's mind actually perceives the targets singly in the pair, and it sees them in what might be described as slow motion.

Certainly, the targets are not going any slower, but they are going relatively more slowly, because the mind has been speeding up. It is at these times that the shooter is most fluid in swings and shots. This must certainly be because the mind is operating so quickly that it is able to relay messages to the muscles many more times a second, so to speak, than normal. This results in every movement of the shooter's body being totally deliberate and "on target."

Rarely does any shooter find himself in this state throughout a shoot. There are too many distracting factors afoot to allow that. However, the more often the shooter can enter this state, the better the shoot will go.

Since the top shooters are good enough to shoot top scores under regular conditions, there really is no need for them to get into the extended mental state to do well. But it is necessary for them to enter it when their minds are otherwise playing tricks on them. It is a form of self-defense against the mind. It is a way to keep from thinking one's way into missing a target.

In such surroundings as this, the shooter may tend to feel a touch of claustrophobia, the walls crowding in.

For those who have not yet developed this kind of ability, one does not merely think one's self into such a state. That's not the way it works. Rather, one concentrates as totally as possible and tries as hard as possible. After doing this repeatedly, the shooter eventually will develop the ability to shut out all unnecessary input.

When should a shooter begin to take the mental game seriously? Whenever it becomes evident to that competitor that targets are being missed which should not be, based upon proven ability and experience. For a beginner, this might seem to come quite early. And at the early stages of shooting development, it is not so critical to be able to control the mind so well. However, it is a great time to begin practicing concentration and focus.

By practicing concentration and focus regularly, the shooter will be able to develop the kind of mental discipline it takes to go to the next level — whatever that level happens to be at the time. Eventually, with practice, the ability will be there — but only if ability is accompanied by a like desire.

And there is a big difference between wanting to shoot well, and really desiring to shoot well. To want is to dream. To desire is to have a mission. And it is the concept of purpose, after all, which turns a game into a competition.

Yes, sporting clays can be a lot of fun. And, it can be much more. It can be as much or as little as the shooter wants to make it. There is always room at the top. Simply put, getting there is simple, although not easy. The secret is: Think straight to shoot straight.

Even during intense competition, there is time for fun in sporting clays. That's what game is about.

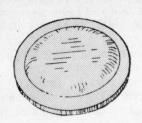

CHAPTER 20

CHEROKEE ROSE

This Georgia Shooting Resort May Be The Finest In The Nation

JUST A short decade ago, sporting clays ranges in this country were about as common as good manners at a punk rock concert. The sport, well established in Europe, was only beginning to make its presence felt on these shores. In the last five years, that situation has changed considerably.

For scattergunners grown bored with the unvarying fare offered by trap and skeet, the first taste of sporting clays was a veritable smorgasbord. Targets zipped by at speeds and angles previously unseen on American target ranges.

Sometimes it would be a single clay leaping from an unseen trap and disappearing behind a screen of brush before the shooter could even react. Just when the gunner felt that target was mastered, the boom of his shotgun would send a second target speeding across his field of view, or two targets would pop out. And, they might be climbing, quartering, falling, or streaking high overhead!

Master those and some sneaky range operator would

The sign at the entrance to Cherokee Rose leaves little doubt as to the purpose of the shooting resort. Georgia club has gained a reputation as one of the world's top courses.

Sandra Bennett, a course guide at Cherokee Rose, is an active competitor, too. All personnel at the club are well versed in sport.

The numerous signs pretty well describe what the shooter can expect to face at Cherokee Rose.

change the angle on the trap, alter the speed, or even move the shooting stand, leaving the hapless gunner to face an entirely new set of challenges.

For many, it was as much fun as you could have legally with a shotgun!

The rapidly growing popularity of sporting clays has prompted the construction of a number of new ranges on which to play the game. In fact, it's a safe bet the majority of new ranges being constructed in this country either are primarily sporting clays oriented or have sporting clays incorporated.

Unfortunately, the sport still is new enough in this country that there are no real hard and fast rules for constructing and operating a world-class facility. You could say it's a "growth industry," and as such there will be those who lead and innovate; there will be others who simply follow and copy. For those who would like to experience the former at its best, we suggest a visit to the Cherokee Rose Shooting Resort.

Although this facility has only been operating in its present guise since June 1990, it already has earned a reputation among veteran sporting clays enthusiasts from

Field Five, the duck pond, is an example of how to cram a lot of variety into one shooting station. A trio of hidden Beomat traps can zip clays across the water from many angles, requiring shooter to stay on his toes.

both sides of the pond as a shining example of what a world-class sporting clays facility can and should be.

Located in Griffin, Georgia, just a short thirty-five minutes south of the Atlanta airport, Cherokee Rose occupies 125 acres of some of the most picturesque hill country in north Georgia. At present, only about fifty acres are in actual use. But, one would be hard pressed to find a more challenging and diverse array of shotgun sports packed into a similar-size area.

"Although known primarily as a sporting clays course, Cherokee Rose offers skeet, a dove tower with five stations, bunker trap, three different flush games, a five-stand sporting clays course operated by a Birdbrain computer, and the only Starshot layout in the Southeast," according to Chris Christian, who we sent to look it over.

"That alone would keep many ranges busy. But at Cherokee Rose, they play a second fiddle to a magnificent ten-field championship sporting clays course."

Designed by well known course designer Gordon Phillip, the course meanders through hills, gullies and across ponds. The initial design made excellent use of existing terrain features and kept their disturbance to a minimum. An all-weather path winds between shooting stations and may be walked or, for the truly jaded, motorized golf carts are available.

The entire course is automated using high-capacity Beomat machines. Simply flipping a switch as one enters the shooting area activates that station, and regular club members — memberships are available as well as non-member shooting — don't even require a course guide.

The course may be shot as a fifty-target affair providing one single, one report pair and one true pair per station. As a one-hundred-bird course, two singles, two report pairs and two true pairs are included.

The course covers the full gamut of sporting clays presentations.

An all-weather path meanders through the course. For the jaded, golf carts offer transportation!

Field One — Whistlin' Bob — simulates flushing quail, with the targets quickly quartering away from the shooter and, just like their namesake, quickly heading for cover.

Field Two — Sneaky Snipe — presents quartering-away shots that often climb at a steep angle. The "window" on this station can be quite small, the target often starting out against a wooded background, zipping through a patch of open sky, then back across a wooded background.

Field Three — Chuckling Chukars — features an elaborate wooden deck built into a hillside with two shooting stations looking into a gully. Each station presents its own unique challenge: One station reduces the angle and can be taken quickly, while the other presents a much longer shot at a hard, crossing angle.

Field Four — Dove Roost — features a tower presentation with two shooting stations that can provide hard crossers or incomers. From either stand, the targets can find some

Natural terrain features are utilized to the maximum at Cherokee Rose's championship course. Well situated trees require shooters not only to swing and pull the trigger, but to consider where they can score.

trees to hide behind fairly quickly, meaning the shooter better react when they appear!

Field Five is the Duck Pond, a shooting station jutting out over a pond, giving the gunner the opportunity to deal with three strategically placed Beomat traps that may offer shots coming from behind the shooter and quartering quickly away, crossers, settling incomers or any combination of the above in report or true pairs. It's a lot of variety from one shooting station!

Field Six — Humpin' Hares — offers movable barriers that can be shifted to increase or decrease the difficulty of the rabbit targets, which can be launched as singles or pairs. As a side bonus, a manual trap often will toss a hard-quartering quail when you least expect it. Talk about tough doubles!

Field Seven — Turbo Woodcock — offers a totally tough ninety-degree right-to-left crosser as a single, with report and true pairs to follow. The targets bear a strong resemblance to a Nolan Ryan fast ball, and if you are one of those laid-back deliberate shooters, it can be a humbling experience.

Field Eight — Redneck Ringnecks — offers a fast,

rapidly climbing target that duplicates the flush of a pheasant, plus another equally steep bird that crosses left to right quartering away. That second target can find the trees real fast on pairs, leaving some shooters to wonder if two targets really did come out.

Field Nine — Darting Doves — offers tower targets coming from behind the shooter, and for a little spice, a springing teal thrown in. Plenty of variety here!

Field Ten — Grouse Gulch — is one of the course's most challenging fields. The two shooting stations are located on a sturdy deck built into a hillside staring down into another gully. The targets are launched below the shooter, from his right, each station providing a different angle and shot. Complicating the matter are a few tall trees left standing right in the middle of the shooting area. The targets are quite adept at ducking behind these just as you decide to pull the trigger.

While the basic layout offers a great deal of variety, shooters shouldn't become too comfortable with it. About the time they do, range manager Marty Fischer is likely to make changes.

Fischer, an accomplished scattergunner, NRA-certified

shotgun coach and one of less than fifty National Sporting Clays Association-certified sporting clays instructors in the country, is a firm believer that variety is truly the spice of life.

"Being able to shift and change your course of fire through the redirection of electrically operated traps, the addition of manual traps, or by incorporating some portable shooting stations is what sets sporting clays apart from other shotgun games, and what attracts shooters," he says.

"Any time you build a course, then sit back and rest on your laurels, you're not being as creative as you could be," he adds. "Veteran sporting clays shooters don't want to see the game become so standardized that people start running 1000 targets straight as a matter of course. The fact that we set up our facility — through the equipment we purchased and the design of the course — to be able to vary the course of fire on a regular basis is part of the reason we have achieved the reputation we have in such a short period of time."

While the championship course grabs most of the headlines, there is another, less publicized course alongside it that Fischer rates as equally important when it comes to running a successful commercial shooting resort.

"One of the first things we did after setting up the big course," he explains, "was to use those shot-fall areas to set up a smaller sub-gauge course. These targets fly a little slower, a little closer and are easier. It was intended originally to allow .410 and 28-gauge shooters to enjoy sporting clays, but it has turned out to be a big asset when dealing with new shooters.

"Our marketing approach," Fischer continues, "is geared to different types of organizations: not just hunters and target shooters, but to anyone who has ever done any type of outdoor recreation. Anyone who enjoys outdoor activities — be it fishing, golf, tennis, as well as shooting and hunting — is a candidate to come to Cherokee Rose and try sporting shotgun games. A good deal of our business is corporate parties, where co-workers are afforded the opportunity to spend recreational time with each other in order to build a better personal bond.

"In the past, many such groups have been sent on golf or fishing outings, even though some of the group many not pursue those sports on their own. We actively solicit such groups and that's where the sub-gauge course proves so valuable."

As is to be expected, not all members of these parties have wingshooting experience, but that doesn't mean that

A stroll through Cherokee Rose is like a walk through a well maintained park with carefully tended paths.

they can't have a good time. "When we get in a group like this, we have certified instructors and top-quality rental shotguns — the Remington 11-87 and the Berreta A303 — and we put the newcomer through a short orientation course as part of the trip package.

"Once that is done, we take them out to the sub-gauge course and each member of that group will break some targets and have a good time. That's the real key."

Fischer feels, "You can't just take a group of novice shooters out and put them through an advanced course. That's a good way to lose that group, because it will be a frustrating experience for them. The future of sporting clays is right there: this group of shooters. We hold that future in our hands. Why screw it up?

"A good indoctrination and a course in which each shooter can experience a sense of satisfaction and accomplishment by breaking at least a few targets is often all it takes to turn first-time visitors into enthusiastic participants. That's the real advantage of the easy course. It provides fun and leaves a positive image in the shooter's mind."

Adding to that "positive image" is another factor about which Marty Fischer feels strongly.

"It's been said," he states, "that you get only one chance to make a first impression and that's true. When someone visits your facility, if he's not impressed, he probably won't be back. That's the reason why, from the moment an individual turns into our driveway, I want him to be impressed!"

To say Fischer accomplishes that goal quite well would

Left: Fifteen-year-old Brad Dameron gets some pointers from gunsmith Art Leckie, who also is an ardent clays shooter. (Below) The rabbit field features movable barriers that can change the shooting situation quickly.

Challenging five-stand and super sporting clays range also is available. Many shooters find it more of a challenge to their talents than championship course.

be a lot like saying Dolly Parton looks good in a tight dress. At best, understatement!

On his investigative trip to Cherokee Rose, in the company of shooting buddy, Jack Mitchell, Chris Christian was informed by Mitchell that it is considered poor form to deposit any trash — even a cigarette butt — on the ground.

A chain smoker, Christian took that as a challenge. He wouldn't throw any on the ground, but he'd sure try to find where someone else had!

"After a trip through the championship course, I still was looking! Every time I felt the need to put out a cigarette, I had only to take a quick look around to find a conveniently located butt kit. When I needed to throw away a film wrapper, there always was a trash can nearby."

"Many shooting ranges," Marty Fischer observes, "are not the best maintained pieces of property around. But, it doesn't take that much effort to have a clean place. Veteran shooters may not really care if they have to wade through three-foot piles of fired hulls to reach their shooting station,

The extensive use of automated machines allows regular club members to shoot the course without a guide. That saves money and makes machines less expensive, in the long run, than manual machines manned by operators.

The Straightshooter pro shop offers all the items needed by the shooter; included are clothing, shells, rental guns.

The center arena has a dove tower, bunker trap, skeet, flush games and the only Starshot layout in the South.

but non-shooters and new shooters do. And, as I said before, they are the future of the sport. It makes sense to try to impress them."

One would have to work hard to be unimpressed on a visit to Cherokee Rose. "It's like walking through a well-maintained park," Christian opines.

Completing the picture of a country club retreat for "regular folks" is a full-service restaurant that, with advanced reservations, can serve everything from man-size sandwiches to a gourmet repast and cocktails. A comfortable rustic lodge provides accommodations for small groups,

with full kitchen facilities or catering. Plans are under way to expand the lodge facilities significantly.

Add to that a well stocked pro shop and a top-notch corps of instructors including — by the time you read this — world champion sporting clays shooter Steve Middleditch. Upon announcing his decision to migrate from England, Middleditch had his pick of every sporting clays facility in America. He chose Cherokee Rose because he thought it was the best. It's not hard to see why Cherokee Rose Shooting Resort has been referred to as "Disneyland for shotgunners."

CHAPTER 21

MINI-COURSE, MAXI-RESULTS

Here's A Plan For Building A Small Sporting Clays Layout That Has All The Advantages And Few Of The Costs Of A Large, Commercial Field!

"**I** CHOKED!

"It was as simple as that. No excuses. No pointing fingers at the slight delay on the target release. No blaming the breeze that angled across the little valley pushing the targets to the left. No nothing. I simply took the apple and blew it!

"I was at station ten on the sliver-like course, slightly behind and to the left of the trap, and needed to break the last pair of curling, going-away targets to set a new hunters class course record. I had shot stations one, two, and three, on the south side, plus stations four and five straight down the middle, about normal."

Barry C. Davis, who spoke those words, is an accomplished shotgunner as well as an outdoor writer. He was one of a group of shooters interested in building a mini sporting clays layout for their own use. Here is his report on what it was all about:

Coming back up the much more treacherous north side

ridge stations, things simply fell into a groove. Settling, passing and quartering targets broke in the openings between the trees at six, seven and eight like they hadn't before. At station nine was the nastiest simulation of a pair of grouse flushing I've ever seen. Here it was necessary to instantly take the first target in one gap, then wait out number two 'til it reached a second gap farther downrange. I broke four out of five rather than the usual two or three.

At station ten, I needed to go straight. The single and first pair broke clean. Intent on getting on the second target of the final pair before it slid behind a downrange tree, I took the lead target for granted. What do they say about counting your chickens before they hatch? The "lost bird" came on the lead target, not the more difficult trailer. But it was still a miss, and the course record, shared by three of us and challenged regularly by some of the wickedest shooting birdhunters to ever pull on a pair of brush pants, stood pat.

"Nice try," said one of my buddies on the squad, feigning sincerity.

"Argh, argh," said another as he grabbed his throat and made choking noises.

"Such is life," said my partner on the trap machine. "Maybe when you get more familiar with that new spaghetti gun — his reference to my Marocchi Avanza Sporting Clays model — you'll have your name at the top of the board all by its lonesome."

"Not likely," said one of the sharers of the record with a grin. "The boy's too erratic. If he had the sense his momma gave him to adapt to the little things that are always changing on this course, then I'd be worried."

If there's any one, universal quality that can be applied to the game of sporting clays, it's adaptability. Unlike other target games in which everything is regulated and specified within a rigid framework, sporting clays is the epitome of elasticity. It requires only a small stretch to say the game can be moulded and manipulated to be anything you want it to be.

Every field and station, in theory, is supposed to be a representation of a real-life hunting situation. Because real life hunting situations are infinitely variable, the course designer's options become equally so, and, in the end, so does the game itself.

It's the American way to make things bigger, faster and always more complex, and that's been a key factor; a negative one in my opinion, in the development of the game since its adaptation here in the States. In those areas of the country where sanctioned sporting clays ranges are sparse, where drives of two or three hours to a course are the norm, it's an unrealistic expectation to count on casual shooters making that trip on a clockwork, weekly basis. In those areas where the game is firmly established, you can see a new madness emerging.

The competition among new and redesigned ranges to be "the biggest and the best" is a double-edged sword with, I'm afraid, one side far sharper than the other. On the dull, plus side, it can lead to more overall shooting "opportunities." On the sharper, far more threatening downside,

Settling targets that come from behind and overhead demand clean gun mount and quick reactions to break them before they can disappear downrange.

it has led to a near lockstep genuflection to technical difficulty, and to country club-quality creature comforts. The belief behind it: both are necessary for success in attracting and holding shooters.

So, what's the problem? The lack of reality, for one. Absurd technical difficulty is a turn-off to shooters who do not consider the game a religion. Even more important, however, is the expense. In a growing number of cases, the need to quickly recover the costs of these "improvements" are pricing the average guy right out of the game before he's even had a chance to become part of it.

We're talking big bucks, folks. For example, only a few years ago, it was possible to build a full-scale, bare-bones sporting clays range, excluding property costs, for $20,000 to $25,000. Today, double it. And we're still talking bare bones. Some of the upscale, new ranges have twenty grand or more sunk into a single field. And their clubhouses are the kinds of places where blue collar shooters and hunters intuitively look for the service entrance.

That's not to say there isn't a place for these types of ranges in the sporting clays hierarchy. There most certainly is. They are gorgeous to walk, and impressive to shoot. But when prohibitive costs virtually wipe out ninety percent of the potential shooter base, it does not bode well for the overall future of the game.

Is there a solution to this quandry at both extremes of the problem; on the one hand, no range close-by, on the other, ranges too expensive to shoot? You bet there is. They're called mini-courses, and in some ways they go right back to the origins of the game.

Mini-courses are flexible and adaptable — there's that word, again — just like the big ranges. The only functional difference is they're compact enough to be fit onto a much smaller piece of land. Even more importantly, the cost to build one is only a fraction of that needed to put together a full-size range — even one without the frills and amenities. With lower costs to build, maintain and operate, mini-courses can charge far less to shoot than the big ranges. By being able to charge bargain rates, the number of shooters able to participate on a regular basis increases dramatically.

What a true mini-course definitely is not, and it's the

Overhead incoming driven grouse targets are a staple at most mini-courses built in wooded terrain. Needed is a shot-proof barrier for the trapper, as well as the simple, basic shooting pad and stand; not fancy, but functional.

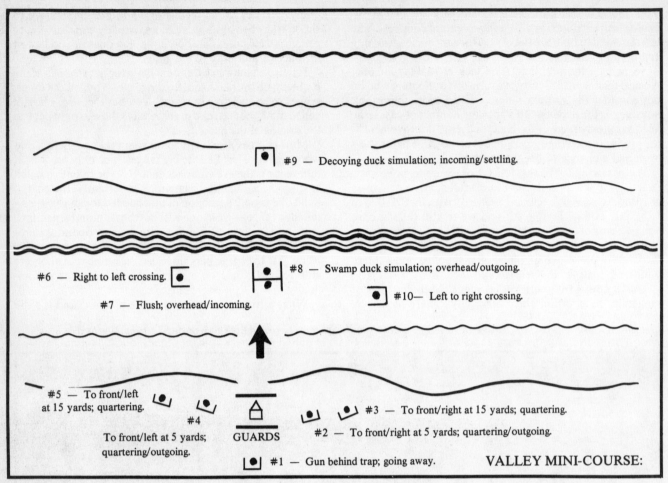

#9 — Decoying duck simulation; incoming/settling.

#6 — Right to left crossing.   #8 — Swamp duck simulation; overhead/outgoing.

#7 — Flush; overhead/incoming.   #10— Left to right crossing.

#5 — To front/left at 15 yards; quartering.

#4   #3 — To front/right at 15 yards; quartering.

To front/left at 5 yards; quartering/outgoing.   GUARDS   #2 — To front/right at 5 yards; quartering/outgoing.

#1 — Gun behind trap; going away.   VALLEY MINI-COURSE:

This valley is only a hundred yards from ridge to ridge. The target direction is to station 9, according to Rick Spivey, who designed the course. He operates Beaver Dam Sporting Clays in Greenville, North Carolina, as a pro.

misconception most shooters have of them before ever setting foot on one, is what some term a "hobby" layout. You know what I mean; a few guys together on a Saturday afternoon at an old stubblefield or pasture and throw a bunch of lazy, wobbly, open-view targets with a cheap, weak-springed thrower. Moving around a bit changes the angles some, but it's really not much of a challenge.

A mini-course, on the other hand, is as real in its presentation of targets as a heart attack. It just isn't as big and fancy. Here's a practical definition: a true mini-course is a formally structured, six- to twelve-station layout, serviced by one or two trap machines; usually single, but sometimes multi-choke in nature. The course is constructed with full consideration given to suiting the purposes of real hunters.

A couple of actual mini-course descriptions can help put the definition into perspective. At the upper end of the scale, a tournament skeet-shooting friend of mine is ready to put the final touches on a "tower" course. In his travels, he found two old automatic skeet machines, bought them for next to nothing, had them refurbished, and set them, one high and one low, on a thirty-foot tower overlooking a fifty-yard-wide wooded ravine. Shooting lanes and seven

stations were cut into and along the edge of the ravine. From each, you can shoot a wide variety of targets, depending on the machine from which they're thrown. Singles, and simultaneous, following and report pairs are all possible. The owner is in love with high, passing shots silhouetted against an open sky, so the tower and upper machine were personal necessities.

Another acquaintance out West has similar "tower"-type plans. However, restricted by a far smaller budget, he's using a single, fully adjustable, manual trap mounted on a swivel stand. The gamebird shots usually found in the open, rangeland terrain in his part of the country are perfectly suited to the types of target presentations possible by using the tower as a hub for the predetermined stations set in an erratic circle around it.

Established gun clubs with combined skeet and trap ranges also are toying with mini-courses before committing to the investment in a full-scale clays layout. By strict definition, however, these are really hybrids, because they lack formal structure. By using temporary barriers to restrict lines of sight, and by placing stations in some of the oddest positions I've ever seen, a wide variety of targets can be thrown from both skeet houses and the trap pit. Some weird combinations of doubles can push the envelope of reality, but the mix of singles is definitely within reason.

The overwhelming majority of mini-courses being built, though, lack towers and automatic machines and any of the other bigger ticket items. Being elaborate or expensive is not the key to being effective. Using the available natural terrain to its best advantage is. A prime example at the bottom end of the budget scale would be the mini-course mentioned in the opening paragraphs.

Built in a narrow, wooded valley, it has one trap machine and ten stations that comprise a fifty-target round of quartering, passing, incoming and outgoing chances at singles and pairs that scream when you're close to the trap and settle deceptively like decoying ducks at the downrange end. Visibility is severely limited by trees at more than half of the stations, and the mental discipline, let alone shooting

skill, necessary to break targets in the available "shooting windows" is a severe test for even the most practiced wingshot. Having exasperated a lot of shooters, from local birdhunters to top sporting clays tournament guys, the course has received a number of nicknames. One of the most charitable is "the little course from Hell."

I know the course well, because a buddy and I built it. By determining exactly what we wanted ahead of time — a real, branch in the face, birdhunters course with no gimmicks or cheap, easy shots — we selected a small chunk of natural terrain that would work to our best advantage. By scrounging around for materials to build protective barriers and shooting stands, doing all of the labor ourselves, we brought it in for less than $1000. That included the trap machine, and a consultation with a professional course designer. The end product, after a tiny bit of fine tuning, is a mini-course that has produced maxi-results.

Following the preliminary laying out of a mini-course, the only way to know where to make adjustments is by throwing some targets down the proposed shooting lanes. Such fine-tuning is a definite must on such a course.

The local cadre of hunters, who never would travel an hour and a half or more to a big range, shoot it regularly, because it's convenient and inexpensive at six bucks a round. And because, in their eyes, the target presentations are as challenging and unforgiving as they experience in the woods and swamps and cutovers. High-overall class tournament shooters have expressed much the same positive feeling. However, nouveau sporting clays aficionados with inflated opinions of their own shooting abilities usually are one-time visitors. The course doesn't cut them any slack, and it rips their egos to be beaten by guys who wouldn't know a Krieghoff from a can opener, shooting scratched, scarred, near wornout field guns.

The point to all of this is that a mini-course can be anything you want it to be — within reason. With one machine, particularly in a fixed position, it's impossible to create the extensive variety of shots offered at a full-scale range. But you can place great emphasis on the types of shots you want, or those that predominate in the "real" hunting you do.

Some mini-courses move the trap around on a trailer or attached to a special Trapboy base (Throw Rite, Inc., 913 Baltimore, Kansas City, MO 64105) that fits on the ball hitch of a pick-up. We've found, with our course, that it's a logistical pain in the neck. It takes up far too much time when one squad is shooting, and another is waiting to take its turn on the course. One other point: mini-courses, by their nature and size, are rarely suitable for more than one squad at a time, particularly from a safety standpoint.

Safety is absolutely critical when you're shooting in such close quarters. Barriers capable of taking a load of shot should be built around the trap machine to protect the trapper. And there should be something at each station, be it a tree trunk, a post driven into the ground, or even a portable stand, to prevent a gun from being inadvertently swung at the trap. There also should be a minimum three hundred-yard shot fall zone surrounding the course in any direction in which you shoot.

From a design standpoint, the keys to creating a successful mini-course are, first, being realistic about your budget. Quality manual sporting clays machines range from less than $400 on the used market to near $1500 in the showroom. About $750 is average. New electric automatics start at around $3000 and go up from there. So, planning a multi-directional tower set-up when you only have cash for a basic machine and the materials necessary to build barriers is a straight road to discouragement — and a quick way to end up with diddly.

Second is determining ahead of time the types of target presentations you desire. It's impossible to be exact, but, for example, if you do a lot of woods and hedgerow hunting, trying to incorporate high, floating crossing targets will only confuse your plans. And, third, having the patience to search for the correct piece of property that will allow you to put all of the pieces together. If you let common sense be your guide, the rest has a habit of falling into place.

Top-quality mini-courses are a genuine challenge even to open class tournament-grade shooters if laid out right.

Above: Fast, angling going-away targets challenge even the best of shooters when trees are in the way. (Left) Rick Spivey introduces wife, Laura, to sporting clays. Because of the mini-course's casual approach, it can be ideal for introducing new shooters to this sport. Spivey designed the courses shown in this chapter.

In the general media, to suit an upscale image and to give added respect to pulling a trigger, sporting clays has been equated to playing golf with a shotgun. If that be the case, then a temporary hobby course or practice field would be equivalent to putt-putt, and a well-designed mini-course would correspond to a par three layout. The best of the mini-courses, however, are as difficult and devious as any PGA tour stop.

Mini-courses are going to be the biggest trend in sporting clays during the next decade, because they're so practical and economically feasible both to set up and to shoot. They are for that great mass of potential hunters and shooters ignored, overlooked or flat-out snubbed by the big-ticket ranges.

If sporting clays is the best thing to happen to shotgun target shooting in a long, long time, then mini-courses that produce maxi-results are certain to advance the cause.

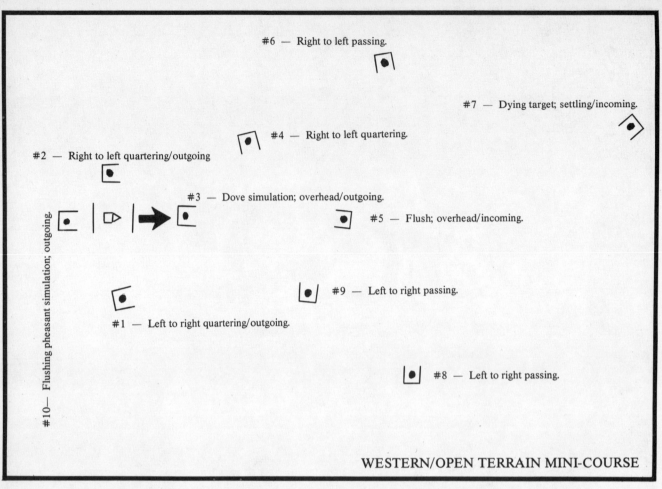

#6 — Right to left passing.

#7 — Dying target; settling/incoming.

#4 — Right to left quartering.

#2 — Right to left quartering/outgoing

#3 — Dove simulation; overhead/outgoing.

#5 — Flush; overhead/incoming.

#10 — Flushing pheasant simulation; outgoing.

#9 — Left to right passing.

#1 — Left to right quartering/outgoing.

#8 — Left to right passing.

WESTERN/OPEN TERRAIN MINI-COURSE

Trap machine is set on flat land, using brush to block the shooter's view. A shot-proof barrier is necessary in front of the trap and in rear if optional station #10 is used. Distances to targets can be varied as necessary.

THERE ARE a host of quality trap machines available to those planning a mini-course. In most cases, a basic manual machine will do the job more than adequately, and, because of the simplicity, hold up under a heavy workload for a long time with minimal maintenance. Look for a three-quarter cock machine, unless you want the added dubious benefit of building your arm muscles to match Arnold Schwarzenegger's. You'll also need a dual target arm to throw pairs, and be sure the machine offers easy adjustment for target elevation.

For those with more pennies in their piggy-bank, the automatics are wonderfully convenient. As this is being written, the word coming through the grapevine has it that there will be two fully automatic sporting clays machines, each capable of throwing true pairs, on the market soon. They are sure to be expensive, but, with remote control, they'll allow someone to shoot a course without assistance.

When it comes to targets, the major brands all offer quality. My only suggestion is to stick with full orange international types for your standard targets. Yellow and white targets, and even orange ones with a black rim, can be difficult to see if your mini-course is set up in thick cover. Using midis on a few stations can make things more interesting, but minis and battues should be used only in an open-terrain layout.

TRAPS:

Boss, P.O. Box 25141, Houston, TX 77265, 713/623-4327.

Cambron Engineering Co., (Redball), 3800 E. Wilder Road, Bay City, MI 48706, 800/626-5377.

Farey USA, Inc., (Farey), Meadows Road, Box 258, Jamaica, VT 05343, 802-874-4395.

G.H. Enterprises, (Twin Trainer), Bag 10 Okotoks, Alberta, Canada, 403/938-6070.

Hunters Pointe Mfg., (Quickfire), 14809 Timberlake Road, Wichita, KS 67230, 316/264-4686.

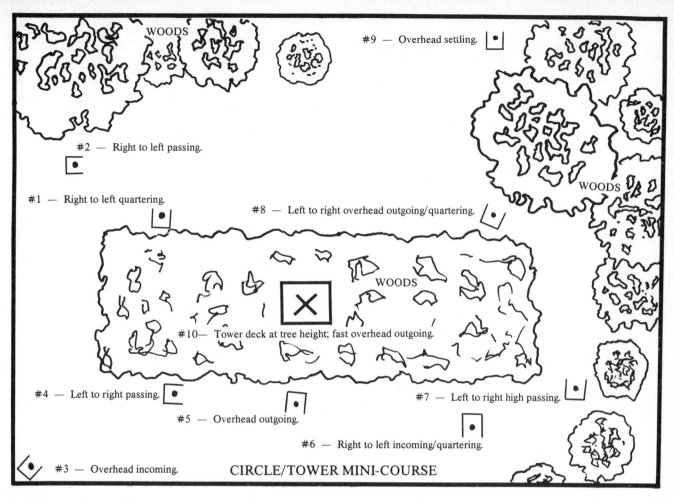

WOODS

#9 — Overhead settling.

#2 — Right to left passing.

#1 — Right to left quartering.

WOODS

#8 — Left to right overhead outgoing/quartering.

WOODS

#10— Tower deck at tree height; fast overhead outgoing.

#4 — Left to right passing.

#5 — Overhead outgoing.

#7 — Left to right high passing.

#6 — Right to left incoming/quartering.

#3 — Overhead incoming.　　CIRCLE/TOWER MINI-COURSE

Best suited for wooded terrain, tower height depends on the tallness of the trees. A two-to-one ratio is typical, a sixty-foot tower being used in thirty-foot trees. The trap machine can swivel 360 degrees and hurl 200 yards.

Listo, Inc., (Serena), Rt. 1, Box 167, Mauk, GA 31058, 912/649-7120.

Northwest Shooters Supply, 10410 Douglas Drive, Tacoma, WA 98499, 206/582-2940.

Outers, (American Sporter), 2299 Snake River Avenue, Lewiston, ID 83501, 800/635-7656.

Quack Decoy Corp., (Quack), 4 Mill Street, Cumberland, RI 02684, 401/723-8203.

Remington, (Remington), Wilmington, DE 19898, 302/773-5291.

Safari Outfitters, (Ibis), 71 Ethan Allen Highway, Ridgefield, CT 06877, 203/544-9505.

Tri-State Trap & Skeet Co., 670 Main Street, North Huntington, PA 15642, 412/864-4235.

Universal (Universal), Unit 5, Dalacre Farm Ind., Wilbarston, Market Harborough, Leic, England, 011-44-536-771-625.

Winchester, (Winchester/LaPorte), East Alton, IL 62024, 618/258-2000.

TARGETS:

Champion/Federal Targets, 232 Industrial Parkway, Richmond, IN 47374, 800/441-4971.

LaPorte Targets, Shooting Academy, RR 1, Box 56-1, Blairstown, MO 64726, 602/585-0882.

Remington Targets, Wilmington, DE 19898, 301/773-5291.

White Flyer, 124 River Road, Middlesex, NJ 08846, 908/469-0100.

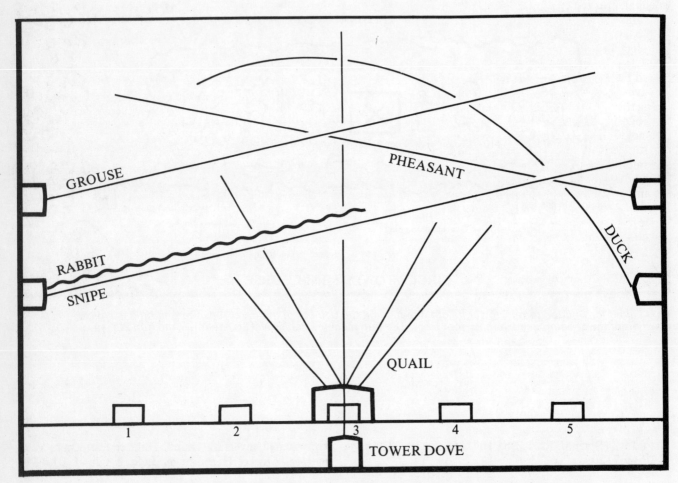

GROUSE

PHEASANT

DUCK

RABBIT

SNIPE

QUAIL

1   2   3   4   5

TOWER DOVE

This is the basic five-stand sporting clays layout that can offer plenty of excitement on minimal acreage.

SPORTING CLAYS is the hottest new shooting game in America, and it's a rare clay target shooter or hunter who isn't itching to give it a try. Unfortunately, at the moment, it's an even rarer scattergunner who has one of these facilities located close-by.

The biggest stumbling block is the amount of land required to construct a good course. Although some might be tempted to equate them with a golf course, it is a bit more complicated, since one must also take into consideration safe fall areas for the shot charge.

Beaning somebody with a golf ball is no big deal. Former President Ford did it all the time, but it is considered exceedingly poor form to do the same thing with a charge of 7½ shot! As a result, sporting clays courses often require more land than is readily available.

Time also is an enemy. As with golf, it takes a fair amount of it to negotiate one's way around the course, and if the foursome in front is a bit laggardly, that time can stretch considerably. Those operating shoot-for-pay ranges frequently find profits less than expected due to the limited number of shooters who can be accommodated.

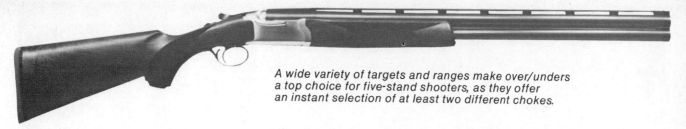

A wide variety of targets and ranges make over/unders a top choice for five-stand shooters, as they offer an instant selection of at least two different chokes.

Lastly, the game is a labor-intensive affair. Safety and common sense dictate that each shooting station have a course guide on hand, especially with novice shooters. If manual traps are employed, somebody has to man them. That takes trained people, who require salaries.

No, sporting clays is not a simple affair. But, thanks to the electronic and computer talents of the National Sporting Clays Association's advisory council member Raymond Forman, it can be made that way.

Five-stand sporting clays is a computer-driven game using the Forman-designed Birdbrain computer. Capable of programming and operating four to eight trap machines, the new game can offer virtually every shot found on a sporting clays course. Yet, the game can be run by one operator, the shooters cycled through as quickly as a fast-paced round of trap, and, best of all, the game can be shot on any existing trap or skeet field!

Some of the country's top range operators feel this new game may be the most significant thing to happen to sporting clays since it arrived from Europe.

"We have found our five-stand sporting clays course to be a major advantage," says Marty Fischer, manager of the Cherokee Rose Shooting Resort in Griffin, Georgia. "Our emphasis is on group entertainment and we needed a field game that could be shot day or night, rain or shine. Five-stand fits that bill beautifully, because with covered shooting stations on a skeet-size field, rain is no problem. Also, the field is small enough to be lighted inexpensively for night shooting.

"Inclement weather can close down a full-size sporting clays course," notes Fischer, "but with the five-stand field we can shoot day or night, twelve months a year. It is a commercial range operator's dream."

While the new game does have a lot of logistic advantages, don't be lulled into thinking of it as just a fast-food version of sporting clays. It is an exciting and challenging game in its own right. In fact, it can be a good bit tougher than full-scale sporting clays!

"There actually are two versions of this new game," continues Fischer. "The original five-stand version utilizes

In five-stand shooting, one may shoot against a wide variety of backgrounds in a confined area.

There may not be the degree of laughing and scratching comraderie in five-stand that one sees in tournament-type sporting clays, but the fun still is there, and the game constitutes a challenge for better shooting.

the Birdbrain computer, and a newer version called super sporting uses a less sophisticated — and less expensive — control box. Each of these control units can operate a minimum of four and a maximum of eight trap machines resulting in a large variety of target angles and presentations."

In the original five-stand game, the computer programs the machine to give each shooter the same shots per station, but in a random order. The shooter does not know which target will come out when he calls for the bird. Level one will see all singles at each station. Level two gives three singles and one true pair, while the toughest setting— level three — offers two true pairs and one single.

At the third level — or even the second — this game is even tougher than regular sporting clays, because you don't know what you will get until the targets actually are in the air.

Fischer finds that degree of difficulty pays dividends in a most unexpected way.

"One of the greatest advantages to five-stand, when it comes to attracting new shooters," he explains, "is that nobody is going to hit them all. Even the best will miss and that is comforting to new shooters. You take a guy with a twenty-eight-inch-barrel modified-choke Remington 870 pump who shoots birds a couple of times a year and doesn't shoot any other time, then put him on a skeet range with some steely-eyed AAA-class shooter toting a $10,000 Kreighoff

On many skeet fields, low house can be used to throw the mallard target that rises quickly, then will settle in the middle of the field, the author found.

On the left side of the field is a machine that can throw a ground-bouncing rabbit or a quartering snipe target singly or as pairs.

who hasn't missed a target in ten years, the newcomer is going to be embarrassed and probably won't come back. Put them both on a five-stand course, however, and things start to even out. The hunter also will get targets in five-stand that really will help him with his field shooting — not always the case with trap and skeet."

The newer super sporting version offers the same targets. The difference is that the shooter does know the order in which the targets will be presented and can set himself for the expected targets. It makes it a little easier and has a major side benefit.

"Super sporting," says Fischer, "is under consideration and undoubtably will be incorporated into the Olympic Games as an exhibition sport. The fact that the targets are known is important here, because television and spectators need to know what is coming next if they are to follow the action.

"That also gives range operators the ability to duplicate the Olympic course of fire and will allow shooters to see how they compare to the Olympic competitors."

What exactly will the Olympic shooters face? The game is new enough — and sufficiently versatile — that a stan-

dardized course really has yet to be developed. Given the option of incorporating four to eight machines per control box, course designers can come up with some interesting shooting situations.

On the five-stand field at Cherokee Rose, shooters enter the field and are faced with five shooting stations under cover, all set in a straight line just like a trap line. Each station has side partitions to limit overswinging and excessive gun travel as is standard in sporting clays. Each shooter is assigned a station and will be presented with five targets at that station. He then will rotate to the next station, as is done in trap. A total of twenty-five targets comprise a round, so more than one box of shells is a wise idea.

On the far left side of the field is trap number 1 which launches a ground-bouncing rabbit target that quarters to the middle of the field. A zipping snipe target follows a similar path through the air. Farther into the field on the left side is trap number 2, the grouse. This can be one of the toughest shots on the field, a quick quartering or long crosser — depending upon the station being shot from — that gets out there in a hurry!

Left: Grouse target can be the toughest on the field. It gets away in a hurry and is easy to miss. (Below) Single-barrel guns give a good account of themselves, if the shooter selects an open choke, more powerful loads.

Sporting clays shooters seem to come in all sizes, age groups and a variety of shapes these days. The game is one that can be enjoyed by almost anyone who enjoys shooting, presenting a special challenge to competitors.

Trap number 3 is a wobbling trap located just forward of and below the shooting line that launches flushing quail targets at a number of different angles. Located on the roof of the shooting station is the dove tower that launches blind to the shooter and sends a high, outgoing target. On the far right is the duck trap, climbing quickly, then settling equally fast in the middle of the field.

Farther into the field, on the right, is the pheasant trap, another fast-climbing flusher, but this one doesn't stop! Additional plans are to include a seventh trap well out into the field, screened by trees, that throws a high-climbing target which reaches its apex, then drops straight down!

Anybody for some blind doubles — true pairs — on level three five-stand? How about a rabbit and a tower dove? Or maybe a snipe and a grouse? Why not a duck and grouse?

These are tough enough to master with repeated practice from one station, but each flight angle changes as the shooter changes stations! You'll never see the same shot twice in a round of five-stand.

Anyone who thinks sporting clays is becoming easy might consider a round of this. Chris Christian, who handled this report, can personally assure you it is a mind-boggling experience and a most humbling one, as well! "On some occasions, when I was thrown doubles, not only

Five-stand or super sporting are ideal games for any commercial range. They require little space, and with a covered shooting line can be played day or night, rain or shine. These variations have their advantages.

did I not see one of the targets, but never even realized it had been thrown until a chuckling Marty Fischer pointed the fact out to me,'' Christian reports. ''This new game compares to standard sporting clays like sporting clays compares to skeet. It could hardly be considered a fast-food version!''

''Five stand and super sporting,'' Fischer feels, ''may have the greatest future of any shooting game I've yet seen. That includes rifle and pistol games, as well. There are millions of shotgun owners out there who want a game more realistic and challenging than trap or skeet, but really don't have anything available.

''These games require no more space than trap and skeet and can be set up quickly on existing fields, even using some of the existing trap and skeet machines.''

Shooters won't be well off, however, utilizing standard trap and skeet techniques. A shooter stepping up to a five-stand or super sporting field for the first time is going to be playing a new game, and that calls for a slight change in tactics.

''If I'm shooting five-stand,'' Fischer explains, ''and I don't know where the target is coming from, I have to take a good deal of care with my foot and starting gun position at each station. Basically, I will align my body to the center of

Unlike full-scale sporting clays, both of these newer games can be controlled by a single operator to cycle shooters through quickly. These fast-paced games are reported to turn profits for range operators.

the field, since every target thrown will pass through it.

"The exception to this," he continues, "is if I know that one of the targets that might be presented on that station could be a problem. On station one, for example, that would be the grouse target. It can come out quickly, and if you are late getting on it, the bird can get out there a long way and become a long, tough quartering target. If this target has not yet been thrown to me at that station, I will hedge a bit toward it in order to help get on it a bit quicker."

In super sporting, where all targets are known, Fischer advises proceeding exactly as you would on a regular sporting clays course: Analyze the target, determine where you want to break it, then set the body up to break it at that point.

The same also can be done in five-stand should you get a broken (no-bird) target out of a trap. The machine will rethrow that target and this is the only time in the game you will know what target is coming when you call for it, and can set the body to break that bird.

As in sporting clays, the low-gun position is used and the gun cannot be mounted until the bird is released. Where you set the initial gun position, however, can play a major role in your success.

"Never start with the muzzle held above the flight path of the lowest target presented (obviously excepting the ground-hugging rabbit)," Fischer cautions. "The reason is that, if your muzzle is above the flight path, you create a blind spot under the gun that can prevent you from picking up that target in time to break it. This applies to any sporting clays course, but is doubly critical here. You don't know what target is going to be thrown next, and you must be able to pick up any target quickly enough to break it.

"If the target goes under the barrel, it is no different than the blind spot most automobiles have. You can't see, and you'll miss the target initially. Now you have to refocus on it, and your timing will be off. You'll usually miss any target — except the rabbit which moves a bit slower than the aerial targets — that comes out under the gun."

Given the wide variety of targets that can be presented, choosing the proper choke for each station might seem a confusing task. According to Fischer, however, it's not.

"The best choke is improved cylinder, and I would suggest it for all five stations," he advises. "More scores are

Because the targets are thrown in random order, Marty Fischer positions his body to cover the center of the field, where the targets must pass, instead of lining up on any one particular trap. Five-stand can be rough!

improved by opening chokes than by tightening them, but this holds true in any sporting clays game. If you're shooting a single-barrel gun, improved cylinder is going to be your most effective choice, since you may get targets ranging anywhere from fifteen to forty yards.

While Fischer doesn't recommend shifting chokes between stands, he does suggest changing shells.

"Most targets can be handled well with a light load of #8s," he observes, "but if you know a long target — thirty-five to forty yards-plus — is likely to come up, it's a good idea to slip in a 3-dram 1⅛ #7½ load, or even one of the newer international loads. From an IC-choked gun, these will break any forty-yard target. Remember, we only have to knock a visible piece off the target; we don't grade them.

The facilities at Cherokee Rose offer a variety of challenges to a broad span of shooters who want to develop their capabilities fully.

Federal's new sporting clays loads in 12, 20 gauges have fiber wads that are biodegradable.

For long-range targets, a new international load is made with 7½ shot.

Changing stations also changes the angle of the target from each house in five-stand. This makes the game an even greater challenge, because it means a shooter will not see the same shot twice in a round, author says.

It's either a hit or a miss and a couple of #7½s from a slightly higher velocity load will get you that visible piece."

Shooters opting for over/unders obviously have a wider range of choke options, but Fischer still feels beginning shooters are better off with open chokes.

While the new game may be challenging, it is not that complicated in terms of the shooter's equipment, nor is the equipment difficult to install.

The original Birdbrain computer provides the option of shooting both five-stand (random targets) and super sporting (known targets). An additional machine being made available through the National Sporting Clays Association

(P.O. Box 680007, San Antonio, TX 78268) plays only super sporting, but is considerably less expensive.

Either control station allows the game to be set up on any skeet or trap field. In fact, NSCA has a turn-key package available that offers a complete setup that can convert standard trap and skeet fields quickly into super sporting.

"That's the real beauty of this game," Fischer has found. "It's a simple setup that can create an exciting and challenging new game. As a range operator, I can attest to the fact that once this game is set up, the shooters will come. It is going to be the hottest shooting game in the country."

Good facilities make a good impression. While building elaborate shooting stations like this one on the five-stand field at Cherokee Rose may seem a lot of trouble, it does pay dividends in the long run, management finds.

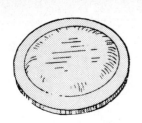

CHAPTER 22

WINNING THE CUSTOMER GAME

Operating a Successful Sporting Clays Range Is More Than Just Throwing Targets!

O N THE surface, sporting clays would seem to be an entrepreneur's dream. As one of the fastest-growing and most popular shooting sports in the country, the game still is new enough that there exists a paucity of places to play it. It certainly would seem that opening such a facility near any reasonably large population center would be enough to keep the targets flying, the guns booming, the cash register ringing.

Unfortunately, that's not always the case, and Marty Fischer knows that quite well.

"Anybody who opens a range, then sits back and waits for customers, probably isn't going to be in business long. Running a successful commercial shooting range is a lot more complicated than just throwing targets," Fischer told Our Man in the South, Chris Christian.

At age 39, this personable Georgia native has a job that many serious shooters would envy. As the general manager of the Cherokee Rose Shooting Resort in Griffin, Georgia, he is tasked with the responsibility of running what many expert sporting clays shooters consider the finest facility of its type in the world.

A certified sporting clays instructor and a top-ranked competitor, Fischer finds plenty of time to enjoy the various clay target games Cherokee Rose offers, whether it is aiding students in sharpening their game, or keeping his own hand in.

A dream job? Yes, but as Fischer has found, one that takes considerable thought and effort. Here are some of the ways Fischer helped turn 125 acres of North Georgia hill country into one of the world's most renowned commercial shooting ranges.

INITIAL SET-UP:

"Building a good sporting clays course can be as expensive and elaborate as one wants to make it," Fischer says. "The most important thing to do before you begin con-

Marty Fischer (right) explains the upcoming field to Jack Mitchell. Fischer feels a personal touch is a requirement if a range is to prove to be successful.

Extra touches to improve the quality of the shooting range don't take that much time and effort. Safety is a facet of operation that must never be ignored.

Fischer's philosophy of buying and building the best is demonstrated with the dove tower set-up. Automated machines offer a wide latitude in shifting the targets.

struction is to make certain local zoning laws allow you to do everything you want to do — and locks you in to allow you to keep doing it.

"If you don't pay attention to this important, but often overlooked item, fifty homeowners that move in around you next week could take away the range you may have spent years building."

It is not uncommon for developers to purchase land next to less-than-desirable neighbors (shooting ranges, small airports, industrial parks) because such land is relatively inexpensive.

A sub-division is built; homes sold to folks looking for cheap property. Then when enough of them gather together, they attempt to change the zoning to remove or restrict the activities of the "neighbor" who was responsible for providing them with cheap property in the first place! It's a common situation nationwide.

"When we first began planning Cherokee Rose, we hired a good attorney who understood what we wanted to do, and got the type of zoning that will grandfather us in down the road if some guy comes in and wants to build a subdivision next door."

Zoning is a boring subject, but a mandatory one. As a side benefit, it is much easier to obtain bank loans for future development if your zoning is rock solid.

SELECTING EQUIPMENT

Here's another area where inattention can hurt in the long run.

"When we decided to fully automate the course," Fischer explains, "we elected to buy what we felt was the best available target presentation equipment, the Swedish-made Beomat machine. It was more expensive initially, but by using all the same machines, we reduced the inventory of spare parts we had to carry and simplified maintenance.

This elaborate shooting station is just one of many custom touches that help to make an all-important first impression. The Cherokee Rose operators have come to know a good first impression means repeat customers.

"Another advantage of automated machines is a tremendous reduction in the number of people required to operate the range; that saves salaries. Top-quality, automated machines have proven to actually be far less expensive in the long run than bargain-priced equipment."

How true! There are examples on the reverse side. One small Florida skeet club felt it was not drawing enough shooters because it lacked trap facilities. The governing board of the club — primarily skeet shooters — decided to buy the cheapest used trap machine they could find. They installed it, but it never worked properly and no one knew how to fix it!

When they put up their new sign saying *Skeet & Trap Club,* trap shooters came — and grew disgusted when every other target came out of the house broken! Targets were wasted, range fees had to be refunded and the club got a bad reputation. Trap shooters don't go there anymore.

It was a money-losing proposition that could have been a money-maker had someone had the foresight to spend a few more dollars initially.

"Just purchasing the best equipment," Fischer cautions, "won't prevent all problems. Anything mechanical can break and we made sure our initial purchase allowed for back-up machines. We also sent some of our people to

school to learn how to repair those machines quickly and properly."

Fischer knows nothing is as frustrating to a paying customer as having to stand around and wait while someone scratches his head trying to figure out how to get a machine to work.

Cherokee Rose also has a number of manual machines — and the people to man them — for such emergencies. In fact, at a recent major tournament, one Beomat did go down, and the broken part was not easily replaceable. It took only minutes to plug in a manual machine and operator and the shoot continued, missing barely a beat!

"Being prepared to handle that type of emergency not only saves customers," Fischer has found, "but it will enhance your reputation and actually gain new customers by word of mouth."

COURSE DESIGN

Securing proper zoning and purchasing top flight equipment requires money and lawyers, but it is what you do with those items that will play a major role in your success.

"I feel one of the biggest problems with many sporting clay ranges," states Fischer, "is in course design. All too

This shooting field is an excellent example of a clean, attractive place to shoot. Note the conveniently located trash can, ice water dispenser. Butt kits also are in the stand, helping to create a good impression.

often, the goal is to make the course tough. In reality, we have found that to be self-defeating.

"Sporting clays is intended to be hunting without blood and feathers, so why present unrealistic and unfair targets? If you are going to present a quail or a snipe target, it should be set at the speed at which those birds actually fly, not at eighty-five miles per hour. Unfortunately, there are many courses that think target speed is a substitute for creativity in the set up of the course.

"You can do much more to impress the shooter by changing angles and presentations than you can with pure target speed."

Fischer feels — and his experience has borne out — that creating a tough course does not necessarily hurt the range operator with the die-hard competitive shooters. They'll shoot anything and consider it a challenge.

But is that the group to whom the successful range operator should cater? Fischer thinks not!

"You can't expect the serious competitive shooter to provide enough business to keep your doors open," he explains. "There simply aren't enough of them, and you probably won't see them, unless you are hosting a tournament — which you can't do seven days a week! To be successful in this business you must appeal to the untapped market."

According to Fischer, that market is threefold:

1. Hunters: "There are millions of wingshooters out there who do not shoot clay targets on a regular basis, but would if they had a game that was more field-realistic and fun than trap and skeet. We can offer that."

A malfunctioning range doesn't make money, chases away repeat customers. This manual trap adds a bit of spice to a functioning field. It could be used to restore a down field to full operation in a matter of minutes.

2. Women: "There are a great many women out there who enjoy physical sports; golf, tennis, jogging, handball or whatever. Sporting clays is a fascinating game that requires hand-eye coordination and the use of equipment. You don't have to have a desire to hunt or kill. This game can be played for its own sake — and a surprising number of women enjoy it."

(Fischer also notes that they often make better students, and become competent — much more quickly than many men!)

3. Children: "This is the biggest overlooked market, yet one of the most important, since they are the future of this sport.

"If you accept this line of reasoning," Marty Fischer continues, "then it doesn't make a lot of sense to offer a course that will challenge the most expert shooter. You will just frustrate your new shooters — and probably lose them."

This philosophy has been a major factor in how Fischer has set up his courses of fire.

"Our championship course was designed by Gordon Phillip, who did a masterful job of utilizing natural terrain features to produce an interesting and attractive course," Fischer states. "All I did was explore the possibilities of making a more varied presentation through the redirection of electronic machines, the use of temporary manual traps and moveable shooting stands."

What resulted is a championship course that can be shifted quickly to produce virtually any degree of difficulty. If a group of steely-eyed competitive shooters show up, the

The course can be adjusted to the talents of individual shooters. A real pro gets a lot of really tough birds.

course can be as "tough" a course as one will find anywhere. If, however, for a group of wide-eyed novices, it can be much more user-friendly.

"The initial decision to purchase top-quality machines," Fischer notes, "allows us a great deal of variation in our course and target presentation. Being able to offer a continually shifting course of fire, with degrees of difficulty appropriate to those shooting the course, is one of the most important factors in being able to please all your customers, from the most veteran competitors down to the first-time shooters."

Fischer, however, goes even further in offering a varied fare.

"Once the championship course was in place, the next thing we did was to use those shot-fall areas to set up a small-gauge course. The targets are closer, slower and

This young lady is not a hunter, but enjoys the challenge of sporting clays. In catering to new shooters, Fischer sees that she gets excellent instruction, as well as advice on obtaining proper equipment, including guns. (Below) After the shot has been made, Fischer discusses what this newcomer did right and what she did wrong.

easier. It allows .410 and 28-gauge shooters to experience sporting clays.

"But that sub-gauge course also has proven to be our biggest asset when it comes to dealing with new shooters. You can't send a first-time shooter out onto a tough course where they can't break any targets. You frustrate them and that is not fun....they don't enjoy the experience and they don't come back."

"The little course is just tough enough to challenge, and just easy enough to reward the novice to the point where one feels a sense of accomplishment and wants to continue.

"That," he grins, "is the single largest factor we have found in turning interested first-time visitors into enthusiastic return customers. Every satisfied return customer you can create makes you that much more successful."

Offering a variety of shooting games is another way to bring shooters back, and the menu at Cherokee Rose is one of the most varied in the country. In addition to two sporting clays courses — a third in the planning stages — they also offer a five-stand sporting clays field, driven by the Birdbrain computer, skeet, a dove tower with five stations, bunker trap, tree flush games, and the only Starshot layout in the southeast!

"The more you can offer shooters," Fischer feels, "the more shooters you are going to attract. In the commercial range business, anytime you don't have shooters on the line, your cash register is not ringing."

It takes money to make money; that's an old axiom that has proved to be true in sporting clays. Building challenges into the game can be a costly proposition, as illustrated by this elevated stand for the shooter.

Simply bringing shooters through the front gate, however, is no guarantee of success. Fischer makes every effort to make certain they come back.

CATERING TO CUSTOMERS

"If you have a good course that runs smoothly, the serious shooters will be coming back, but the real key," Fischer claims, "is to create a new shooter from the curious first-time visitor.

"To do that, you can't simply point them in the direction of the range and tell them to have a good time. You have to help them find the fun!"

When novice shooters arrive at Cherokee Rose, they are greeted by a top-quality instructor who puts them through a brief but comprehensive indoctrination course. Among items covered are proper, safe gun handling, basic shooting instruction (with more advanced courses also offered), tips for shooting sporting clays, as well as checking the customer's gun fit and even determining which is the master eye! If the shooters arrive sans guns, Cherokee Rose has Remington 11-87 and Beretta A303 rental guns on hand.

"If that sounds like a lot of unnecessary effort," Fischer states, "think about this: How many people go to a golf course for the first time and have the club pro come up and

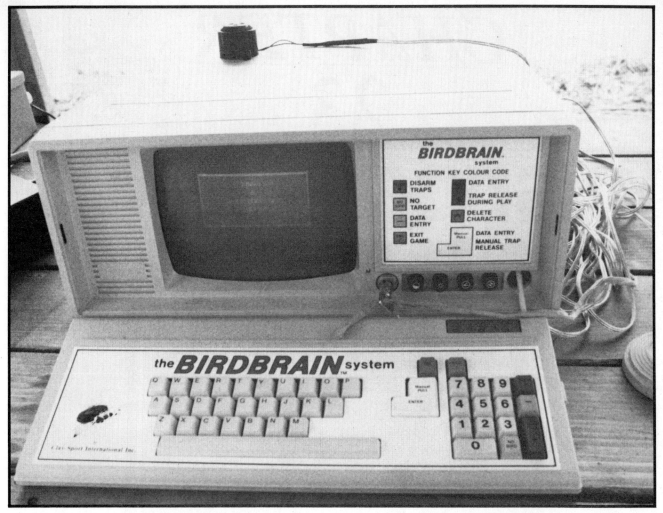

The electronic age has entered sporting clays and the Birdbrain computer can be programmed to operate course. The various challenges to the shooter can be altered by a change in the computer program; it's done periodically.

give them a free lesson? Not many! But, we have found this approach brings many of these people back looking for more."

Once the indoctrination is over, the instructor also has a pretty good idea of which course to send the shooters through to make sure they enjoy their trip.

"As a commercial range operator," Fischer feels, "you not only hold the future of your business in your hand, but the future of the sport itself. Why screw it up if it only takes a little more effort to do it right?"

Doing it right, according to Fischer, also encompasses a few things many ranges ignore.

"If you can't impress shooters on the first visit, there is a good chance they won't make a second visit. Impressing a shooter with your facilities goes far beyond simply having a variety of interesting shooting courses."

Fischer is convinced the majority of shooting ranges are not the most well-maintained pieces of property around. Trash, cigarette butts, fired hulls and general course litter may not make an unfavorable impression on die-hard shooters, but it does turn-off some new shooters....the group most range operators fail to accommodate!

"It doesn't take a lot of thought and effort to put out butt kits and trash cans, letting shooters know you expect they

be used. Actually, they appreciate the fact you are going to those lengths to offer them a clean, well-maintained facility.

"And it doesn't hurt to make certain the staff adheres to a uniform dress code, even if you have to provide them with club T-shirts.

"We stress to our personnel," Fischer states, "that the customers they deal with are the most important people they will meet that day. Without those customers, none of us would have a job!

"That doesn't mean they let customers walk all over them and do whatever they want on the course," Fischer notes. "We insist on safety first and fun second. Course guides will be firm with those who fail to understand that. All of our course guides are qualified to administer those rules, because they have been through an approved hunter safety course, as well as passing our own written tests regarding firearms safety and the rules of sporting clays.

"Still," he adds, "your on-the-scene personnel can make a major impact on customers. The more time you take to select and train your people, the better the impression they will make."

That sums up Fischer's "Guide For Running a Commercial Range."

CHAPTER 23

WISDOM FROM A CHAMPION

"KK" Kennerknecht Offers His Thoughts On The Right Way To Win, The Wrong Way To Try!

Kennerknecht, on a shooting stand, is ready to call for the target, gun positioned.

AS MUCH as timing makes all the difference in hitting targets, timing played a pivotal role in the making of one of sporting clays' true American champions. Rick "KK" Kennerknecht of Lomita, California, shot up through the ranks of sporting clays following his first exposure to the then-new game in 1987. Within a matter of months, he became one of the really consistent performers at the world level. His credits and accomplishments continue to grow in both number and stature, and he can be found at almost every really major event around the world.

Through his own experiences, KK can help others who are interested in furthering their efforts in sporting clays — whether they are interested in becoming serious competitors, or just interested in shooting their best recreationally. He is also happy to share a host of helpful "tips" and "secrets" which contribute to making a champion a champion. For KK, as has been the case with shotgunners through the years, his shooting career began as a hunter. In the traditional manner, Kennerknecht's father, Dick (Papa KK), introduced Rick to hunting when Rick was a young child. And his father has played an important role in supporting Rick's shooting through the years. KK also credits much of his success to support from other members of his family — mother Sharon and sister Karon.

"Howard Otamura and I were doing some off-season, springtime work at the Denvo Duck Club in Southern California, just across the Santa Ana River from Dan Carlisle's Shotgun Sports sporting clays facility," KK recalled as he thought back to the time he first learned about sporting clays. "I had shot just a little bit of registered skeet back in 1982, and that was it, when it came to any kind of competition."

Carlisle, at that time, had recently entered civilian life after having completed a world championship career as a shooter with the U.S. Army's Marksmanship Training Unit at Fort Benning, Georgia. An Olympic medalist and world record holder in clay target shooting at that time, Carlisle was chief instructor nationally for the U.S. Sporting Clays Association and one of the recognized leaders in the growing sport. Hence, KK's first exposure to the new game was via input from one of the finest shotgunners in the world today.

But serious competition in sporting clays was not even a possible dream for KK that day when he first was exposed to it.

"In fact, I hadn't even played any kind of competitive sports in high school," KK continued as he thought back to that day at the duck club. "Howard and I heard all that shooting, so we hopped into the car and drove over to Carlisle's. He had a tournament going in which the top five scorers were going to be able to go over to England to compete in sporting clays, representing the United States. That was to be the first team which ever competed in England

On this sporting clays course, an actual goose pit has been constructed, giving realism to the challenge.

from the United States and it was to be composed of winners from that tournament.

"The winners and members of that first team were Dan Carlisle, Tom Strunk, Alan Owens, Dan Reeves and Jay Braccini," KK remembered. "Howard and I stayed there for about an hour and watched those guys shoot, and thought it looked like a lot of fun. So, the next weekend when we went out to the duck club, we took our guns with us and took some time out to go over to Carlisle's course and have a go at it."

That was the beginning, and Rick Kennerknecht, then 26 years old, got into the game seriously and quickly. He shot his first tournament in July, 1987. It was called the Golden State Sporting Clays Open, which was the equivalent of the first California State Sporting Clays Championships. KK took high overall, hitting 83 of the 100 targets in the event. In all, about eighty shooters competed in that event at the Carlisle facilites, which were located on the grounds of the Raahauge's Pheasant Hunting Club in Norco, California.

The next tournament he entered was six months later — the Southwest Sporting Clays Open, which was a regional championship. In that shoot, he took high overall, as well. With those two initial wins, KK was well on his way to

making a name for himself in the early days of the fastest growing of the American shooting sports.

"Dan Carlisle had an influence on me at that time, encouraging me to go out and shoot other courses," KK explained, noting that until then, he had not shot sporting clays at any other range. It was during a meeting with Carlisle and two other range operators — Dick Haldeman and Mike Raahauge — that the map for KK's shooting future was laid out.

"A group of us Americans went over to England to shoot in the Beretta World Championships held at the Apsley Shooting Grounds," he explained, noting that there had been a warm-up tour of some of the other shooting facilities in England before the Americans entered the main event at Apsley.

"We fielded three teams, and one of them took the bronze medal in the team event," KK continued, but he was not a member of that team. Important to the young competitor then, however, was the learning experience. The target presentations over there were so different from those he had experienced in the United States that it gave KK a real insight into what to start practicing for and what to expect at national and international level events.

"Once you shoot internationally, you'll never be the

same," noted KK, who has competed internationally in four European countries every year since 1988.

"There are really no hard-and-fast rules for learning how to shoot," KK advises. "Certainly, you want to shoot all of the regional, state and national championships. Basically, you need to begin with a desire to get out there and do the best that you can, and shoot at as many different courses as you can.

"Most of those who are shooting really well are competing just about every weekend. These days, there are tournaments you can go to about every week, so you are never at a loss to be able to shoot in a tournament under competitive conditions. You can pretty much go through the association magazines like *Sporting Clays* magazine of the NSCA and *Shotgun Sports* magazine of the USSCA and see which of the shoots are going to be high visibility and high intensity. It is easy to tell that by how much prize money they're offering, who is sponsoring it or what sort of championship is at stake. Those usually will be the shoots where you can compete against the other guys who are at the top.

"The confidence you can build by beating these shooters you once thought were unbeatable — the guys who were always at the top — does a lot for your confidence and that will reflect in better scores, no matter where you shoot.

"Practice is important. Practice with people who are better shots than you are. You can learn a lot from shooting with champions. Watch their techniques and try them for yourself. You may not be able to shoot exactly the way they do, but you can derive your own technique and mould what you've learned into your own style.

"Most good shots are willing to help out. There also are coaches who can help you in your game, but pick your coach wisely. Get several recommendations before you make your decision. There are a lot of shooters who think they are coaches, but have no business coaching. Talk to some of their students, or call the National Sporting Clays Association at (800) 877-5338 and ask for the certified coach nearest to you. Picking the wrong coach could be a costly mistake.

"You should also practice before a tournament. I know a lot of people who try to go out and burn up three hundred or four hundred rounds in practice the day before a tournament. I think you actually can shoot yourself out. What I mean by that is that you can shoot too much all at once at the last minute, and if you develop a bad habit or something like that, it's kind of hard to get out of it one or two days before a tournament.

"If you practice a couple of hundred targets during the week before the tournament, you will be in better shape for

Kennerknecht is ready to shoot a crossing pair of targets, whether coming from the right or left.

the actual competition. One or two days before a tournament, I try not to shoot more than one hundred rounds. During a major tournament, there are a lot of re-entry events which are side games like flurry shoots. A little bit of practice on something like that is helpful, just to get your game going during the actual tournament.

"Even with all of this, it is possible, and probably predictable that any shooter will go into a slump from time to time. It is this way in any sport. The best way to get out of a slump, if you find that you're into it for more than a week or two, is to get some expert you trust to analyze your shooting to see what you are doing wrong.

ment. A lot of people, when they hear the word "tournament," are nervous and feel they can't handle much pressure. The more tournaments you shoot, the more you are able to deal with tournament pressure.

"If you get out there and you don't feel any tournament pressue — and you are a high-level shooter — there is something wrong. I think you have to have that little butterfly in your stomach when shooting. If you don't, then you are not concentrating enough. It sounds funny, but it is true.

"After a certain point, you have to be able to read all the targets — at least have an idea of how you are reading the

Although sporting clays is shot from the low-gun position, low is a matter of interpretation, as seen.

"A lot of people try to shoot themselves out of a slump by shooting and shooting and shooting. Sometimes, if you are not careful, you could be simply reinforcing bad habits by doing that. These bad habits can be little things you are not sure why you are doing them — or you may not be aware you are doing them at all. So, instead of just trying to shoot your way out of it, get with a friend or with a fellow shooter who knows what he's doing and can tell you what you are doing wrong, and help you get out of it. You save a lot of time and a lot of money by doing it like that.

"There is one way to help maintain the competitive edge over time. Get out there and shoot tournaments. Shooting a tournament is good practice for shooting another tourna-

targets — and have a good, working knowledge of the sport. Then it comes down to the mental part of the game, and how much you can concentrate and remember what you are supposed to be doing.

"Reading targets, or figuring out exactly how they are going through the air in relation to the shooting stand is critically important. Terrain, landscape, trees and bushes will be deceptive a lot of times. A good course owner can throw deceptive targets on his course. Targets, for example, may look like they are crossing and rising when actually they are crossing but falling. Or targets that actually are going downhill may look like risers. Others that look like risers may be falling off. There are all sorts of different ways this can be done. Hence, if you go ahead and shoot the shot while deceived, you are going to miss. Reading targets is extremely important.

"There also is a need for top shooters to be able to take advantage of the various shooting techniques. I use quite a few of them. A good, overall knowledge of the come-from-behind technique, the sustained lead (move, mount, shoot), and sometimes even a spot shot technique are important. A good, working knowledge of how to execute all of those techniques will come in handy, and each can be used in a lot of different instances. Here is where reading targets comes into play again. The better you can read a target and know exactly what it is doing, the easier it is to decide which technique will work best and most consistently.

"Having a goal also is highly important for anyone who is a top shooter — or who would like to be one of the best. If you want to become an All-American or to become a Team USA member, setting a realistic goal for yourself is important. Keeping that goal in mind at all times while you're shooting gives you an incentive to work harder, and to get to the point where you want to be. Once you get to that point, you may want to re-set your goal higher, or you may want to set your goal to maintain your current status. For example, since there are two sporting clays associations in the United States, you might first decide to become an All-American in one of them. Once you achieve that goal, you might want to become an All-American in the other group, as well. So, having a goal is terribly important.

"There are some who really do shoot just for fun, even though they shoot a lot and are in the major competitions. You're going to find a lot of people who shoot tournaments just for fun.

"I would guess only about ten to twenty percent of the people who shoot sporting clays ever register any targets. And this also can be a goal — to shoot in certain tour-

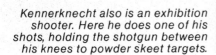

Kennerknecht also is an exhibition shooter. Here he does one of his shots, holding the shotgun between his knees to powder skeet targets.

One Kennerknecht trick is to turn his back to the targets to shoot, holding gun with only his right hand. It requires muscle!

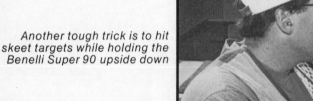

Another tough trick is to hit skeet targets while holding the Benelli Super 90 upside down

naments, even if you never intend to try to be a champion. There is a lot more to winning than just a score. Winning is fulfillment, and that can mean different things to different people. Sporting clays has room for every kind of person, and each person needs to look within himself or herself, decide what the sport means personally, then go out and do what is necessary for it to have a personal meaning.

"After a certain point, sponsorships become a matter for consideration by many of the better shooters. The sport is expensive; there are no two ways about it. The better you get, the more you want to get out and travel. When you go to the big shoots, you have airfare to pay, you have the expenses of hotels, car rentals, entry fees.

"Entry fees alone can run $250, and if you want to play all the options, you can easily pay another $200 on the options as well. It's easy to get to $2000 or $2500 if you go across the United States to shoot someplace in a major tournament. Add to this the cost of ammunition and all of the other things which come up, and the sport stays expensive. So anytime you have sponsorship, it helps. It's important to be able to afford to continue to shoot against the other shooters who you're trying to win against.

"A good gun and good stock fit are really important. A lot of people don't bother to get a stock to fit properly. Even I didn't do that until just about a year and a half ago. Many times people wonder why a gun is beating them up, or recoiling too hard. Good stock fit will help you break a couple of extra targets or more in a given shoot.

"The kind of gun you use can be most important. There are a couple of top shooters, including Dan Carlisle, who use semi-automatics, but probably ninety-five percent or more of the top shooters use over/unders. Why? Balance, for one thing. And, with an over/under, you have a selection of barrels so you can shoot either the top barrel or the bottom barrel first. Also with an over/under, you have the opportunity to shoot two different chokes during those times when there is a close target and a distant target in a particular presentation. That way, you can put in an open choke for the close target and a tight choke for the distant target. This is something you can't do with a single barrel gun.

"Reliability is another factor. A lot less can go wrong with an over/under mechanically than with a semi-automatic, simply because there are fewer moving parts. If something does go wrong with a gun, it breaks your concentration, and you want to avoid any such possibilities. The game is complicated enough without adding more problems."

Kennerknecht has been a three-time Sporting Clays All-American — every year since 1989 — and was a Team USA member in 1988 and 1989.

To be an All-American in the United States Sporting Clays Association, a shooter must shoot a minimum number of registered targets — 1200 at this time — at a minimum of five different facilities. He or she must shoot the nationals, and maintain an AA classification average each year. To be classified AA, the shooter must break at least seventy-eight percent of all registered targets.

For the National Sporting Clays Association, the formula is more complex, but also reflects top performance at major shoots on the state, regional and national level.

Outdoor Life magazine has sponsored the USSCA All-

With Alps as a backdrop, Kennerknecht holds his Perazzi Sporter with which he competed in Switzerland in 1980.

Left: The Californian shoots English sporting clays at Mid-Norfolk Shooting Grounds. Art Smith keeps score.

Kennerknecht shot in 1988 Beretta World Championships held at the famed Apsley Shooting Grounds in Britain.

Bob Allen shot with Kennerknecht during the 1991 Flash Cup shoot. This event was conduclted in Poitiers, France.

The 1990 Team USA members took the gold medal at the Internationaux de Nantes. From left are: Jon Kruger, Doug Fowler, C.C. Hoagland, Dan Reeves, Kennerknecht.

American team since its inception in 1988. Kennerknecht is one of only four people who have maintained All-American status since 1989.

The first Team USA was selected in 1989 from among USSCA members with international competition experience who were considered to be goodwill ambassadors for the sport. This procedure continued for the first two years, then a more complex selection procedure was initiated, requiring All-American status as well as a high performance record for the previous year.

Kennerknecht urges any serious shooter to keep good records. "Keep a record of your accomplishments," he insists. "Retain copies of all the media exposure (written and electronic) that you receive for your accomplishments. Construct a Shooter's Bio (resume) and keep it updated. This is a great reference for potential sponsors, and it gives you the incentive to add wins to it."

Although the write-ups and videotapes covering Kennerknecht's accomplishments fill more than one file cabinet, his Shooter's Bio is both mind-boggling and short — just two pages. It represents a good example of the kinds of things, and order of information, which should be maintained by each serious shooter:

RICK "KK" KENNERKNECHT
SHOOTING RESUME
POSTAL BOX 1586
LOMITA, CA 90717-5586
PHONE: (213) 325-0102
FAX: (213) 325-0298
REVISED AS OF 9/05/1991

DOMESTIC SHOOTING EXPERIENCE:

An avid competitive shotgunner, conservationist, photographer and hunter since 1972, holding life memberships in the NRA, USSCA; founding committee and staff member of the Verdugo Hills (SoCal) Chapter of Ducks Unlimited; and a member of: NSCA, ATA, QU (Quail Unlimited) and DU. Also a graduate of the International Shootists Inc. (ISI) practical pistol course taught by Mickey Fowler and Mike Dalton.

INTERNATIONAL SHOOTING EXPERIENCE:

I have extensive international experience, shooting under the instruction of such greats as John Bidwell, U.K. ('88 World Champion), A.J. "Smoker" Smith, U.K. ('87, '89 World Champion) and other British shooting greats such as Barry Simpson, Michael Rose and Les Bradley. I am a member of the Canadian Sporting Clays Association and the Clay Pigeon Shooting Association of Great Britain. I have competed on several occasions in Great Britain and France and have shot in the European Championships (Oporto, Portugal), and the World Championships (Villars, Switzerland). See competition experience.

Rick Kennerknecht (right) was introduced to hunting by his father. Photo is circa 1973.

NOTABLE COMPETITION ACHIEVEMENTS:

Classified AA in NSCA & USSCA Sanctioned Sporting Clays Competitions. Three-time member of the Outdoor Life "All American Team" '89, '90, '91. Two-time USSCA TEAM USA member during 1988 & 1989. Consistently placed in the top 10 to 20 in the nation. (National NSCA/USSCA Tournaments 1988-91).

NOTABLE TOURNAMENT ACHIEVEMENTS
1987-1990:

1987 HOA (High Overall) CHAMPION Golden State Sporting Open (CA State)

1988 HOA CHAMPION Southwest Sporting Clays Open (Regional)

1988 TEAM REMINGTON TOUR placing consistently in the Top 10.

1989 AMERICAN OUTDOORSMAN OF THE YEAR 9th OVERALL and FIRST PLACE in the bolt action rifle event.

1989 WORLD FITASC CHAMPIONSHIPS, Villars, Switzerland, placing 6th in the team event.

1990 FFTP/USA PROFESSIONAL CLAY TARGET CHAMPIONSHIPS, Nantes, France. First Place Team Member.

1990 FRANCIADE OPEN DE FRANCE 90 DE BALL TRAP PRO, Chateau de Chambord, France. Placed 1/8 finale.

1990 USSCA NATIONAL CHAMPIONSHIPS, 3rd PLACE, 28 gauge event.

1990 USSCA CALIFORNIA STATE CLASS AA CHAMPION.

1991 USSCA CALIFORNIA STATE CLASS AA CHAMPION.

1991 NSCA ZONE 7 CHAMPIONSHIPS, 2nd place AA class.

1991 FLASH CUP '91, lst place USA/FRENCH Team Championships in Portier, France (FFTP).

1991 USSCA NATIONALS, 3rd place Corporate Team Event.

1991 DU SILVER DOLLAR CLASSIC, Reno, Nevada, AA CHAMPION.

INDUSTRY FIRSTS:

1987 — First Perfect Starshot Score recorded on the West Coast and most perfect scores recorded in the United States.

1988 — Member of the first Remington Corporate Sporting Clays Team.

1989 — Member of the first U.S. FITASC Team to compete at European Championships in Oporto, Portugal.

1989 — Member of the first U.S. FITASC Team to compete at the World Championships in Villars, Switzerland.

1990 — Member of the first team to compete and win in the French Ball Trap Pro in Nantes, France.

1991 — Captain, Team Perazzi (Perazzi's first National Sporting Clays Team).

MEDIA COVERAGE:
Appears in numerous articles in national and international sporting newspapers and magazines, including a cover photo Western Outdoor News*; featured in Ron Shearer's* Great American Outdoors, *a two-part Cable TV Series on sporting clays. Appeared in* Sporting Clays World *TV Series and* Woods 'n Water *TV show; as well in an exhibition shooting segment for Charlton Heston Celebrity Invitational taped for TV. Appeared on Portuguese, Swiss and French TV in shooting segments. Performed in shooting exhibitions in the U.S. and Europe.*

NATIONAL LISTING: Marquis Who's Who in the West, *23rd Edition*

NATIONAL ADVISORY POSITIONS:
1988-1990, USSCA Rules & Ethics Committee.
1991-Date, NSCA National Advisory Council.
1991-Date, NSCA National Advisory Council.
1991-Date, Winchester Shooters Advisory Council.

PERSONAL BEST SPORTING CLAYS SCORES:
96/100 and 181/200 Peppermill Sporting, Mesquite, Nevada, 11/90.

HOME SPORTING CLAYS COURSE: *Moore-N-Moore Sporting Clays, San Fernando, California.*

GUNS PREFERRED: *Perazzi Mirage Special Sporting.*

AMMUNITION PREFERRED: *Winchester AA.*

GUNSMITHING SUPPLIES: *The Shotgun Ship.*

GUN CASES BY: *Americase.*

SHOOTING GLASSES: *Eagle 475.*

SHOOTING VESTS: *Perazzi, ADS, Bob Allen*

Meanwhile, Rick "KK" Kennerknecht is fully involved in the shooting sports. He owns and operates KK Awards Manufacturing in Lomita, California, which makes and markets trophies and medals for the shooting sports. When he is not in the office, or shooting on a sporting clays range, he serves as a consultant in various aspects of the sport, including course design, course products (traps, et cetera), awards recognition, shooting exhibitions and events and coaching referrals.

The champ started as a hunter and still is, as evidenced by bobwhite limit.

WHERE TO SHOOT

National Sporting Clays Courses

All the clubs, layouts and sites listed below are dues-paying members of the NSCA and offer sporting clays shooting and competition. All are associated with the National Sporting Clays Association in an official capacity at the time of publication. For further information on clubs in your area, contact the NSCA at 1-800-877-5338.

ALABAMA
DIXIELAND PLANTATION
P.O. BOX 168
HATCHECHUBBEE, AL 36858
205/667-7876

GREENFIELD SPORTING CLAYS
P.O. BOX 174
PITTSVIEW, AL 36871
205/855-9118

MOBILE SHOOTING CENTER
710 DYKES RD.
MOBILE, AL 36608
205/633-8629

SELWOOD HUNTING PRESERVE
RT 1, BOX 230
ALPINE, AL 35014
800/522-0403

ARIZONA
ARIZONA HUNT CLUB
P.O. BOX 1021
MAYER, AZ 86333
602/632-7709

BLACK CANYON TRAP
& SKEET CLUB
49 W McLELLAN
PHOENIX, AZ 85013
602/258-1901

PHOENIX TRAP AND SKEET CLUB
12450 W. INDIAN SCHOOL RD.
LITCHFIELD PARK, AZ 85340
602/935-2691

RIVER'S EDGE SPORTING RETREAT
HCR BOX 742
BENSON, AZ 85602
602/321-7096

ARKANSAS
CROWLEY RIDGE SHOOTING RESORT
RT 1, BOX 350
FORREST CITY, AR 72335
501/633-3352

SUGAR CREEK SPORTING CLAYS
RT 4, BOX 326
BENTONVILLE, AR 72712
501/273-0848

THUNDER VALLEY SPORTING CLAYS
P.O. BOX 2401
BATESVILLE, AR 72501
501/793-4563

CALIFORNIA
5 DOGS RANGE
BOX 16
GRANITE STATION
BAKERSFIELD, CA 93308
805/399-7296

BIRDS LANDING SPORTING CLAYS
P.O. BOX 5
BIRDS LANDING, CA 94512
707/374-5092

GREEN HEAD HUNTING CLUB
P.O. BOX 552
PINE VALLEY, CA 92062
619/473-8668

MOORE-N-MOORE SPORTING CLAYS
12651 N LITTLE TUJUNGA CYN RD.
SAN FERNANDO, CA 91342
803/890-4788

RAAHAUGE'S SHOTGUN SPORTS
5800 BLUFF ST.
NORCO, CA 91760
714/735-7981

RIVER ROAD SPORTING CLAYS
P.O. BOX 3016
GONZALES, CA 93926
408/675-2473

SANTA BARBARA SPORTING CLAYS
P.O. BOX 3306
SANTA BARBARA, CA 93130
805/965-9890

WEST VALLEY SPORTING CLAYS
P.O. BOX 257
GUSTINE, CA 95322
209/854-6265

COLORADO
AMERICAN SPORTING CLAY CLUB
3818 S HELENA WAY
AURORA, CO 80013
303/693-1065

HIGH COUNTRY GAME BIRDS
33300 ROAD 25
ELIZABETH, CO 80107
303/646-3315

INDIAN CREEK FARM
5111 E CO RD 62
WILLINGTON, CO 80549
303/568-7796

MT. BLANCA GAME BIRD & TROUT
P.O. BOX 236
BLANCA, CO 81123
719/379-3825

RENEGADE GUN CLUB, INC.
3570 WELD COUNTY RD 23
FT. LUPTON, CO 80621
303/857-6000

THE BROADMOOR SHOOTING
GROUNDS
1 LAKE CIRCLE
COLORADO SPRINGS, CO 80906
719/635-3438

VAIL ROD & GUN CLUB
225 WALL ST.
VAIL, CO 81658
303/476-2662

WESTERN COLORADO SPORTING CLAY
3172 GLENDAM DR.
GRAND JUNCTION, CO 81504
303/434-0906

FLORIDA
BIG D SPORTING CLAYS
RT 2, BOX 294C
LAKE CITY, FL 32055
904/752-0594

EVERGLADES SPORTING CLAYS
4701 COUNTY RD. 951 SOUTH
NAPLES, FL 33962
813/793-0086

INDIAN RIVER TRAP & SKEET CLUB
389 ISLAND CREEK DR.
VERO BEACH, FL 32963
407/231-1783

PALM BEACH TRAP & SKEET CLUB
2950 PIERSON RD.
WEST PALM BEACH, FL 33414
407/793-8787

TAMPA SPORTING CLAYS, INC.
7716 VAN DYKE RD.
ODESSA, FL 33556
813/986-7770

TRAIL GLADES SPORTING CLAYS
P.O. BOX 557912
MIAMI, FL 33255
305/226-1823

WHITE OAKS HUNTING CLUB
13511 NW 3 STREET
PLANTATION, FL 33325
305/474-3613

GEORGIA
BURGE PLANTATION
31 IVY CHASE
ATLANTA, GA 30255
404/787-5152

CALLAWAY GARDENS GUN CLUB
P.O. BOX 464
PINE MOUNTAIN, GA 31822
404/663-5129

CAT CREEK SPORTING CLAYS
P.O. BOX 2475
VALDOSTA, GA 31604
912/686-7700

CHEROKEE ROSE SHOOTING RESORT
P.O. BOX DRAWER 509
GRIFFIN, GA 30224
404/228-2529

FOREST CITY GUN CLUB
9203 FERGUSON AVE.
SAVANNAH, GA 31406
912/352-8613

LITTLE PACHITLA SPORTING CLAYS
P.O. BOX 421
NEWTON, GA 31770
912/835-3044

MILL POND CHAMPIONSHIP SPORTING
RT 1
DESOTO, GA 31743
912/874-6721

MILLROCK CLAY BIRD CLUB, INC.
2855 OLD ATLANTA RD.
CUMMING, GA 30130
404/889-2936

MYRTLEWOOD CHAMPIONSHIP
SPORTING
P.O. BOX 32
THOMASVILLE, GA 31799
912/228-6232

PIGEON MOUNTAIN SPORTING CLAYS
197 CAMP RD.
CHICKAMAUGA, GA 30707
404/539-2287

PINETUCKY SKEET & TRAP CLUB
P.O. BOX 204690
AUGUSTA, GA 30917
404/592-4230

RIVERVIEW CHALLENGE
RT 2, BOX 515
CAMILLA, GA 31730
912/294-4904

SOUTH RIVER GUN CLUB
157 N SALEM RD. NE
CONYERS, GA 30208
404/786-9456

THE MEADOWS NATIONAL GUN CLUB
P.O. BOX 377
SMARR, GA 31086
912/994-9910

WOLF CREEK
3070 MERK RD. SW
ATLANTA, GA 30349
404/346-8382

IDAHO
BUZ FAWCETT'S SHOOTING
GROUNDS
2090 S MERIDIAN RD.
MERIDIAN, ID 83642
208/888-3415

ILLINOIS
DIAMOND S SPORTING CLAYS, INC.
27211 TOWNLINE RD.
TREMONT, IL 61568
309/449-5500

INDIAN RIDGE SPORTING CLAYS
RR 1, BOX 209
LACON, IL 61540
309/246-3366

NORTHBROOK SPORTS CLUB
P.O. BOX 766
GRAYSLAKE, IL 60030
708/223-5700

ROCK RUN SPORTING CLAYS
2708 EDGEWOOD DR.
ROCKFORD, IL 61111
815/633-8870

SENECA HUNT CLUB LTD.
P.O. BOX 824
SENECA, IL 61360
815/357-8080

TRAIL OF TEARS SPORTSMAN'S CLUB
RT 1, OLD CAPE RD
JONESBORO, IL 62952
618/833-8697

INDIANA
BUSH COUNTRY SPORTING CLAYS
RT 1, BOX 101-A
CAMPBELLSBURG, IN 47108
812/755-4760

EVANSVILLE GUN CLUB
RT 2, BOX 89-D
HAUBSTADT, IN 47639
812/768-6370

SHOTGUN HOLLOW
RT 1, BOX 105
CLOVERDALE, IN 46120
317/795-3999

IOWA
BLACKHAWK SPORTING CLAYS
RR 1
JANESVILLE, IA 50647
319/987-2625

FLOOD CREEK HUNTING PRESERVE
RR 2, BOX 58
NORA SPRINGS, IA 50458
515/395-2725

GRISWOLD SPORTING CLAYS CLUB
BOX 249
GRISWOLD, IA 51535
712/778-4459

LAZY H HUNTING CLUB
RR 2
WOODBINE, IA 51579
712/647-2877

RIVER VALLEY SPORTING CLAYS
BOX 117
SIOUX RAPIDS, IA 50585
712/283-2342

SPRING RUN SPORTSMAN'S CLUB
BOX 8364A
SPRIIT LAKE, IA 51360
712/336-5595

TIMBER RIDGE SPORTING CLAYS
RR
CASTANA, IA 51010
712/353-6600

KANSAS
CEDAR HILL GUN CLUB
RT 3
BLADWIN, KS 66006
913/843-8213

CIMARRON SPORTING CLAYS, INC.
BOX 575
CIMARRON, KS 67835
316/855-7050

COKELEY FARMS
RT 1, BOX 149
DELIA, KS 66418
913/771-3817

FLINT OAK
RT 1, BOX 262
FALL RIVER, KS 67047
316/658-4401

HORSESHOE BEND SPORTING CLAYS
RR 1, BOX 13
OAKLEY, KS 67748
913/672-4111

LYNBROOKE SPORTING CLAY, INC.
1900 STATE ST.
AUGUSTA, KS 67010
316/775-7583

QUAIL VALLEY SPORTING CLAYS
RR 1, BOX 134
MOUNDRIDGE, KS 67107
316/345-8368

KENTUCKY
BLUE GRASS SPORTING CLAYS CLUB
2101 NICHOLASVILLE RD.
LEXINGTON, KY 40503
606/293-1529

BUSH ROAD SPORTING CLAYS, INC.
888 BUSH RD.
CADIZ, KY 42211
502/522-6193

GROUSE RIDGE SPORTING CLAYS
RR 1, BOX 755
LOAD, KY 41144
606/473-7400

HUMMIN' BIRDS SPORTING CLAYS
9110 WALL RD.
UTICA, KY 42376
502/785-9429

JEFFERSON GUN CLUB
10100 DIXIE HWY.
LOUISVILLE, KY 40272
606/937-4766

KENTUCKY SPORTSMAN'S CLUB
25 FOUNTIN PLACE
FRANKFORT, KY 40601
502/223-8806

MUDLICK GUN CLUB SPORTING CLAY
223 HIGHLAND AVE.
CYNTHIANA, KY 40131
606/234-4535

SHOOT-FIRE SPORTING CLAYS
290 KOOSTRA RD.
BOWLING GREEN, KY 42101
502/781-9545

TRIPLE - S SPORTING CLAYS
RT 5, BOX 46-A
MORGANFIELD, KY 42437
502/389-3580

LOUISIANA
AMERICAN HUNTER
2009 HWY 190 BY-PASS
COVINGTON, LA 70433
504/892-2521

HIGH POINT SHOOTING GROUNDS
P.O. BOX 790
BELLE CHASSE, LA 70037
504/656-7575

THE SHOOTOUT SPORTING RANGE
P.O. BOX 660
HAUGHTON, LA 71037
318/949-2548

WILD WINGS SPORTING CLAYS
P.O. BOX 26
DOWNSVILLE, LA 71234
318-982-7777

MARYLAND
CHESAPEAKE GUN CLUB
RT 1, BOX 76B
HENDERSON. MD 21640
301/758-1824

DELMARVA - SPORTING CLAYS
RT 1, BOX 59
MARDELA SPRINGS, MD 21837
301/742-2023

HOPKINS GAME FARM
RT 298
KENNEDYVILLE, MD 21645
301/348-5287

IZAAK WALTON LEAGUE OF AMERICA
6300 WALHONDING RD.
BETHESDA, MD 20816
301/229-6502

J & P SPORTING CLAYS
P.O. BOX 111
BENTON CREEK RD.
SUDLERSVILLE, MD 21668
301/438-3832

PRINCE GEORGE'S SHOOTING CENTER
10400 GOODLUCK RD.
GLENN DALE, MD 20769
301/577-7178

SINGLETREE SPORTING CLAYS
RD 1, BOX 140
SUDLERSVILLE, MD 21668
301/438-3479

MASSACHUSETTS
FALMOUTH SKEET CLUB, INC.
P.O.BOX 157W
WAQUOIT, MA 02586
508/540-3177

MICHIGAN
BLENDON PINES SPORTING CLAYS
8455 88TH AVE.
ZEELAND, MI 49464
616/875-7545

DETROIT GUN CLUB
2775 OAKLEY PARK RD.
WALLED LAKE, MI 48088
313/624-9647

HUNTERS RIDGE HUNT CLUB
3921 BARBER RD.
OXFORD, MI 48371
313/628-4868

SOUTH HAVEN ROD & GUN CLUB
68611 8TH AVE.
SOUTH HAVEN, MI 49090
616/637-8001

SUPERIOR SPORTING CLAYS
859 VAN BUSKIRK
IRONWOOD, MI 49938
906/932-3646

THE OUTDOORSMAN
SHANTY CREEK-SCHUSS MT. RESORT
BELLAIRE, MI 49615
616/533-8621

WHISKY RIVER HUNT CLUB
4555 CAMBRIA RD.
HILLSDALE, MI 49242
517/357-4424

MINNESOTA
GAME FAIR SHOOTING GROUNDS
8404 161ST AVE.
ANOKA, MN 55303
612/427-0944

LAC QUI PARLE SPORTING CLAYS
RR 5 , BOX 68
MONTRVIDEO, MN 56265
612/269-9769

LITTLE SWAN SPORTING CLAYS
10734 HELSTROM RD.
HIBBING, MN 55746-8112
218/262-5388

MINNESOTA HORSE & HUNT CLUB
2920 220TH ST.
PRIOR LAKE, MN 55372
612/447-2272

RICE CREEK HUNTING & RECREATION
RT 5, BOX 213
LITTLE FALLS,MN 56345
612/745-2232

ROYAL FLUSH SHOOTING CLUB
RT 5, BOX 228
LITTLE FALLS, MN 56345
612/745-2522

VALHALLA HUNT CLUB
RR 1, BOX 225
ALBERT LEA, MN 56077
507/377-7225

WILD MARSH SPORTING CLAYS, INC.
13767 COUNTY RD 3
CLEAR LAKE, MN 55319
612/662-2021

WINDSOR FIELDS SPORTING CLAYS
6835 HILDA RD.
TOWER, MN 55790
218/741-5837

MISSISSIPPI
PLANTATION SPORTING CLAY
P.O. BOX 1082
PICAYUNE, MS 39466
601-798-6919

MISSOURI
GAME HILL HUNTING CLUB
18480 HWY P
WESTON, MO 64098
816/431-5057

HAZEL CREEK SPORTING CLAYS
RT 2, BOX 167
GREENTOP, MO 63546
816/949-2689

OZARK SHOOTERS GUN CLUB
1719 COLLEGE
SPRINGFIELD, MO 65806
417/820-3766

POND FORT ESTATE HUNT CLUB
8860 HWY "N"
O'FALLON, MO 63366
314/327-5680

ROCKY RIDGE SPORTING CLAYS
RR 2, BOX 71
CHILLICOTHE, MO 64601
816/636-5276

TWIN LAKES SPORTING CLUB, INC.
RT 1, BOX 203
MEXICO, MO 65265
314/581-1877

UNITED SPORTSMEN'S CLUB
P.O. BOX 7148
COLUMBIA, MO 65201
314/474-0557

MONTANA
PERRY HUNTS & ADVENTURES
BOX 355
FT. BENTON, MT 594432
406/622-5336

SPORT MONTANA
9430 PRYOR RD.
BILLINGS, MT 59101
406/252-8188

NEBRASKA
GRAND ISLAND SPORTING CLAYS
1221 SOUTH SHADY BEND RD.
GRAND ISLAND, NE 68801

MIDLAND SPORTSMAN'S CLUB
801 "P" STREET
LINCOLN, NE 68508
402/477-9249

PHEASANT HAVEN SPORTING CLAYS
P.O. BOX 529
ELKHORN, NE 68022
402/779-2608

SUMAC SPORTING CLAYS
P.O. BOX 189
HOMER, NE 68030
712/251-1882

NEVADA
BIRDELLO GUN CLUB, INC.
336 THOMA ST.
RENO, NV 89502
702/322-1006

FLYING M HUNTING CLUB
70 PINE GROVE RD.
YERINGTON, NV 89447
702/463-5260

LAZY FIVE GUN CLUB
P.O. BOX 1566
RENO, NV 89505
702/673-1370

PEPPERMILL/ARVADA GUN CLUB
P.O. BOX 360
MESQUITE, NV 89024
800/621-0817

SAGE HILL CLAY SPORTS
11500 MIRA LOMA RD.
RENO, NV 89511
702/851-1123

TOPAZ SPORTSMAN'S CLUB
3851 HWY 208
WELLINGTON, NV 89444
702/266-3381

NEW HAMPSHIRE
SKAT SPORTING CLAYS
P.O. BOX 137
TEMPLE RD.
NEW IPSWICH, NH 03071
603/878-1257

NEW JERSEY
QUINTON SPORTSMENS CLUB
P.O. BOX 397
QUINTON, NJ 08072
609/748-2244

WEST CREEK SPORTING CLAYS
RD 1, STIPSON ISLAND RD.
ELDORA, NJ 08270
609/861-2760

NEW YORK
CATSKILL PHEASANTRY & SPORTING
P.O. BOX 42
LONG EDDY, NY 12760
914/887-4487

CEDAR HILL SPORTING CLAYS
RD 2, BOX 261
GERMANTOWN, NY 12526
518/828-9360

MASHOMACK PRESERVE CLUB
P.O. BOX 308
PINE PLAINS, NY 12567
518/398-5151

MID HUDSON TRAP & SKEET
411 N OHIOVILLE RD.
NEW PALTZ, NY 12561
914/255-7460

MORRIS CREEK FISH &
GAME PRESERVE
RD 1, BOX 122
SOUTH NEW BERLIN,
NY 13843
607/263-5238

SANDANONA SPORTING CLUB
P.O. BOX 800
MILLBROOK, NY 12545
914/677-9701

TACONIC TRAP CLUB
RT 82
SALT POINT, NY 12578
914/266-3788

WHALEBACK FARM
3700 EAST AVE.
ROCHESTER, NY 14618
716/554-3967

NORTH CAROLINA
ADAMS CREEK SPORTING CLAYS
6240 ADAMS CREEK RD.
HAVELOCK, NC 28532
919/447-6808

CENTRAL CAROLINA SPORTING CLAY
P.O. BOX 1101
BISCOE, NC 27209
919/428-2529

DEEP RIVER SPORTING CLAYS
P.O. BOX 18066
RALEIGH, NC 27619
919/774-7080

PINEHURST GUN CLUB
P.O. BOX 4000
PINEHURST, NC 28374
919/295-6811

POWER PACKED RANGES
1125 HWY 16 SOUTH
DENVER, NC 28037
704/483-3528

SHANE'S SPORTING CLAYS
6319-A HWY 158
SUMMERFIELD, NC 27358
919/643-7168

SMOKE RISE FIELD CLUB
P.O. BOX 1069
CASHIERS, NC 28717
704/743-5799

NORTH DAKOTA
DAKOTA HUNTING CLUB & KENNELS
BOX 1643
GRAND FORKS, ND 58206-1643
701/775-2074

OHIO
BEAVER CREEK CLUB
472 ROCK CREEK RUN
AMHERST, OH 44001
216/988-8884

BUCKEYE VALLEY SPORTING CLAYS
12507 SHELLBEACH RD.
THORNVILLE, OH 43076
614/467-2868

ELKHORN LAKE HUNT CLUB
4154 KLOPFENSTEIN RD.
BUCYRUS, OH 44820
419/562-1471

GRAND VALLEY RANCH
10198 PENNIMAN RD.
ORWELL, OH 44076
216/437-6440

HIDDEN HAVEN SPORTING CLAYS
9291 BUCKEYE RD.
SUGAR GROVE, OH 43155
614/746-8568

HIGHFIELD SHOOTING SPORTS CLUB
1835 WEST MAIN ST.
ZANESVILLE, OH 43701
614/849-3144

HILL-N-DALE CLUB
3605 POE RD.
MEDINA, OH 44256
216/725-2097

JUNGLE SPORTING CLAYS
3856 BARNETT RD.
NEW CONCORD, OH 43762
614/826-7284

LANGUILLE RIVER HUNT CLUB
P.O. BOX 18337
FAIRFIELD, OH 45018
501/633-8195

OHIO CLAY TARGETS ASSN.
P.O. BOX 8949
CINCINNATI, OH 45208
513/871-1328

PHEASANT VALLEY FARM
11625 BELOIT SNODES RD.
BELOIT, OH 44609
216/584-6828

PINEBROOKE SHOOTING SPORTS
26110 BIG PINE RD.
ROCKBRIDGE, OH 43149
614/385-4299

RUFF SHOT SPORTING CLAYS
3333 PERRON RD. SE
CARROLLTON, OH 44615
216/739-6597

SCIOTO RIVER HUNTING CLUB
P.O. BOX 1588
LIMA, OH 45802
513/464-6560

OKLAHAMA
J & J SPORTING CLAYS
6606 NW 26TH
BETHANY, OK 73008
405/387-2990

SOUTHERN RANCH HUNTING CLUB
RT 2, BOX 75
CHANDLER, OK 74834
405/258-0000

OREGON
BRIARWOOD SPORTING CLAYS
31180 LANES TURN RD.
EUGENE, OR 97401
503/942-2021

HULSE SPORTING CLAYS
60277 TYGH RIDGE RD.
DUFUR, OR 97021
503/467-2513

JEFFERSON STATE SHOOTING ASSN.
1505 MADISON SP81
KLAMATH FALLS,
OR 97603
503/882-2778

PENNSYLVANIA
BACKWOODS SPORTING CLAYS
P.O. BOX 447
CLARION, PA 16214
814/764-3722

CACOOSING GUN CLUB
P.O. BOX 293
BIRDSBORO, PA 19508
215/640-6072

CARLISLE FISH & GAME ASSN.
491 PINE RIDGE CIRCLE
LEWISBERRY, PA 17339
717/938-2043

CHESTNUT RIDGE SPORTING CLAYS
P.O. BOX 547
YOUNGSTOWN, PA 15650
412/539-2070

FACTORYVILLE SPORTSMEN CLUB
RD 1, BOX 1440
FACTORYVILLE, PA 18419
717/378-2593

FOREST HILL SPORTING CLUB
RD 2, BOX 389
MIFFLINBURG, PA 17844
717/966-9419

HILLSIDE HUNTING PRESERVE
P.O. BOX 128
BERLIN, PA 15530
814/267-3945

HOLLIDAYSBURG SPORTSMEN'S
RD 2, BOX 259
TYRONE, PA 16686
814/695-8138

PINEWOOD HUNTER CLAYS
RD 3, BOX 436
KUTZTOWN, PA 19530
215/376-6721

THE BUSTED FLUSH
RD 3, BOX 57
SHREVE RD.
TITUSVILLE, PA 16354
814/827-4030

THURSTON HOLLOW SPORTING CLAYS
RR 2, BOX 72-30
TUNKHANNOCK, PA 18657
717/836-4143

TOHICKON SPORTING CLAYS
RT 611
PIPERSVILLE, PA 18947
215/766-7520

RHODE ISLAND
ADDIEVILLE EAST FARM
BOX 248
MAPLEVILLE, RI 02839
401/568-3185

SOUTH CAROLINA
BROXTON BRIDGE PLANTATION
P.O. BOX 97
EHRHARDT, SC 29081
803/866-2218

CAROLINA DREAMIN' SPORTING CLAY
P.O. BOX 943
WINNSBORO, SC 29180
803/635-2562

CAROLINA SPORTING CLAYS
RT 3, BOX 455-H
NICHOLS, SC 29581
803/392-1401

CEDAR BRANCH SHOOTING CLUB
P.O. DRAWER 418
AIKEN, SC 29802
803/648-0067

OKATIE GUN CLUB
RT 1, BOX 67A
BLUFFTON, SC 29910
803/757-5180

SOUTH DAKOTA
DAKOTA SHARPSHOOTER
RR 3, BOX 167
MADISON, SD 57042
605/256-3636

WILLOW CREEK SPORTING CLAYS
HCR 33, BOX 24
FT. PIERRE, SD 57532
605/223-3154

TENNESEE
BEECH HILL SPORTING CLAYS
RR 4, BOX 40002
WINCHESTER, TN 37398
615-962-0540

GRINDERS SWITCH SHOOTING ESTATE
1608 CHICKERING RD.
NASHVILLE, TN 37215
615/373-8340

UPPER CUMBERLAND SPORTING CLAYS
RT 3, BOX 195-C
CROSSVILLE, TN 38555
615/484-1624

TEXAS
ALPINE RANGE SUPPLY CO.
5482 SHELBY RD.
FT. WORTH, TX 76140
817/478-2881

AMERICAN SHOOTING CENTERS
P.O. BOX 820368
HOUSTON, TX 77282
713/556-1597

BLUE GOOSE SPORTING CLAY RANGE
P.O. BOX M
ALTAIR, TX 77412
409/234-3597

CHAMPION LAKE GUN CLUB
5615 HILTONVIEW
HOUSTON, TX 77086
713/893-5868

CLEAR CREEK GUN RANGE
306 CRYSTAL
LEAGUE CITY, TX 77573
713/337-1722

CYPRESS VALLEY PRESERVE
P.O. BOX 5783
AUSTIN, TX 78763
512/825-3396

DALLAS GUN CLUB
P.O. BOX 292848
LEWISVILLE, TX 75029-2848
214/462-0043

DRY FORK SPORTING CLAYS
RT 3, BOX 174
HICO, TX 76457
817/796-2148

GREATER HOUSTON GUN CLUB
P.O. BOX 97
MISSOURI CITY, TX 77459
713/437-6025

JOSHUA CREEK RANCH
HCR 7, BOX 2469
BOERNE, TX 78006
512/698-1007

KAT CREEK SPORTING CLAYS
P.O. BOX 987
HENDERSON, TX 75652
903/854-2232

LA PALOMA SPORTING CLUB
P.O. BOX 160516
SAN ANTONIO, TX 78280
512/980-4424

LAGUNA VISTA INTERNATIONAL
P.O. BOX 44
COOMBES, TX 78535

NATIONAL SPORTING CLAYS ASSN.
P.O. BOX 680007
SAN ANTONIO, TX 78268
512/688-3371

ONE IN ONE HUNDRED GUN CLUB
RT 1, BOX 1021
KOUNTZE, TX 77625
409/755-9903

RE-BOB ENTERPRISES
903 MISTLETOE
BRECKINRIDGE, TX 76024
817/559-9578

RUSTIC RANGE SPORTING CLAYS
P.O. BOX 6743
LUBBOCK, TX 79493
806/745-8087

SAN ANGELO CLAYBIRD ASSN.
P.O. BOX 61211
SAN ANGELO, TX 76906
915/658-1986

SPORTING CLAYS INTL. OF DALLAS
RT 1, BOX 118
ALLEN, TX 75002

WEST TEXAS SPORTSMAN'S CLUB
P.O. BOX 14214
ODESSA, TX 79768
915/561-9379

UTAH
PORCUPINE ADVENTURES
8660 SOUTH 300 WEST
PARADISE, UT 84328
801/245-4555

UTAH SHOOTING SPORTS
1966 SOUTH II75 EAST
BOUNTIFUL, UT 84010
801/298-8343

VIRGINIA
CHARLES CITY CLAYS
501 SHIRLEY PLANTATION RD.
CHARLES CITY, VA 23030
804/829-6270

SUSSEX SHOOTING SPORTS
P.O. BOX 1752
PETERSBURG, VA 23805
804/834-3200

THE HOMESTEAD SHOOTING CLUB
P.O. BOX 1000
HOT SPRINGS, VA 24445
703/839-7787

THOMPSON VALLEY SPORTING CLAYS
P.O. BOX 4285
RICHLANDS, VA 24641
703/963-9369

WASHINGTON
BREMERTON TRAP & SKEET CLUB
4956 STATE HWY. 3 SW
PORT ORCHARD, WA 98366
206/674-2438

LANDT FARMS
SPORTING CLAYS
W16308 FUR MOUND RD.
NINE MILE FALLS,
WA 99026
509/466-4036

PALOUSE RIVER SHOOTING SPORTS
826 SOUTHVIEW
COLFAX, WA 99111
509/397-3670

R & M GAME BIRDS SPORTING CLAYS
495 FISHER HILL RD.
LYLE, WA 98635
509/365-3245

SUNNYDELL KENNELS
160 DRYKE RD.
SEQUIM, WA 98382
206/243-6653

TURKEY RIDGE SPORTING CLAYS,
RT 1, BOX 281
EVANS, WA 99126
509/684-2735

WISCONSIN
COLUMBIA COUNTY SPORTSMAN'S
W7144 N OAKRIDGE CT.
POYNETTE, WI 53955
608/635-7149

CUR-SAN'S CLAYS & KENNEL
RR 1, BOX 87
HANCOCK, WI 54943-9730
715/228-5151

GENEVA NATIONAL HUNT CLUB
555 HUNT CLUB COURT
LAKE GENEVA, WI 53147
414/245-0250

HARTLAND SPORTSMEN CLUB
1701 PEWAUKEE RD.
WAUKESHA, WI 53188
414/547-7070

J & H HUNT CLUB
RT 1, BOX 221
SHIOCTON, WI 54170
715/758-8134

PHEASANT CITY HUNT CLUB
RT 1, BOX 272
MARKESAN, WI 53946
414/324-5813

TOP GUN SPORTING CLAYS
N3249 RIVER VIEW RD.
JUNEAU, WI 53039
414/349-8128

WERN VALLEY SPORTSMAN'S CLUB
536W29903 WERN WAY
WAUKESHA, WI 53188
414/968-2400

WILDERNESS RIDGE HUNT & HORSE
RT 1, BOX 162B
CASCADE, WI 53011
414/528-7335

WOODHOLLOW SPORTING CLAYS
517 COPELAND AVE.
LA CROSSE, WI 54603
608/784-0482

DOMINICAN REPUBLIC
CASA DE CAMPO SHOOTING CENTER
P.O. BOX 140
LA ROMANA
DOMINICAN REPUBLIC
809/523-3333

CANADA
ORILLA GUN CLUB
RR 2
HOWKESTONE-ONT-CAN
L0L 1T0
705/689-2102

SCARBORO ROD & GUN CLUB
c/o BOX 96
HAMPTON-ONT-CAN
L0B 1JO
416/226-6202

CLUB ROUE DU ROY
882 QUEST RD.
HEMMINGFORD-QUE-CAN
J0L 1H0
514/247-2882

ROSE RANCHES SPORTING ASSO.
RR 1
WINTERBURN-ALTA-CAN
T0E 2N0
403/962-1323

SILVER WILLOW PHEASANT FARM
BOX 974
CARSTAIRS-ALTA-CAN
T0M 0N0
403/337-2490

WILD WINGS SPORTSMANS CLUB
RR 4
INNISFAIL-ALTA-CAN
T0M 1H0
403/227-1232

United States Sporting Clays Association

This organization is headquartered in Huston, Texas, and has its own associated sporting clays clubs and ranges. It should be noted, however, that some of the installations also serve the National Sporting Clays Association in an official capacity. All are dues-paying members of the USSCA and offer sporting clays shooting. For further information on clubs in your area contact the USSCA at 713-622-8048

ARKANSAS
L'ANGUILLE RIVER HUNT CLUB
RT 2 , BOX 107
FORREST CITY, AR 72335
501/633-8195

MID -AMERICA SPORTING CLAYS
CROWLEY RIDGE SHOOTING RESORT
FORREST CITY, AR 72335
50l/633-3352

NEVADA GAMEBIRDS
RT 1, BOX 171
BUCKNER, AR 71827
501/899-2902

SUGAR CREEK SPORTING CLAYS
RT 4, BOX 326
BENTONVILLE, AR 72712
501/273-0848

CALIFORNIA
ANTELOPE VALLEY SPORTSMAN'S CLUB
45408 160TH ST.
WEST LANCASTER, CA 93536
805/724-1291

BIRDS LANDING SPORTING CLAYS
2099 COLLINSVILLE RD.
BIRDS LANDING, CA 94512
707/374-5091

GREEN VALLEY SPORTING ESTATES
HWY. 33 STAR RT 1, BOX 149B
MARICOPA, CA 93252
213/371-1128

PACHMAYR HUNT SCHOOL
1875 SO. MOUNTAIN AVE.
MONROVIA, CA 91760
818/357-7771

RAAHAUGE'S
5800 BLUFF ST.
NORCO, CA 91760
714/735-2361

RIVER ROAD SPORTING CLAYS
P.O. BOX 3016
GONZALES, CA 93926
408/675-2473

SACRAMENTO SPORTING CLAYS
2787 PLEASANT GROVE RD.
PLEASANT GROVE, CA 95668
916/656-2544

WINCHESTER CANYON GUN CLUB
P.O. BOX 3306
SANTA BARBARA, CA 93130
805/965-9890

COLORADO
BROADMOOR SHOOTING GROUNDS
1 LAKE AVE.
COLORADO SPRINGS, CO 80906
719/635-3438

GLENARM SPORTING CLAYS
68202 TROUT RD.
MONTROSE CO, 81401
303/249-6490

HIGH COUNTRY GAME BIRDS
33300 COUNTY RD. 25
ELIZABETH, CO 80107
303/646-3315

MT. BLANCA GAME BIRD & TROUT
SMITH RESERVOIR RD.
(3 1/2 MI S.W. OF BLANCA)
BLANCA, CO 81123
719/379-DUCK

ROCKY MOUNTAIN ROOSTERS
21171 RD. 78, RT. 1
CALHAN, CO 80808
719/635-3257

CONNECTICUT
CONNECTICUT TRAVELERS
SPORTING CLAYS
91 PARK LANE RD.
NEW MILFORD, CT 06776
203/354-9351

MADISON ROD & GUN CLUB
P.O. BOX 1333
MADISON, CT 06443
203/245-3515

DELAWARE
OMMELANDEN RANGE
1205 RIVER RD.
NEW CASTLE, DE 19720
302/328-2256

FLORIDA
ROCKY COMFORT
RT 4, BOX 373
QUINCY, FL 32351
904/627-8074

INDIAN RIVER TRAP & SKEET CLUB
5925 82ND AVE
VERO BEACH, FL 32963
407/231-1783

SANDESTIN
EMERALD COAST PARKWAY
DESTIN, FL 33592
904/267-8111

TAMPA SPORTING CLAYS
15720 APACHE RD.
THONOTOSASSA, FL 33592
813/985-2783

GEORGIA
BEAR SPORTS CENTER
P.O. BOX 1698
THOMASVILLE, GA 31792
912/228-0209

CHEROKEE ROSE PLANTATION
895 BAPTIST CAMP RD.
GRIFFIN, GA 30224
404/228-CLAY

HEARTBREAK RIDGE SPORTING CLAYS
1107 8TH AVE.
ALBANY, GA 31707
912/435-1555

HUNT CLOSE PLANTATION
P.O. BOX 191
GAY, GA 30218
404/538-6352

MYRTLEWOOD PLANTATION
CAMPBELL ST.
THOMASVILLE, GA 31792
912/228-6232

PIGEON MOUNTAIN SPORTING CLAYS
197 CAMP RD.
CHICKAMAUGA, GA 30707
404/539-2287

SOUTHERN WINGS PLANTATION
RT 1, BOX 495
HARRISON, GA 31035
404/446-7737

HAWAII
SCHOFIELD ROD & GUN CLUB
1726 S. KING ST., #24
HONOLULU, HI 96826
808/955-0771

ILLINOIS
DIAMOND S SPORTING CLAYS
RT 1,
TREMONT, IL 61658
309/449-5500

MIDWEST SHOOTING SPORTS
P.O. BOX 166
HARRISBURG, IL 62946
618/982-2906

SENECA HUNT CLUB
P.O. BOX 306
MAYWOOD, IL 60153
708/681-2582

TROUT & GROUSE SHOOTING GROUNDS
300 HAPP RD.
NORTHFIELD, IL 60093
708/501-3111

INDIANA
SHOTGUN HOLLOW
RT 1, BOX 103
CLOVERDALE, IN 46120
317/653-4586

WEST CREEK S.C. &
HUNTING PRESERVE
15547 W. 169TH AVE.
CEDAR LAKE, IN 46303
219/696-6101

IOWA
BLACKHAWK SPORTING CLAYS
2410 W. LONE TREE RD.
CEDAR FALLS, IA 50613
319/987-2625

LAZY H HUNTING CLUB
RR #2
WOODBINE, IA 51579
712/647-2877

SOUTHERN IOWA SPORTING CLAYS
RR 2, BOX 91
MOULTON, IA 52572
515/642-3256

THE OUTPOST SHOOTING CLAYS COURSE
RR 1, BOX 211
LOGAN, IA 51546
712/644-2222

TRIPLE H RANCH HUNTING RESERVE
& SPORTING CLAYS RANGE
RT 2 , BOX 165
BURLINGTON, IA 52601
319/985-2253

KANSAS
FLINT OAK RANCH
RR 1
FALL RIVER, KS 67047
316/658-4401

MARAIS DES CYGNES SPORTING PARK
2201 E, 15TH
OTTAWA, KS 66067
913/242-SHOT

KENTUCKY
SHOOT-FIRE SPORTING CLAYS
KOOSTRA FARMS
290 KOOSTRA RD.
BOWLING GREEN, KY 42101
502/781-9545

LOUISIANA
HIGH POINT SHOOTING GROUNDS
BAYOU RD @ WALKER RD
P.O. BOX 790
BELLE CHASE, LA 70037
504/656-7575

WILD WINGS SPORTING CLAYS
RT 2, BOX 290
HWY 5531
DOWNSVILLE, LA 71234
318/981-7777

MAINE
FOGGY RIDGE GAME BIRD & FARM
P.O. BOX 211
WARREN, ME 04864
207/273-2357

MARYLAND
BERETTA-PRINCE GEORGE
TRAP & SKEET
I04 GOOD LUCK RD.
GLENN DALE, MD 20769
301/577-1477

FAIRFIELD SHOOTING GROUNDS
RT 3, BOX 245A
CHESTERTOWN, MD 21620
301/758-1824

HOPKINS GAME FARM
RT 298
KENNEDYVILLE, MD 21645
301/348-5287

J&P SPORTING CLAYS
BENTON CORNER RD.
SUDLERSVILLE, MD 21668
301/438-3832

THE CHESAPEAKE GUN CLUB
P.O. BOX 609
CHESTERTOWN, MD 21620
301/758-1824

MASSACHUSETTS
WALPOLE SPORTSMEN'S ASSN.
53 REBECCA RD.
SCITUATE, MA 02066
617/545-4725

FALMOUTH SKEET CLUB
205 CARRIAGE SHOP RD.
WAQUOIT, MA 02536
508/540-3177

MICHIGAN
BOYNE SPORTING CLAYS CLUB
841 HIGHLANDS RD.
HARBOUR SPRINGS, MI 49740
616/526-7911

GRAND BLANC HUNTSMAN CLUB
9046 S. IRISH RD.
GRAND BLANC, MI 48439
313/636-7261

HUNTERS RIDGE HUNT CLUB
& SPORTING CLAYS
3921 BARBER RD.
OXFORD, MI 48051
313/628-4868

MINNESOTA
CLEAR CREEK OUTDOORS
RT 1, BOX 53A
WRENSHALL, MN 55797
218/384-3670

CROOKSTON GUN CLUB
BOX 259
CROOKSTON, MN 56716
218/281-5143

LEBLANC'S RICE CREEK HUNTING
RT 5, BOX 213
LITTLE FALLS, MN 56345
612/745-2451

MINNESOTA HORSE & HUNT CLUB
2920 220TH ST.
PRIOR LAKE, MN 55372
612/447-2272

ROYAL FLUSH SHOOTING CLUB
RT 5, BOX 228
LITTLE FALLS, MN 56345
612/745-2522

WILD MARSH SPORTING CLAYS
13767 COUNTY RD. 3
CLEAR LAKE, MN 55319
612/662-2292

MISSISSIPPI
QUIALWOOD PLANTATION
P.O. DRAWER 1296
OXFORD, MS 38655
601/357-2660

WILDERNESS WEST
5455 KAYWOOD DR.
JACKSON, MS 39211
601/956-4762

MISSOURI
BLACKHAWK VALLEY
HUNTING PRESERVE
RT 1, BOX 108
OLD MONROE, MO 63369
316/665-5459

OZARK SHOOTERS GUN CLUB
HWY. 65
BRANSON, MO 65616
417/831-2376

POND FORT KENNELS & HUNT CLUB
8860 HWY. N
O'FALLON, MO 63366
314/327-5680

TRAIL RIDGE
RT 1
BLAIRSTOWN, MO 64726
816/885-3632

WILDWOOD HUNTING & SPORTING
CLAYS OF SEDALIA, MO
RT 1, BOX 144
HOUSTONIA, MO 65333
816/879-4451

MONTANA
ROYAL BIGHORN LODGE
P.O. BOX 206
ST. XAVIER, MT 59075
406/666-2340

SPORT MONTANA
4930 PRYOR RD.
BILLINGS, MT 59101
406/252-8188

NEBRASKA
GRAND ISLAND SKEET &
SPORTING CLAYS
1221 SOUTH SHADY BEND RD.
GRAND ISLAND, NE 68801
402-463-8580

NEVADA
FLYING M HUNTING CLUB
70 PINE GROVE RD.
YERINGTON, NV 89447
702/463-5260 OR 5261

PEPPERMILL'S ARVADA RANCH
P.O. BOX 360
MESQUITE, NV 89024
602/347-5200

TOPAZ SPORTSMEN'S CENTER
3851 HWY. 208
WELLINGTON, NV 89444
702/266-3512

NEW HAMPSHIRE
SKAT HUNTING PRESERVE
P.O. BOX 137
NEW IPSWICH, NH 03071
603/878-1257

NEW JERSEY
BUCKSHORN SPORTSMEN CLUB
507 FRIENDSHIP ROAD
SALEM, NJ 08079
609/935-9805

OLDMAN'S CREEK FARM &
SPORTING CLUB
OLDMAN'S TOWNSHIP - RT 130
PEDRICKTOWN, NJ 08067
215/647-7973

WEST CREEK SPORTING CLAYS
STIPSON ISLAND RD.
WOODBINE, NJ 08270
609/861-2760

NEW MEXICO
CIRCLE DIAMOND RANCH
BOX 182
TINNIE, NM 88351
505/653-4957

NEW YORK
DUTCHESS VALLEY ROD &
GUN CLUB
AIKENDALE RD.
PAWLING, NY 12564
914/855-5014

GOOSE CREEK HUNT CLUB
RT 1, BOX 479B
ASHVILLE, NY 14710
716/782-CLAY

HENDRICK HUDSON FISH &
GAME CLUB
AVERILL PARK, NY 12018
518/674-5184

MID-HUDSON TRAP &
SKEET PRESERVE
411 NORTH OHIOVILLE RD.
NEW PALTZ, NY 12561
914/255-7460

MORRIS CREEK FISH & GAME
WELLS RD.
SOUTH NEW BERLIN, NY 13843
607/263-5238

PAWLING MOUNTAIN CLUB
P.O. BOX 573
PAWLING, NY 12564
914/855-DUCK

PECONIC RIVER SPORTSMAN'S CLUB
RFD 389, RIVER RD.
MANORVILLE, NY 11949
516/727-5248

ROCHESTER-BROOKS GUN CLUB
926 HONEOYE FALL ROAD #6
RUSH, NY 14543
7 1 6/533-9913

SANDANONA SPORTING CLAYS
P. O. BOX 800, SHARON TURNPIKE
MILLBROOK, NY 12545
914/677-9701

NORTH CAROLINA
ADAMS CREEK SPORTING CLAYS
RT 1, BOX 119
HAVELOCK, NC 28532
919/447-7688

BEAVER DAM SPORTING
CLAY RANGE
RT 4, BOX 97M
GREENVILLE, NC 27834
919/758-2266

DEEP RIVER SPORTING CLAYS
P.O. BOX 18066
RALEIGH, NC 27619
919/774-7080

OHIO
HILL-N-DALE
3605 POE RD.
MEDINA, OH 44256
216/725-2097

OKLAHOMA
SOUTHERN RANCH LODGE &
HUNTING CLUB
RT 2, BOX 75
CHANDLER, OK 74834
918/377-4226

OREGON
BRAIRWOOD SPORTING CLAYS
31180 LANESTURN RD.
EUGENE, OR 97401
503/344-7224

TREO CORPORATION
RT 1, BOX 3171
HEPPNER, OR 97836
503/676-5840

PENNSYLVANIA
FAYETTE SHOOTING SPORTS
138 LANGLEY RD.
UNIONTOWN, PA 15401
412/438-4526

GAP-VIEW SPORTING CLAYS
P.O. BOX 577
CAMP HILL, PA 17011
717/761-7779

HUNTING HILLS HUNTING PRESERVE
RD 1, BOX 385
DILLINER, PA 15327
412/324-2142

LAUREL HILL HUNTING PRESERVE
RT 2, BOX 162
ROCKWOOD, PA 15557
814/352-7063

T.N.T. HUNTING PRESERVE
RT 1, BOX 147
SMOCK, PA 15480
412/677-2609

RHODE ISLAND
ADDIEVILLE EAST FARM
BOX 248, 200 PHEASANT DRIVE
MAPLEWOOD, RI 02839
401/568-3185

SOUTH CAROLINA
BRAYS ISLAND PLANTATION
P.O. BOX 30
SHELDON, SC 29941
803/525-6303

CHARLESTON SPORTING CLAYS
P.O. BOX 773
MT. PLEASANT, SC 29464
803/884-6194

RIVER BEND SPORTSMAN'S RESORT
1000 WILKIE BRIDGE RD.
P.O. BOX 625
INMAN, SC 29349
803/592-1348

THE OAKS GUN CLUB LTD.
RT 2, BOX 196-A
GEORGETOWN, SC 29440
803/527-1861

SOUTH DAKOTA
DAKOTA SHARPSHOOTER
SKAT COURSES
RR 3, BOX 167
MADISON, SD 57042
800/351-1477 EXT. 415

VALLEY WEST TRAP &
SPORTING CLAY RANGE
RR 3, HWY. 17
P.O. BOX 88045
SIOUX FALLS, SD 57105
605/361-3173

TEXAS
CHAMPION LAKE GUN CLUB
5615 HILTONVIEW
HOUSTON, TX 77086
713/893-5868

CIRCLE BAR SPORTING CLAYS
HCR 69, BOX 20
FLUVANNA, TX 79517
915/573-7469

CLEAR CREEK GUN RANGE
FM 1266
LEAGUE CITY, TX 77573
713/337-1722

CYPRESS VALLEY PRESERVE
P.O. BOX 5783
AUSTIN,TX 78763
512/825-3396

DALLAS GUN CLUB
P.O. BOX 292848
LEWISVILLE, TX 75029
214/462-0043

HONEY CREEK SPORTING CLAYS
RT 3, BOX 174
HICO, TX 76457
817/796-2148

KAT CREEK SPORTING CLAYS
S OF FM 1798, OFF US 79
HENDERSON, TX 75652
214/854-2232

LA PALOMA SPORTING CLAYS
P. O. BOX 160516
SAN ANTONIO, TEXAS 78280
512/438-4424

ONE IN ONE HUNDRED GUN CLUB
P.O. BOX 7794
BEAUMONT, TX 77726
409/755-9903

RE-BOB ENTERPRISES
FM 578
BRECKENRIDGE, TX 76024
817/559-9578

SPORTING CLAYS INTL. DALLAS
RT 1, BOX 118
ALLEN, TX 75001
817/659-4811

TIERRA COLINAS
RT 5, BOX 162B
WEATHERFORD, TX 76086
817/594-5001

UPLAND BIRD COUNTRY
FM 637, P.O. BOX 1110
CORSICANA, TX 75151
214/872-5663

VIRGINIA
EASTERN SHORE SPORTING CLAYS
BOX 37
JAMESVILLE, VA 23398
804/442-6035

WASHINGTON
WESTERN WASHINGTON
SPORTING CLAYS
N.E. 137TH ST.
DUVALL, WA 98019
206/333-4138

WEST VIRGINIA
FOXY PHEASANT HUNTING
PRESERVE
RT 1, BOX 437
KEARNEYSVILLE, WV 25430
304/725-4963

WISCONSIN
RIVER WILDLIFE
444 HIGHLAND DR.
KOHLER, WI 53044
414/457-0134

TOP GUN SPORTING CLAYS
BOX 44
WOODLAND, WI 53099
414/349-3108

TROUT & GROUSE
SHOOTING GROUNDS
11110 110TH ST.
KENOSHA, WI 53142
414/857-7232

WYOMING
PHEASANT MEADOWS GUN CLUB
P.O. BOX 1044
DOUGLAS, WY 82633
307/358-5212

CANADA
CLUB ROUE DU ROY
882 QUEST RD.
HEMMINGFORD, QUEBEC JOL180
514/247-2882

SPRING LAKE COUNTRY CLUB
BOX 495
SUNDRE, ALBERTA, CAN
TOM IX0
403/638-2040

DOMINICAN REPUBLIC
CASA DE CAMPO
P.O. BOX 140
LA ROMANA, DOMINICAN REPUBLIC